Managing Knowledge Work

Managing Knowledge Work

Sue Newell
Maxine Robertson
Harry Scarbrough
Jacky Swan

palgrave

First published 2002 by
PALGRAVE
Houndmills, Basingstoke, Hampshire RG21 6XS and
175 Fifth Avenue, New York, N. Y. 10010
Companies and representatives throughout the world

PALGRAVE is the new global academic imprint of
St. Martin's Press LLC Scholarly and Reference Division and
Palgrave Publishers Ltd (formerly Macmillan Press Ltd).

ISBN 0–333–96299–0

This book is printed on paper suitable for recycling and made from fully managed and sustained forest sources.

A catalogue record for this book is available from the British Library.

Library of Congress Cataloging-in-Publication Data
Managing knowledge work / Sue Newell... [et al.].
       p.   cm.
   Includes bibliographical references and index.
   ISBN 0–333–96299–0 (pbk.)
   1. Knowledge management.   2. Knowledge workers.   3. Information
technology—Management.   I. Newell, Susan.
HD30.2 .M366 2002
658.4'038—dc21   2001060275

10   9   8   7   6   5   4   3   2   1
11   10   09   08   07   06   05   04   03   02

Printed and bound in Great Britain by
Creative Print & Design (Wales), Ebbw Vale

Contents

List of figures and tables

Figures

Tables

Preface

Aims of this book

This book is aimed at a wide readership encompassing the diverse range of groups who are involved in teaching, studying, practising and managing knowledge work. In recent years, a number of different management concepts have attempted to address the design and management of knowledge work. Approaches such as BPR (Business Process Reengineering), the Learning Organization and most recently Knowledge Management have sought to increase organizations' ability to exploit knowledge as a resource. The main problem with these approaches is that they have focused on defining a specific recipe for success. This has helped to make them fashionable for a certain period, and has helped to sell the tools and methods that they promote. It has not, however, greatly advanced our understanding of the peculiar characteristics of knowledge work or the distinctive challenges that it throws up for management.

In this text, we have sought to step back from the ebb and flow of management fads to set out a coherent account of the management of knowledge work which is based on an extensive body of research and analysis, including our own. Whereas management fads often treat knowledge and learning as if they were something abstracted from the way people work, our concern here is to put knowledge back into work – to show that knowledge work ultimately depends on the behaviours, motivations and attitudes of those who undertake and manage it. The idea that knowledge can be managed simply through the right process design or by codifying it in information and communication technology (ICT) systems is, we argue, illusory. A large volume of research evidence shows this to be the case. Our aim therefore is not so much to offer recipes for success, but to highlight the different behavioural and organizational conditions under which knowledge can be managed effectively. The focus is on improving the reader's understanding of knowledge work by outlining the different perspectives which have been applied to it. We believe that managing such work is enhanced not by clinging on to particular recipes, but by improving our ability to analyse its distinctive implications for management.

The historical and critical context for this book

This is not the first and it certainly will not be the last book on the management of knowledge work. It is easy to forget that the notion of knowledge work has been around at least since the late 1960s when it was popularized in the work of Peter Drucker and then given added legitimacy by Daniel Bell's analysis of the rise of the post-industrial society. Many authors see the emergence of knowledge workers as a consequence of this broader shift from an industrial to a post-industrial society. Reich (1991), for example, uses the term 'symbolic analysts' to refer to the knowledge work occupations created by this shift. This group is broadly defined to encompass the ranks of R&D experts, designers, marketers, advertisers, consultants, financiers and investment analysts.

As Reich's selection of occupations suggests, however, the task of identifying the distinctive features of the management of knowledge work is made more complicated by the definitional problems which attach to this concept. Depending on our parameters, the term can be applied to a wide range of different occupational settings. As many writers have pointed out (for example, Manwaring and Wood, 1985), even the most routinized jobs still demand tacit knowledge from employees, so at some level all work is arguably knowledge work. But, even if we set aside this argument and focus strictly on work which is characterized primarily by the application of knowledge rather than physical effort, there are still debates about the best way of characterizing such work. A recurring question here is whether knowledge work can be equated with the work of 'professional' groups. Historically, work based on abstract knowledge has often been regulated through professional structures, where practitioners are licensed to practise on the basis of state recognition for the profession. This has given professionals a degree of autonomy from business organizations and consumers alike. The professional label is typically applied to groups such as lawyers and doctors, but some would also include 'organizational professionals' such as R&D scientists. In fact, some writers argue for the continuing relevance of the notion of professionalism, and suggest that we are moving towards the 'professional society' (Freidson, 1994).

In focusing on the management of knowledge work, we are not denying that some of the issues associated with professionalism remain valid – for example, knowledge workers are indeed similar to professional groups in the sense that they typically exercise a significant degree of autonomy in their work. On the other hand, the professional model seems increasingly strained by a series of developments in advanced economies which seem to demand a more inclusive account of the way in which knowledge is applied to work (Crompton, 1992). These developments can be summarized as follows:

1. The decline of the professional model itself

The professional model has only ever been fully realized in the USA and the UK. Increasingly the spread of market forces and globalization is diluting the role of the profession as the main way of regulating abstract knowledge. Public sector professionals have lost much of their autonomy, and other groups such as R&D scientists and IT experts are increasingly subject to market pressures through the development of 'outsourcing' (Whittington, 1991).

2. The rise of managerialism

The private sector business firm has increasingly become the model for all kinds of work organization. At the same time, the growing importance of competitive pressures and market forces has given much greater power to managerial groups to determine the design and performance standards of organizations. Management practices to do with controlling resources and setting targets have spread to encompass a wide range of occupational and employee groups (Scarbrough, 1998).

3. The technicization of work

The advance of new ICTs is a major contribution to the development of knowledge work. This operates partly by making it easier to transfer codified forms of knowledge between different groups. As a recent OECD report notes:

> ICTs allow for increased codification of knowledge, that is its transformation into 'information' that can easily be transmitted . . . through codification knowledge takes on more and more the properties of a commodity. (OECD, 1996, p. 13)

The impact of ICTs on the flow of knowledge within and between organizations occurs in many different ways. Broadly speaking, however, ICTs are important in making it easier to encode tacit and embodied knowledge into symbolic forms which can be transmitted digitally. This means that knowledge can be manipulated and combined with other packaged forms of knowledge more easily. Such changes serve, in turn, to open up new possibilities for the organizational forms through which knowledge can be managed. Advances in ICTs have encouraged the emergence of looser and more spatially distributed organizational forms. The traditional ways of acquiring and controlling knowledge – in particular, the professional model described earlier – are thus increasingly displaced in favour of networking and market-style arrangements. Overall, the advance of ICTs can thus be seen as part of a general tendency for all work to become more technical in nature (Barley and Orr, 1997). As Zuboff (1988) argues, 'intellective skills' to do with the manipulation of symbols are displacing manual skills in a range of occupations.

We argue that the development of knowledge work needs to be seen in terms of these widespread and convergent patterns of change in the nature of work which cut across existing occupational categories, changing existing roles and creating new ones. This is not to adopt the post-industrial thesis uncritically, of course. One of the features of these changes is the way in which certain groups have become subject to greater management control, and others are increasingly expected to manage themselves. We also recognize the numerous criticisms of the whole concept of knowledge work. For one, knowledge workers are not a discrete occupational group and most of the descriptions of such workers tend to lump together a variety of occupations and roles (for example, Davenport *et al.*, 1996). There is also the argument that the concept of knowledge work is politically loaded, because it gives an upbeat gloss to the processes of industrial change (Knights *et al.*, 1993). And, by the same token, we acknowledge that it would be grossly inaccurate to pretend that anything more than a fraction of the jobs even in the advanced economies correspond to the kind of knowledge work roles highlighted here. We note, for instance, that much actual and forecast job growth in both the USA and the UK is occurring in routine service jobs to do with guarding, cleaning and nursing which are outside the 'high-tech' or knowledge-intensive sectors (*Labour Market Trends*, 2000; Crouch *et al.*, 1999).

But, even accepting these criticisms, we believe that subsequent chapters of this text demonstrate the growing importance of the management of knowledge work as a response to these wider changes in advanced economies. This is not to ignore the wider pattern of growth in routine McJobs or even Mac-Jobs in the service sector. But knowledge work in the terms used here denotes a trend rather than a discrete set of occupational groups. It involves some of the characteristics of professional work, but is primarily driven by business and organizational needs rather than occupationally-defined norms and practices. In so far as knowledge workers ostensibly display some of the features of the classic professional – for instance, retaining some autonomy and self-management in their working practices – this is to do with their labour-market position and the nature of the work they do rather than the institutional power of any profession. This is also reflected culturally in the balance of power between experts and users. Where professionals deal with clients, knowledge workers have to satisfy managers and customers.

It follows that, in the discussion developed here, groupings of 'knowledge workers' are identified not so much by their affiliation to occupational norms as by the work that they do. This is work which is relatively unstructured and which involves the manipulation of symbols through the use of a range of tools, including ICT systems. As reflected in the range of occupational groups highlighted by subsequent chapters, the characteristic feature of such work is not the industrial context or the specific skills being applied so much as the centrality of various kinds of knowledge in the work process of these groups. For knowledge workers, knowledge is simultaneously an input, medium and output for their work.

This broadly-based definition of knowledge work is aimed at reflecting the widespread changes in the work process described above. It is a dynamic definition in that it captures broad trends in the work process affecting a range of occupational groups rather than specific shifts within or between such groups. At the same time it underlines what we believe to be important areas of convergence in the work experience of a range of different groups. These include, first, the growing importance of ICT systems and networked organizational forms as means of knowledge production for these groups. ICT systems, in particular, are increasingly widespread as enabling technologies for the processing of knowledge; furnishing knowledge *inputs* in the form of software systems; providing the *medium* for knowledge work through the development of e-mail, groupware and intranet technologies; and becoming the means for capturing the *output* of knowledge work in the shape of ICT-based artefacts and representations. Second, we can also observe a critical convergence in the locus of knowledge production. Thus, in knowledge work we see knowledge being created and applied not through the profession or the discipline but in the immediate context of its use (Gibbons *et al.*, 1994).

Structure of the book

The book is organized around the major perspectives which have been applied to the management of knowledge work. By presenting a wide array of perspectives, we are highlighting the multifaceted nature of that task and the need for a more holistic approach to it. Thus the Introduction outlines the key debates in this field, and some of the problems of managing knowledge within a historical grounding. Chapter 2 deals with some of the most developed settings for knowledge work – so-called 'knowledge-intensive firms' – and draws out the lessons for management more generally. Chapter 3 deepens our understanding of knowledge work itself by focusing on its practice. Much knowledge work takes place within teams, and the way teams operate, so effective management involves understanding the dynamics of teams and the trust they engender. This usefully sets the scene for Chapter 4 which places these behavioural conditions for knowledge work into the arena of Human Resource Management (HRM), where the relative advantages of different HRM approaches and policies can be fully debated.

Only once we have reviewed the wide range of organizational conditions for knowledge work is it appropriate to focus specifically on the role of ICTs. It is relatively easy to dispose of the idea that ICTs represent a solution to the problems of managing knowledge. It is more difficult, however, to analyse the interaction between the technical and behavioural dimensions of managing knowledge work. In highlighting these interactions, Chapter 5 leads us on naturally to discuss in Chapter 6 one of the major vehicles through which knowledge is created and shared in work settings – the 'community of practice'. Such communities are increasingly seen as a vehicle for leveraging employees' tacit knowledge. They are also an important means of applying ICT systems more effectively to Knowledge Management.

The final chapters of the book help to integrate many of these observations about the interplay of technical and behavioural issues by providing a broad framework for analysing the management of knowledge work. Chapter 7 does this by showing the different demands upon knowledge work posed by the process of innovation. This is a critical context for the management of knowledge work, and one which is least amenable to the application of simplistic recipes. The following chapter, Chapter 8, then provides a concluding synthesis of the main arguments and debates developed in the text, and supplies a final coda on the challenges which knowledge work continues to pose for management.

Using the text: case studies and role-play

One of the implications of the approach we have taken to this topic is the importance of understanding the different contexts in which knowledge is managed. Evidence shows that there is no one best way to manage knowledge work, as what is effective depends very much on the history and type of organization, the employees involved, the form of it employed, and so on. It follows that we are keen not to generalize about knowledge work as something abstracted from context. Rather, we aim to shed some light on the different conditions which influence knowledge work and inhibit or facilitate its management. To do this, and to develop the holistic understanding of context which our approach involves, we have incorporated, in Chapters 2 to 6 and in Chapter 8, case-study accounts of the management of knowledge work. Each of these has been selected to highlight particular dilemmas which confront managers seeking to direct or exploit knowledge work. Where theoretical models often present a one-dimensional view, the advantage of these cases is that they show the problems of managing knowledge work to be a messy admixture of different issues and aspirations. These are rarely resolved through a single solution, but call on the reader's ability to recognize and evaluate the different trade-offs confronting management.

In this spirit, the case analyses which supplement the cases are designed to highlight a particular way of reading the case, but are not presented as complete solutions in themselves. These case analyses can be found on the tutor website www.palgrave.com/business/newell2. Indeed, the corollary of incorporating cases within the text is really to disrupt rather than advance the view that particular models and concepts can provide an all-encompassing guide for practice. Our analyses are thus a heuristic means of helping the reader/student explore the case – an incentive to address these issues from a range of perspectives – rather than prescriptive guidance for management.

In Chapter 7, we have taken this approach even further by incorporating a role-play exercise within the case study. The role-play can be used in a variety of ways, and there are extensive notes on www.palgrave.com/business/newell2 to assist in using it for teaching purposes. The aim here is not only to present the specific dilemmas posed by the management of knowledge work, but also to show how these dilemmas are perceived and experienced differently by a range of groups within an organization. This helps to unpack the notion of 'management' as a monolithic entity, and shows how there are different political factions and personalities within the management structure which impact on the conduct of knowledge work. This is a further reminder, if one were needed, that whatever nostrums are generated for management practice (and no doubt we are guilty of presenting some here) the outcomes of such practice are in the final analysis a product of managerial agency itself; the actions of particular managers being the medium through which these issues are addressed.

References

Barley, S.R. and Orr, J.E. (1997) *Between Craft and Science: Technical Work in US Settings*. ILR Press: London, p. 5.

Crompton, R. (1992) Professions in the current context. *Work, Employment and Society*, Special Issue, *A Decade of Change*, pp. 147–66.

Crouch, C., Finegold, D. and Sako, M. (1999) *Are Skills the Answer? The Political Economy of Skill Creation in Advanced Industrial Economies*. Oxford: Oxford University Press.

Davenport, T.H., Jarvenpaaa, S.L. and Beers, M.C. (1996) Improving knowledge work processes. *Sloan Management Review*, Summer: 53–65.

Freidson, E. (1994) *Professionalism Reborn: Theory, Prophecy and Policy*. Cambridge: Polity Press.

Gibbons, M., Limoges, C., Nowotny, H., Schwartzman, S., Scott, P. and Trow, M. (1994) *The New Production of Knowledge*. London: Sage.

Knights, D., Murray, F. and Willmott, H. (1993) Networking as knowledge work: a study of interorganizational development in the financial services sector. *Journal of Management Studies*, 30: 975–96.

Labour Market Trends (2000) June. London: ONS.

Manwaring, T. and Wood, S. (1985) The ghost in the labour process. In D. Knights, H. Wilmott and D. Collinson (eds) *Job Redesign: Critical Perspectives on the Labour Process*. Farnborough: Gower.

OECD (1996) *Technology, Productivity and Job Creation*, Vol. 1, *Highlights*. Paris: OECD.

Reich, R. (1991) *The Work of Nations: Preparing Ourselves for 21st Century Capitalism*. London: Simon & Schuster.

Scarbrough, H. (1998) The unmaking of management? Contemporary shifts in the meaning of management. *Human Relations*, 51(6): 691–716.

Whittington, R. (1991) Changing control strategies in industrial R&D. *R&D Management*, 21: 43–53.

Zuboff, S. (1988) *In the Age of the Smart Machine*. Oxford: Heinemann.

Acknowledgements

We would like to acknowledge the support of the UK Economic and Social Research Council (ESRC) for funding the research associated with the LiftCo, Globalbank cases and the Oakland Furniture role play exercise. We would also like to acknowledge the Engineering and Physical Sciences Research Council (EPSRC), which funded the research associated with the Profteam and Midlands Hospital cases. We would like to acknowledge Linda Edelman and John Preston, both of whom were involved in the research for these cases. Our special thanks go also to Dr Donald Hislop and Dr Shan Ling Pan who produced original versions of the Liftco and Buckman Labs cases which are featured here in an adapted form. All of this research was carried out with the IKON Research Unit based at Warwick Business School. IKON was established to advance understanding of the interactions between innovation, knowledge and networking, and is itself a networked research unit with the Universities of Leicester and Royal Holloway. We would also like to acknowledge Professor James Fleck for his contribution to the Oakland Furniture role play. Finally we would like to thank the two anonymous reviewers for their helpful comments on early versions of this book.

1 Introduction

1

Learning outcomes

At the end of this chapter students will be able to:

■ Understand and distinguish between different types of knowledge and relate these to practices of knowing.

■ Understand the importance of managing knowledge in organizations since the introduction of Scientific Management at the turn of the twentieth century.

■ Understand the nature and characteristics of knowledge work and the role of knowledge workers within organizations.

■ Understand the broad issues critical to the management of knowledge and knowledge workers, which will be explored in depth in the remainder of the book.

Introduction

Managing knowledge and knowledge workers is arguably the single most important challenge being faced by many kinds of organizations across both the private and public sectors in the years to come. Knowledge Management, for example, has been heralded as an important and new approach to the problems of competitiveness and innovation confronting information-based organizations in the 'knowledge era'. Where is the impetus for this surge of interest in Knowledge Management and knowledge work? Here in this chapter we will describe the context and problems that have generated this widespread recognition of the importance of managing knowledge and knowledge work in contemporary organizations. This context includes at least three main areas:

● The restructuring of work in the 'Information Age' or 'Knowledge Era'
● Shifts in sources of wealth creation in society
● The centrality of knowledge work and knowledge workers

Looking at this wider context and considering how it has changed since the days of Scientific Management provides a historically grounded understanding of the challenges facing management in the new knowledge-based organization.

We start this chapter, however, by developing a rudimentary understanding of knowledge from frameworks that have been developed in the 1990s and we relate types of knowledge to practices of knowing. We are not going to engage here in a deep philosophical debate about the precise nature of knowledge. Instead, we intend to briefly outline some of the frameworks that have been developed in the field of organizational theory and strategy which help inform our understanding of what it is that firms are trying to do when they claim to be 'managing knowledge'.

What is knowledge?

It is evident from the literature that 'knowledge' is an intrinsically ambiguous and equivocal term. As a useful starting point it is important to consider the distinctions that can be made between information and knowledge. Nonaka (1994), for example, emphasizes that it is the semantic aspects of information that create knowledge, that is, it is the way in which information is conveyed and the meaning that the individual infers from the information that create knowledge. What an individual infers from information is related to their cognitive capacity and interpretive schema. It is reasonable therefore to suggest that different people may infer different things from the same information, which could lead to the creation of new and different knowledge. It is also evident that information and knowledge are distinguishable and information, whilst heavily context-dependent, contributes to the creation of knowledge and vice versa.

Definitions and debates about the nature of knowledge have appeared in philosophical literature since the classical Greek period. Whilst in this book we are focusing on managing knowledge within contemporary organizations, it is interesting to note that much of the recent literature about knowledge and managing knowledge is grounded in Polanyi's (1962) work, which draws on Plato's original definition of knowledge as 'justified true belief'. Knowledge as justified true belief is, however, an individual, somewhat cognitive definition that does not translate particularly well to the level of the organization. For example, in an organizational context beliefs may be false and the truth may not be believed. Furthermore, the truthfulness of something can only be judged in relation to personal belief (Nonaka, 1994) and therefore someone could be provided with full justification for something and still choose not to believe it. These definitional problems draw our attention to the highly contextual, situated nature of knowledge that needs to be addressed when attempting to manage knowledge within organizations. This theme will be revisited throughout this book.

Types of knowledge – the structural perspective

If we adopt a structuralist perspective on knowledge, one that perceives knowledge as a discrete, objective, largely cognitive entity, then there are basically two types of knowledge – tacit and explicit knowledge. Tacit knowledge resides *within* the individual, known but extremely difficult or in some cases impossible to articulate or communicate adequately. Polanyi (1962) suggests, for example, that we know more than we can articulate. Tacit knowledge is often referred to as 'know-how'. It resides in our heads and in our practical skills and actions. For example, many of us 'know' how to ride a bike. However, explaining or writing down for someone else exactly *how* to ride a bike would be extremely problematic. If we actually attempted to do this and a novice tried to follow our instructions they would inevitably fall off the bike. It is in fact the individual's experience of learning to ride a bike for themselves that leads to that individual possessing the knowledge of (or knowing) how to ride a bike. Explicit knowledge, on the other hand, can be readily codified and communicated to others.

If we adopt this distinction then tacit knowledge is distinguishable from explicit knowledge in terms of its relative incommunicability. Other researchers (Boisot, 1995; Nahapiet and Ghoshal, 1998) have, however, suggested that tacitness can be considered to be a variable where the degree of tacitness is a function of the extent to which knowledge can be communicated. These debates around types of knowledge highlight in fact that tacit and explicit knowledge are mutually constituted (Tsoukas, 1996). If we reconsider the bike-riding example, we can see that in order for a novice to be able to ride a bike it would be a useful starting point for the novice to receive some instructions (explicit knowledge) from someone else who knows how to ride a bike. By combining this explicit knowledge with the tacit knowledge or 'know-how' only the novice possesses with regard to balance, hand–eye co-ordination and so on, the novice in fact develops knowledge (creates new tacit and explicit knowledge) of how to ride a bike.

Frameworks for understanding different types of knowledge

If we adopt the structuralist perspective on knowledge, that is, that knowledge is something that people (and organizations) possess (Cook and Brown, 1999), there are a number of frameworks that have been developed recently that help us to understand what types of knowledge are involved in processes of knowledge creation and under what organizational conditions different types of knowledge are applied and created.

Nonaka (1994), Spender (1996, 1998) and Blackler (1995) have all developed frameworks which attempt to:

● Explain the process by which knowledge is created and the way in which knowledge is used within an organization (see Nonaka, 1994; Spender, 1998)

● Map shifts over time in organizing and dominant forms of organizational knowledge at the macro level (see Blackler, 1995)

We shall take each of these frameworks in turn.

(i)   Nonaka's framework (1994)

Nonaka identifies four different processes through which knowledge is created: tacit/tacit through a process of socialization; tacit/explicit through a process of externalization; explicit/tacit through a process of internalization; and explicit/explicit through a process of combination. Because Nonaka believes that individual cognition plays an important part in knowledge creation, he suggests that knowledge creation can only occur at the level of the individual. If we take the socialization process, for example, individuals interacting with others in a social (organizational) context create new tacit knowledge. If we accept that knowledge creation occurs at the level of the individual then even explicit codified knowledge may mean something qualitatively different to different people, dependent on what those individuals might infer from that explicit knowledge. Therefore, according to Nonaka, organizational knowledge cannot exist that has the same meaning to everyone. This emphasis on knowledge existing only at the individual level is a fundamental difference between Nonaka's framework and the other frameworks that are discussed in this chapter. This is not to suggest, however, that organizations and management in particular do not have a role to play in knowledge creation. Nonaka stresses that creative individuals need to be supported in their endeavours and management needs to provide the necessary context for such individuals to share and create knowledge. This theme is addressed in Chapter 2.

(ii) Spender's framework (1996, 1998)

Spender's framework differs from Nonaka's in that Spender highlights an important distinction between individual and social knowledge. His framework provides a 'contrast between the explicit knowledge that individuals feel they possess and the collective knowledge on which this explicit knowledge actually stands, and the interaction of the two' (Spender, 1998; p. 238).

Spender suggests that individual explicit knowledge and social (organizational) knowledge are qualitatively different but there could be some common agreement across members of an organization as to what constitutes explicit organizational knowledge. Spender therefore highlights four different types of knowledge (i) individual/explicit (conscious); (ii) individual/implicit (automatic); (iii) social/explicit (objectified); and (iv) social/implicit (collective). Spender suggests that all four different types of knowledge interact and are created within organizations. This framework therefore acknowledges that forms of social knowledge do exist that in themselves are created and understood (perhaps differently) by individuals within the organization and, in addition, serve to interact with individual types of knowledge to create new knowledge at both the individual and organizational level.

Strategically, Spender argues, collective knowledge is the most useful because this is a type of knowledge that other firms would find difficult to understand and imitate. The idea supports the view that a firm's core competencies are a crucial strategic resource in today's turbulent and complex business environment. Spender's notion of collective knowledge, highly situated and embedded within the organization, also mirrors Brown and Duguid's (1991) concept of 'communities of practice'. These are groups of individuals who regularly work together, developing collective knowledge and shared 'sense-making' (Weick, 1979) of what the 'community' does, how it does it and its relationship with other 'communities'. The idea of communities of practice and the implications for managing knowledge within communities of practice are discussed in Chapter 6.

What this framework does not highlight, however, which Nonaka's framework makes explicit, are the processes that promote the creation of these four different types of knowledge. Therefore Nonaka's framework, whilst not acknowledging that organizational knowledge might exist, is useful for developing our understanding of the processes through which different types of individual knowledge are created.

(iii) Blackler's framework (1995)

Blackler suggests that there are in fact five types of knowledge that can exist in organizations – embrained, embodied, encultured, embedded and encoded knowledge:

> Embrained knowledge is knowledge that is dependent on conceptual skills and cognitive abilities. Embodied knowledge is action oriented and is only partly explicit. Encultured knowledge refers to the process of achieving shared understanding, through the development of an organizational culture. Embedded knowledge is knowledge that resides in systemic routines. It can be analysed by considering the relationships between technologies, roles, procedures and emergent routines. Finally, encoded knowledge is information conveyed by signs and symbols either in manual or electronically transmitted form. (Blackler, 1995, pp. 1024–5)

Blackler's framework suggests that different types of knowledge exist at either the individual or collective level. For example, embrained knowledge equates to Nonaka's notion of tacit knowledge and encultured knowledge equates to Spender's collective (social/implicit) knowledge. Embedded knowledge could be either tacit or explicit knowledge. For example, routines may be formal articulated policy and procedures or informal routines that are tacitly known by everyone in the firm. What Blackler tries to illustrate with his framework, which distinguishes this framework from the others we have considered here, is that different types of knowledge dominate in different types of organizations. For example, he suggests that a highly bureaucratized organization will rely predominantly on knowledge embedded in organizational routines and rules. More dynamic and innovative firms will rely on either encultured knowledge if they are a communication-intensive firm or embrained knowledge if they are primarily dependent on the knowledge, skills and expertise of the individual's employed. This is typical in knowledge-intensive firms which are described in Chapter 2. Blackler's framework is therefore a useful starting point when considering the problems of managing knowledge because it suggests that the type of knowledge that dominates within the firm should to some extent influence the way in which knowledge is managed in the firm. The case studies presented throughout this book will illustrate this important idea.

The relationship between knowing and knowledge – the process perspective

All of these frameworks provide a preliminary answer to the question 'What is knowledge?' However, they are all rooted in the structuralist perspective. Recently some researchers have begun to adopt a process perspective on knowledge, suggesting that in order to understand what knowledge is we should focus our attention on processes or practices of knowing. The process perspective emphasizes that knowledge is socially constructed, that is, knowledge is inherently social and embedded in practice. Spender recognized the limitations of his own framework when he stated:

> Knowledge comprises theoretical statements whose meanings and practical implications depend on their use and on the framework in which they are deployed . . . These days knowledge is less about truth and reason and more about the practice of intervening knowledgeably and purposefully in the world. (Spender, 1996; p. 64)

Spender's definition of knowledge is therefore actually grounded in a processual perspective. It avoids the notion of truth and instead emphasizes context and defines knowledge in dynamic terms, regarding it as a practice of doing or *knowing* rather than something static or objective – *knowledge* which a person possesses. This definition suggests that the process of knowing is as important as knowledge itself. Therefore processes of knowing and knowledge are inextricably linked. As Cook and Brown more recently have highlighted:

> Individuals and groups clearly make use of knowledge, both explicit and tacit, in what they do; but not everything they know how to do, we argue, is explicable solely in terms of the knowledge they possess. We believe that . . . individual and group action requires us to speak about both knowledge used in action and knowing as part of the action. (Cook and Brown, 1999, p. 382)

A substantial part of individuals' tacit knowledge will always remains tacit, resistant to articulation or codification. This tacit knowledge only exists as conscious experience and behaviour which are rooted and manifest in processes of knowing and action. This book aims to address the way in which knowledge can be managed in organizations. In so doing our aim is to focus more upon practices of knowing and ways in which these practices might be managed rather than the management of knowledge as a discrete, objective entity. Whilst in Chapter 5 we do address the role of information and communication technologies in managing knowledge, the emphasis throughout is on managing knowledge through managing people and the interaction between people.

Table 1.1   The structural and processual perspectives compared

Structural perspective	Processual perspective
Knowledge is a discrete cognitive entity that people and organizations possess	Knowledge is rooted in practice, action and social relationships
Knowledge is objective and static	Knowledge is dynamic – the process of knowing is as important as knowledge
Knowledge exists at the individual and collective level	Knowledge exists through the interplay between the individual and the collective level
Different types of knowledge dominate in particular types of organization	Organizations will be characterized by different types of knowledge and practices of knowing
Knowledge is created via specific social processes	Knowing occurs via social processes

The case studies and role-play presented in Chapter 7 serve to illustrate good and bad practice in this respect. Table 1.1 distinguishes between the structuralist and processual perspectives on knowledge.

In the next section, we develop a historical grounding of firms' attempts to manage knowledge in organizations. We initially consider the context for the development of Scientific Management. We then focus on the underlying principles of Scientific Management with particular reference to their relationship with managing knowledge. We then consider how these principles were applied to the development of the production line, which led to the embodiment of knowledge in machines leading to the rise of the mass production process. Finally, in developing this historical account we consider the relationship between the underlying principles of Scientific Management and the contemporary discourse of Knowledge Management.

The context for and underlying principles of Scientific Management

The relationship between knowledge, work and wealth creation and hence the importance of managing knowledge has long been recognized. As long ago as 1890 Alfred Marshall suggested that knowledge was the most powerful engine of production. Whilst then this relationship was recognized, it was not really until the advent of Scientific Management at the beginning of the twentieth century that firms began to explore how to manage knowledge of work processes. Frederick Winslow Taylor developed the principles of Scientific Management and published them in 1911. This new approach to the organization of work – in particular, manual work – had a very dramatic and profound effect on the management and organization of work at this time, many features of which have endured to the present day. Some sectors such as the fast food and customer service (call centre) sectors still, to a significant extent, adopt the principles of Scientific Management for the organization of major work processes. What was the context then for the development of Scientific Management?

It was at the turn of the twentieth century that a number of countries including the United States were undergoing significant industrialization and experiencing the rise of the mass production system. Managers of large organizations at this time were grappling with the problems of controlling production carried out by a largely untrained workforce that was made up of immigrants from Europe or native American workers who had come from the agricultural regions of the USA. These workers were generally unskilled in factory work, many had little understanding of the English language and the majority had little or no experience of working in a factory environment.

Not only was the workforce largely inexperienced and untrained, but Taylor also believed that the existing system of production was highly inefficient for another important reason. In principle, groups of workers were supervised; however, in practice it was largely left to the groups of workers themselves to plan and carry out work tasks as they saw fit. Hence, the knowledge concerning the way work should be planned and carried out only resided within 'the head and the hands' of the workers. Effectively, management did not have control of this knowledge of work processes. This, Taylor suggested, led almost naturally to systematic soldiering – the deliberate slow pacing of work and restriction of output because, Taylor believed, it was not in workers' interests to work efficiently when there was no financial motive to do so.

Taylor was working as a supervisor at the Midvale Steel Company at this time. To overcome these problems and thus boost efficiency, productivity and discipline, Taylor believed work processes should be organized differently with an emphasis on *standardization*. Taylor argued that it should be the task of engineer managers to observe work processes and then determine the organization and planning of the work process in the most efficient manner possible. This would involve standardizing work processes into tasks which could be divided up into highly prescribed, simple sub-tasks. Workers would therefore no longer be responsible for planning the organization of work; instead they would only be required to carry out these simple, standardized sub-tasks in an efficient manner. Hence, an underlying principle of Scientific Management is the separation of the planning of work and the execution of work, the idea here being that the knowledge required to plan work processes should be developed and managed by those supervising the major work tasks so that work could be carried out as efficiently (and therefore productively) as possible.

Taylor recognized that within the existing system of work organization, the knowledge required to carry out work tasks resided in the 'head and the hands' of the workers. However, engineer managers could, Taylor believed, effectively extract and capture the knowledge required to standardize work processes by observation so that these could be carried out in the most efficient manner possible. During the process of determining the most efficient way to conduct the work process these engineer managers were in fact attempting to manage the knowledge of the work process.

The 'one best way' and worker selection

In determining the most efficient or 'one best way' to accomplish tasks, the notion of standardization was emphasized. Work processes were to be broken down into standardized, basic tasks that were simple to perform. Workers could then be selected 'scientifically' (Taylor, 1911) according to the task(s) they were to perform. This approach to selection emphasized suitability (generally premised on physical build) rather than acceptability (workers up to this point had tended to find work through friends and acquaintances). Appropriate workers could then be trained to carry out their allotted tasks in the most efficient way possible. Importantly, Taylor adopted an instrumental view of human nature, believing that workers were purely rational, economic beings directly motivated by monetary incentives. He therefore believed that if firms adopted the principles of Scientific Management, management–labour relations could actually be improved because workers would have the opportunity to earn more (but not excessively more) money in return for the efficiency gains that were created.

Scientific Management – the first studies

Having developed these underlying principles at the Midvale Steel Company, Taylor carried out some of his first studies around 1898 at the Bethlehem Steel Corporation in the USA, where he was employed as a management consultant to apply his ideas to the handling of pig-iron. At the start of his studies, 75 men were loading an average of twelve and a half tons per man per day. Taylor selected a Dutch labourer called Schmidt who he believed was a simple but 'high-priced' man – one who placed a high value on money for his experiments. Schmidt followed Taylor's simple but detailed instructions regarding when to load the pig-iron and walk and when to sit and rest with no interaction with other workers. By following these instructions specifically, Schmidt increased his output to 47½ tons per day. He was able to maintain this output for three years of studies and received a 60 per cent increase in wages compared to the other men he worked alongside. Other workers were selected to be trained to carry out the work in this way; however, perhaps not surprisingly, only one in eight were physically capable of handling this amount of pig-iron (Taylor, 1911).

Following the impressive results at the Bethlehem Corporation, other firms were keen to apply Scientific Management principles. However, the improvements in productivity were accompanied by widespread hostile reactions from workers. Work organized along Scientific Management principles was inherently boring, and fragmented because fundamentally it required the application of little or no skill or knowledge. In addition, in many firms management often chose to introduce the principles selectively in order to reduce the number of workers required and actually cut wages. This selective approach to the adoption of Scientific Management principles often led to strikes and the Federation of Labor rapidly developed vehement opposition to Scientific Management. This led to the establishment in 1911 of a House of Representatives Committee to investigate Taylor's methods. In 1912, the Committee concluded that Scientific Management did provide useful techniques for the management and organization of work. However, because of continued hostility and significant concerns about the potential for industrial unrest in arms factories in wartime, Congress banned the adoption of the approach in the defence industry.

The Ford mass production system

This did not however deter Henry Ford from applying the principles of Scientific Management in the development of the production line for cars. Ford started by applying the principles of work rationalization – allocating simple tasks to each worker to promote efficiency. At the turn of the century highly skilled craftsmen had been employed to build cars using hand–crafted parts that had been manufactured on general-purpose machines. These workers had developed their craft skills through an apprenticeship system lasting several years. However, with the introduction of Scientific Management principles and rationalization at the Ford automotive plant, single-purpose machines were introduced on which anyone could be easily trained to produce standardized parts. The knowledge and many of the skills required to build a car had in effect been *embodied* in the machine. Ford developed these machines again primarily by observation – by filming the work process of the skilled craftsmen. Skilled craftsmen were no longer needed and a productive division of labour was achieved. All that was needed were assemblers to carry out simple assembly tasks.

Despite these dramatic changes in the organization of work, the workers still controlled the speed of production. It was not therefore until Ford developed the concept of the production line – where the car moved past the men, instead of men moving past the car – that Ford was able to achieve what he considered to be total control of the production process. The principles and application of Scientific Management as exemplified in the development of the production line were therefore fundamentally about extracting and capturing the knowledge of workers and using it to develop standard work practices, procedures and performance targets against which workers could be judged and rewarded. In addition, by embodying the knowledge required to perform tasks in machines, mass production processes were rendered efficient.

Whilst the approach naturally led to worker dissatisfaction and high absenteeism as boredom and fatigue set in, Taylor and others like Ford believed that the offer of higher wages would compensate. Ultimately, however, there were significant problems with the quality of the goods produced. Worker fatigue often led to mistakes in the production process and there also continued to be significant industrial unrest. The Human Relations school led by the pioneering work of Elton Mayo at the Hawthorne plant of the Western Electric Company led to the development of different approaches to the organization of work which was characterized by group work and group responsibility for work tasks. The Human Relations approach to work organization recognized that workers are motivated by more than just pay. Elton Mayo demonstrated that workers have social needs and a motivational requirement to interact with others. Workers are not motivated solely by tangible rewards such as money. They are also motivated by intangible rewards such as job satisfaction and recognition of a job well-done.

Scientific Management principles applied in contemporary organizations

Despite the evident problems associated with Scientific Management, we have not witnessed the complete demise of a Taylorist approach to work organization. The underlying principles are still applied within and across sectors, particularly where productive efficiency and cost minimization are the basis on which the firm competes. The problems around quality when using this approach to the organization of work, whether it be quality of product or, increasingly, quality of services, are now addressed technologically. With recent technological advancements contemporary firms that still choose to employ Scientific Management principles tend to cope with the quality problems by building surveillance and quality control into the core technologies that are used by workers (Sewell and Wilkinson, 1992). For example, service call centres across a range of sectors use sophisticated information technology to monitor the number of calls taken by workers and the content of the service interaction between caller and worker.

This description of the emergence and rise of scientific Management reinforces the notion that managing knowledge of work processes has been considered to be of fundamental, strategic importance to firms operating in competitive environments since the turn of the twentieth century.

Restructuring work and occupations in the 'Information Age'

Whilst there has always been a recognition that managing knowledge is important in organizations, more recently there has been a resurgence in this idea. Managing knowledge is now recognized as an important strategic issue and the idea has gained significant momentum across organizations regardless of the sectors in which they operate. This resurgence in interest can be located in wider debates about the organization of work, the sources of wealth creation in contemporary society and the management of knowledge workers. These include specific concerns with issues such as: the learning organization; the strategic management of core competencies; the management of research and development; the nature of knowledge-based organizations and knowledge-intensive firms; Knowledge Management; and the value of intellectual and social capital. The specific labels used come and go but by examining the wider context surrounding attention to these issues, we are able to see that they are sending out similar signals about the fundamental problems confronting organizations in the twenty-first century. The inescapable conclusion is that specific terms (for example, Knowledge Management) will eventually fade away to be replaced by another set of 'buzzwords'. For example, a review of the Knowledge Management literature on the ABI/Inform database which holds articles from more than 1500 journals indicates that interest in Knowledge Management (represented by total number of articles in journals) peaked in 1999. By 2000 the number of article had almost halved to 289 from a peak in 1999 of 462. The emergence and demise of these management fads is itself however a testimony to the phenomena which they seek to address, that is, the growing knowledge-intensity of business, the impact of information and communication technology (ICT) on patterns of work and relationships, and the importance of change and innovation for organizations facing increasingly turbulent environments. These factors are not the product of fashion but of history – a convergent set of forces which are unleashing fundamental patterns of change on advanced industrial economies.

These forces have been examined in a number of different studies looking at patterns of industrial, occupational and organizational change. In 1969, Drucker emphasized that knowledge had become the crucial resource of the economy. Work by Daniel Bell (1973) also described the potential for the development of a post-industrial society dominated by knowledge workers operating in knowledge-intensive firms. It would be a society organized around knowledge for the purpose of economic development, social control and institutional innovation and change. More recent work by Drucker (1988), Gibbons *et al.* (1994) and Manuel Castells (1996) has indicated the extent of such changes in advanced economies since the days when Scientific Management principles were first introduced into organizations at the turn of the twentieth century. What all of this work highlights are important shifts in industrial society, in particular a significant decline of traditional manual trades and blue-collar work and the growing importance of the emergence of knowledge work across occupations. As discussed earlier this is work which is relatively unstructured and which involves the manipulation of symbols through the use of a range of tools, including ICT systems. The characteristic feature of such work is not the industrial context or the specific skills being applied so much as the centrality of various kinds of knowledge in the work process of these groups. For knowledge workers, knowledge is simultaneously an input, medium and output for their work. This is perhaps most apparent in professional and specialist service occupations (Frenkel *et al.*, 1995). However, as emphasized earlier, the centrality of knowledge work cuts right across occupational groupings. Thus the knowledge economy is one where economic value is found more in the intangibles, such as new ideas, software, services and relationships, and less in tangibles, like physical products, tons of steel or acres of land.

These commentators also note how the convergence of computing and communications technology has led to a new generation of *information* technologies – with the emphasis on information, not just technology – that have major impacts on the structuring of work and occupations. These changes have been characterized by a variety of terms – the 'Post-Industrial Era', the 'Information Age', the 'Knowledge Society' and the 'Knowledge Economy'. These terms focus on the importance of knowledge as the defining characteristic of this new age. Organizations, it is argued, will have little choice but to become knowledge-based. Drucker captures this trend in his observation that 'as advanced technology becomes more and more prevalent, we have to engage in analysis and diagnosis – that is, in information – even more intensively or risk being swamped by the data we generate' (1988, p. 46).

Changing organizational structures

A significant impact of these changes is visible changes in organization structures. Organizations, it is argued, are shifting away from the traditional command and control structures of Scientific Management and the classic bureaucracies of Weber towards flatter, decentralized structures and more flexible, fluid, networked, integrated processes. If we look at the high-technology sector today, the emerging organizational system within this sector tends to resemble a 'federation' or a 'constellation' of business units that are interdependent, relying on one another for critical skills and knowledge. If we take, for example, Apple Computers:

> Its main line units – although varying in size, scope, and style – have a peer-to-peer relationship with one another and with the center. The heads of the line units – Apple Products, Apple USA, Apple Europe, and Apple Pacific – are represented on its top management team together with the leaders of corporate functions – finance, human resources, and legal and administrative services. Members of the different units collectively participate in setting and implementing the corporate direction: worldwide meetings (held twice a year) of the top 400 or so executives provide focussed opportunities for discussing critical challenges; and the extensive movement of people between the units ensures that personal relationships are forged to enhance inter-unit cooperation. (Bahrami, 1998, p. 189)

Networked organizations (networks of strategic alliances sometimes referred to as polycentric organizations) and virtual modes of organizing, whereby workers do not have a physical place of work but instead work remotely from home using information and communication technologies, illustrate the extent to which organizational structures have evolved.

This restructuring of organizations is facilitated and promoted by the use of ever more sophisticated information and communication technologies (ICTs) that break down traditional boundaries of time and space. At the same time, these new technologies and structures create their own problems. Information technology is debureaucratizing, decentralizing but also depersonalizing. It can 'informate' or upskill workers (Zuboff, 1988) but also extends the possibilities for surveillance and control as described earlier. Flatter structures and teamwork improve task cooperation but also undermine the acquisition and retention of deeper forms of knowledge and expertise. Whole layers of middle management expertise were lost, for example, through the introduction in the early 1990s of business process reengineering (BPR) initiatives, a fact that only became apparent as the concept and approach to organization redesign became widely applied throughout organizations in the United States and Europe. Whilst BPR was acknowledged by many as an effective approach for cutting costs and increasing efficiency by the removal of functional divisions within firms and the introduction of horizontal process teams, the implications of the loss of knowledge to the organization were simply not recognized initially. Organizations only discovered that they had 'lost' valuable knowledge when the knowledge required for critical organizational processes could no longer be located within the organization. For example, the senior management team responsible for a shipyard in the north of England believed they had successfully reengineered organizational processes leading to significant efficiency improvements in the time needed to build a ship, until it came to launching the newly built ship. Only then did the realization dawn on senior management that the knowledge required to launch a ship had in fact been lost with the downsizing that had taken place as part of the reengineering programme. It has been suggested in fact that one of the reasons Knowledge Management initiatives became so popular in the late 1990s was because they were seen as an antidote to the knowledge loss firms had experienced following the successful implementation of BPR programmes in the mid-1990s.

As businesses are stretched across time and space, reorganized along process or product lines and restructured around virtual teams and networks, they also inevitably lose opportunities for casual sharing of knowledge and learning induced by physical proximity. As Prusak puts it (1997): 'If the water cooler was a font of useful knowledge in the traditional firm, what constitutes a virtual one' (p. xiii). In other words, the importance of managing knowledge can be seen as a response to some of the profound organizational problems posed by IT systems and flatter structures in information-based organizations.

Knowledge Management

A reflection of this recognition of the importance of knowledge in contemporary organizations has been a surge of interest at the end of the 1990s in Knowledge Management practices. These are many and varied in nature but tend to be focused on improving the ways in which firms facing highly turbulent environments can mobilize their knowledge base (or leverage their knowledge 'assets') in order to ensure continuous innovation. The emphasis in Knowledge Management is on identifying, extracting and capturing the 'knowledge assets' of the firm so that they can be both fully exploited and fully protected as a source of competitive advantage. For example, Dow Chemical, which earns a high income through technology licensing, replaced a data archive described as 'a disorganized mess of intellectual capital' with a widely accessible database to keep track of their many patents. These systems and processes have been introduced to exploit the company's intellectual or knowledge assets. The use and limitations of information and communication technologies for managing knowledge are discussed in detail in Chapter 5.

It can be argued therefore that managing knowledge, which recently has been commodified under the rubric term of 'Knowledge Management', is really nothing new. The underlying aim of Knowledge Management is fundamentally the same as the underlying themes of Scientific Management – to capture the knowledge that resides in 'the heads and the hands' of the workers. One of the reasons that managing knowledge has more recently come to the fore in organizations is the restructuring of work and organizations in an 'Information Age'. However, the task of extracting and capturing the knowledge of work processes 'held' in the heads of workers has become far more complex as traditional forms of work have gradually been replaced by what is referred to as knowledge work. The rise in knowledge work and corresponding decline in more traditional forms of work can be related to shifts in the major sources of wealth creation.

Shifts in major sources of wealth creation in society

Peter Drucker claims the credit for coining the notion of 'knowledge work', which he contrasted with more traditional forms of work such as service work and manual work. He offers a historical account of the relationship between knowledge and wealth creation. The period of industrial development from the eighteenth through to the early twentieth century, he argues, saw a shift in the dominant ways in which wealth was created. This shift was away from knowledge being applied to tools, processes and products (for example, through the development of technologies, patents and craft skills in the pre-industrial era), and towards knowledge being applied to human work (for example, through work analysis and time–motion studies at the turn of the twentieth century in the form of Scientific Management). Now, as we turn to the post-industrial or knowledge economy with the decline of manual work, knowledge displaces capital as the driver of competitive performance. Productivity is increasingly reliant on knowledge being applied to knowledge itself in order to create new knowledge relevant for innovation – that is, on knowledge work. In other words, wealth creation in contemporary society is increasingly dependent on innovation through the application and development of new knowledge to existing knowledge and, therefore, on the contribution of know-ledge workers to this process.

This is not to say that knowledge was ever insignificant in industrial development. As seen, ever since the Industrial Revolution and the onset of Scientific Management, science and technology have played a crucial role in industrial change. What is distinctive about the current period, however, is the extent to which knowledge is free from the old material, physical and institutional constraints. Knowledge is no longer necessarily tied to physical equipment and machinery as it was with the development of the production line. Nowadays knowledge now acts upon itself in an accelerating spiral of innovation and change. Castells summarizes the shift as follows:

> What characterises the current technological revolution is not the centrality of knowledge and information but the application of such knowledge and information to knowledge generation and information processing/communication devices, in a cumulative feedback loop between innovation and the uses of innovation ... New information technologies are not simply tools to be applied but processes to be developed. Users and doers may become the same ... For the first time in history, the human mind is a direct productive force, not just a decisive element of a production system. (Castells, 1996, p. 32)

This is, in short, not simply a matter of the increased application of know-ledge but of a change in the way knowledge itself is produced. Gibbons *et al.* (1994) highlight this change in the mode of knowledge production by con-trasting what they refer to as conventional Mode 1 model of knowledge production, where knowledge is produced in ivory-tower, disciplinary-based institutions such as the professions, with the new model (Mode 2) in which knowledge is transdisciplinary and actually produced at the points of applica-tion. The different dimensions of these modes of knowledge production are summarized in Table 1.2.

This shift towards Mode 2 knowledge production has interesting implications for traditional professional work which to date has largely been characterized by Mode 1 knowledge production and leads to a questioning of the future role of traditional professions in society. This is beyond the scope of this text but if we are witnessing a fundamental shift towards Mode 2 knowledge production we may also begin to witness a fundamental restructuring of the traditional professions in the near future.

Table 1.2   Mode 1 and Mode 2 knowledge production

Mode 1 knowledge production	Mode 2 knowledge production
Problems defined by academic and professional communities	Knowledge produced in context of application
Disciplinary knowledge	Transdisciplinary knowledge
Homogeneity	Heterogeneity
Hierarchical and stable organizations	Heterarchical and transient organizations
Quality control by the 'invisible college'	Socially accountable and reflexive

Source: Adapted from Gibbons *et al.* (1994).

The extent of this change in the scope of knowledge production is also not confined to those sectors typically labelled knowledge-intensive. As Prusak notes:

> This shift is more apparent in research labs, consulting firms and software vendors, but as all products are increasingly 'smart' and flexible production processes need to process higher levels of information about changing customer requirements, delivery times, and so on it arguably applies right across the board. Firms describing themselves as in the knowledge business range from BP which drills for oil to Senco which makes nails. (Prusak, 1997, p. xv)

The centrality of knowledge work and specialist knowledge workers

All work requires the application and use of some knowledge, however simple the task, and we have argued that the rise of knowledge work cuts across occupational groupings. However, often the term 'knowledge work' tends to be used to refer to specific occupations which are 'characterized by an emphasis on theoretical knowledge, creativity and use of analytical and social skills' (Frenkel *et al.*, 1995, p. 773). 'Knowledge work' in these terms encompasses both what is traditionally referred to as professional work, such as accountancy, scientific and legal work, and more contemporary types of work, such as consultancy, software development, advertising and public relations. Crucially this type of knowledge work does not lend itself particularly well to knowledge capture and standardization because there is a significant reliance on the application of both explicit and tacit knowledge. Therefore those engaged in these types of work need to be left to make their own decisions about what and how to do their work. The nature of the work they conduct demands autonomy over the major work processes. These knowledge workers are characterized as individuals with high levels of education and specialist skills combined with the ability to apply these skills to identify and solve problems.

What is significant about these types of knowledge workers is that unlike earlier kinds of workers, knowledge workers 'own' the organization's primary means of production – that is, knowledge. In Taylor's time the knowledge used by workers in their daily tasks was relatively easily 'extracted' – primarily by observation because the workers were engaged in relatively simple manual tasks. Their knowledge was not necessarily the direct productive force of the firm. Nowadays the management of knowledge workers assumes greater importance for sustaining productivity than the management of machines, technologies or work processes. This is consistent with other writers (for example, Earl, 1996) who present the management of knowledge and not information or data as the main challenge for firms in contemporary society. Such workers resist the command and control structure of Taylorist times and demand a new form of management and organization more reminiscent of the orchestra than the traditional manufacturing firm. Like musicians, Drucker sees such employees exploring outlets for their creative abilities, seeking interesting challenges, enjoying the stimulation of working with other specialists. This, he argues, poses new challenges for management in knowledge-based organizations in terms of:

● Developing rewards, recognition and career opportunities
● Giving an organization of specialists a common vision
● Devising a management structure for coordinating tasks and task teams
● Ensuring the supply and skills of top management people

These issues will be dealt with specifically in Chapters 2 and 4 where the management of knowledge workers is addressed.

Conclusions

In this chapter the term 'knowledge' has been broadly defined. Both the structural and processual perspectives on knowledge have been presented. Three different frameworks for understanding different types of knowledge and the way in which knowledge is created have been discussed. The chapter went on to consider the context for and underlying principles of Scientific Management as developed by Frederick Winslow Taylor at the start of the twentieth century. These principles were refined and subsequently used in the development of the Ford mass production system. Similarities were drawn between the underlying principles of Scientific Management and firms' current preoccupation with managing knowledge and leveraging knowledge assets. A number of reasons were given as to why managing knowledge in organizations is now considered to be of critical strategic importance. These included the restructuring of work and occupations in the 'Information Age';

changing organizational structures; the development of sophisticated ICTs; and fundamental shifts in the major sources of wealth creation in society. This led on to an introductory discussion as to why knowledge workers and knowledge work are now considered to be central within and across all industrial sectors.

Although the terms 'knowledge work' and 'knowledge worker' have been developed and refined by other writers subsequently, the main themes of Drucker's analysis continue to influence the debate. Knowledge work cuts across occupations and is qualitatively different from some of the traditional, manual occupations of the old industrial economy. The traditional bureaucratic command and control structure will have to be jettisoned in favour of more flexible team- and project-based management approaches. Managers will need to abandon traditional styles and structures and act more like conductors who coordinate the activities of knowledge workers. Managing knowledge within the knowledge-based organization is, therefore, more about the management of the people employed in these firms, typically organized in teams, than about the development of information and communication technologies to extract and capture this knowledge. In the next chapter we focus on the management of knowledge-based or knowledge-intensive firms, as they tend to be referred to in the literature. The management of knowledge-intensive firms presents some distinctive challenges. Using the case of ScienceCo we explore the distinctive structural and cultural conditions that developed in the firm over time, which effectively promoted and facilitated knowledge work processes.

Summary of key learning points

■ Knowledge is highly contextual and situated – thus distinguishing it from information.

■ Different types of knowledge exist – the major distinctions being between tacit, explicit, individual and collective knowledge. Tacit knowledge is difficult or impossible to communicate; explicit knowledge is easy to communicate or codify.

■ The processual perspective suggests that knowledge is rooted in action and social practice – thus knowing is as important as knowledge.

■ The principles of Scientific Management were developed in response to inefficiencies in mass production systems that had begun to develop at the turn of the twentieth century. These include:

● The separation of planning and execution of work
● The determination of the 'one best way' of performing work processes
● Simplification and standardization of work tasks

■ The principles of Scientific Management are still applied today in sectors such as fast food and service (call) centres.

Summary of key learning points continued

- An industrial shift has occurred at the turn of the twenty-first century – to the 'Information Age' or 'Knowledge Era' – and we have witnessed a decline in traditional manual work in conjunction with the emergence of knowledge work across occupations.

- Organizational structures are shifting towards flatter, more decentralized structures.

- Coordination in these restructured firms is facilitated by sophisticated ICTs.

- BPR initiatives of the early 1990s led to the loss of organizational knowledge.

- Knowledge Management was seen as a means of coping with the developments and changes that were occurring in the late twentieth century.

- The underlying principle of Knowledge Management – to extract and harness the knowledge of the individual worker – is similar to the underlying theme of Scientific Management.

- There is a shift towards Mode 2 knowledge production as wealth creation increasingly relies on innovation.

- The management of knowledge workers is of strategic importance to firms competing on the basis of innovation.

References

Bahrami, H. (1998) The emerging flexible organization: perspectives from Silicon Valley. In C. Mabey, G. Salaman and J. Storey (eds) *Strategic Human Resource Management: A Reader*. London: Sage, pp. 185–99.

Bell, D. (1973) *The Coming of Post-industrial Society*. New York: Basic Books.

Blackler, F. (1995) Knowledge, knowledge work and organizations: an overview and interpretation. *Organization Studies*, 16(6): 1021–46.

Boisot, M. (1995) *Information Space: A Framework for Learning in Organizations, Institutions and Culture*. London: Blackwell.

Brown, J. and Duguid, P. (1991) Organizational learning and communities-of-practice: towards a unified view of working, learning and innovation. *Organization Science*, 2: 40–57.

Castells, M. (1996) *The Rise of Network Society*. Oxford: Blackwell.

Cook, S. and Brown, J. (1999) Bridging epistemologies: the generative dance between organizational knowledge and organizational knowing. *Organization Science*, 10(4): 381–400.

Drucker, P. (1969) *The Age of Discontinuity: Guidelines to our Changing Society*. London: Heinemann.

Drucker, P. (1988) The coming of the new organization. *Harvard Business Review*, Summer, 53–65.

Earl, M. (1996) *Information Management: The Organizational Dimension*. Oxford: Oxford University Press.

Frenkel, S., Korczynski, M., Donoghue, L. and Shire, K. (1995) Re-constituting work: trends towards knowledge work and info-normative control. *Work, Employment and Society*, 9(4): 773–96.

Gibbons, M., Limoges, C., Nowotny, H., Schwarzman, S., Scott, P. and Trow, M. (1994) *The New Production of Knowledge: The Dynamics of Science and Research in Contemporary Societies*. London: Sage.

Nahapiet, J. and Ghoshal, S. (1998) Social capital, intellectual capital, and the organizational advantage. *Academy of Management Review*, 23(2): 242–66.

Nonaka, I. (1994) A dynamic theory of organizational knowledge creation. *Organization Science*, 5(1): 14–37.

Polanyi, M. (1962) *Personal Knowledge*. Chicago, Ill.: University of Chicago Press.

Prusak, L. (1997) *Knowledge in Organizations*. Oxford: Butterworth-Heinemann.

Sewell, G. and Wilkinson, B. (1992) Someone to watch over me: surveillance, discipline and the just-in-time labour process. *Sociology*, 26: 271–89.

Spender, J.-C. (1996) Organisational knowledge, learning and memory: three concepts in search of a theory. *Journal of Organisational Change and Management*, 9(1): 63–78.

Spender, J.-C. (1998) Pluralist epistemology and the knowledge-based theory of the firm. *Organization*, 5(2): 233–56.

Taylor, F.W. (1911) *The Principles of Scientific Management*. New York: Harper.

Tsoukas, H. (1996) The firm as a distributed knowledge system: a social constructionist approach. *Strategic Management Journal*, 17 (Winter Special Issue): 11–25.

Weick, K. (1979) *The Social Psychology of Organizing*. Reading, Mass.: Addison-Wesley.

Zuboff, S. (1988) *In the Age of the Smart Machine*. Oxford: Heinemann.

2

Knowledge-intensive organizations

Learning outcomes

At the end of this chapter students will be able to:

- Understand the structural and cultural conditions relevant to the management of knowledge-intensive firms.

- Understand the different ways in which these structural and cultural conditions interact in support of knowledge work.

- Appreciate the importance of achieving a 'fit' between structure and cultural conditions for the successful management of knowledge workers.

Introduction

The first chapter introduced and explained the notion of 'knowledge work' and 'knowledge worker'. Here we focus our attention on firms where the majority or even the whole of the workforce consists of knowledge workers – hence the term 'knowledge-intensive firm' – and consider the distinctive management challenges posed by this particular type of 'expert' workforce. Knowledge workers are a relatively scarce resource within the labour market (Luker and Lyons, 1997). Their particular skills and expertise are not generally widely available in the labour force and in a post-industrial, global economy these skills are now much in demand. Knowledge workers therefore tend to have considerable choice and latitude regarding their place of work and therefore management needs to find ways of retaining an expert workforce.

Knowledge-intensive firms tend to be service-based organizations often competing in their respective sectors based on their ability to solve complex problems and provide solutions for clients. Law firms, accountancy practices, management consultancies, architectural practices, advertising and public relations agencies are all good examples of knowledge-intensive firms These firms tend to organize in distinctive ways in order to (a) attract and retain knowledge workers and (b) promote innovation and in some instances creativity. Sustaining an expert workforce is crucial if knowledge-intensive firms are to achieve competitive advantage in the long term. Knowledge-intensive firms do not rely on physical capital for competitive advantage; they rely on human capital – more precisely the intellectual capital of their expert workforce. It is the workforce in these firms that owns the means of production. Developing and, more importantly, *sustaining* an expert workforce is therefore possibly the most important strategic issue that confronts management within these firms.

In this chapter we are going to consider the structural and cultural conditions which, in combination, support the management of knowledge work and facilitate the recruitment and retention of knowledge workers. We illustrate the importance of the interaction and integration of these organizational elements through the case of ScienceCo. The distinctive organizational arrangements that developed in this firm, characterized by a strong yet ambiguous culture, serve as a useful example of the importance of creating an appropriate organizational environment for the conduct of knowledge work – particularly core work processes involve creativity and innovation.

Types of knowledge-intensive firm

The term 'knowledge worker' is used to encompass both professionals and others with either disciplined–based knowledge or more esoteric expertise and skills. It follows then that different types of firm employ different types of knowledge workers. Lowendahl (1997), for example, suggests that the crucial strategic difference between knowledge-intensive firms is the role of the professionals employed, that is, the characteristics of the resource base and the types of project targeted. She identifies three generic types of knowledge-intensive firm premised on the firm's strategic focus (see Table 2.1).

The term 'knowledge-intensive firm' is therefore used generically to encompass many different types of firm operating across sectors. Traditional professional service firms such as law and accountancy firms, for example, tend to be seen as a subset of knowledge-intensive firms and have existed as long as the organized professions. These types of firm generally organize along partnership lines with recognized codes of practice and clearly defined 'up-or-out' career paths. Despite the changing nature of some of the established professions (Anderson-Gough *et al.*, 2000), the majority of professional service firms still tend to be structured and organized along similar lines – often referred to as the professional bureaucracy (Mintzberg, 1979) or P2 form (Greenwood, Hinings and Brown, 1990). The professional bureaucracy is characterized by a hierarchical, partnership structure and well-defined career paths, and the management of this type of firm is already well-documented in the management literature.

Table 2.1   Types of knowledge-intensive firm

	Strategic focus	*Resources*	*Examples*
Client-based	Client relations	Individually controlled	Law and accountancy practices
Problem-solving	Creative problem-solving – innovation	Team-based	Advertising agencies, software development firms
Output-based	Adaptation of ready solutions	Controlled by the organization	Some large management consultancy firms

Source: Adapted from Lowendahl (1997).

Some knowledge-intensive firms, in particular large consultancy firms, are also often loosely referred to as professional service firms. The way in which the very large, global consultancies such as Accenture, Cap Gemini Ernst & Young and KPMG organize does tend to resemble that of the traditional professional service firm (although they tend to be output-rather than client-based). However, whilst these categories overlap, the features of knowledge-intensive firms are broader and, importantly, some of the features ascribed to the traditional professions are not necessarily apparent in knowledge-intensive firms. For example, codes of ethics, strong professional affiliations and specific educational entry requirements leading to restricted access need not, and do not, exist in many knowledge-intensive firms.

More contemporary forms of knowledge-intensive firms emerged in the latter part of the twentieth century including advertising and public relations agencies, software development companies, and other high-tech and specialist consultancy firms. Very recently we have seen an addition to this broad categorization with the emergence of the dot.coms. It is the issues around organizing and managing within knowledge-intensive firms operating in these contemporary sectors that are going to be specifically addressed here in this chapter.

Not surprisingly, a precise definition of a knowledge-intensive firm is elusive and it is clear from the term itself that it is a socially constructed, broad-ranging and yet quite ambiguous concept. Alvesson (2001) describes knowledge-intensive firms as 'companies where most work can be said to be of an intellec-tual nature and where well-educated, qualified employees form the major part of the workforce' (p. 863). However, the skills and expertise required to work in some types of knowledge-intensive firm are not necessarily acquired through formal education and qualifications. For example, many skills encompassed within the field of Information Technology (IT), such as soft-ware development, web page design and so on, are skills that are often largely self-taught and almost develop intuitively for those individuals with a particular interest in the IT field. In many instances it is simply not necessary to have a degree in computer science in order to become an expert software or web developer. It is therefore quite difficult to give a precise, relatively objective definition of a knowledge-intensive firm.

From a critical perspective, Alvesson (1993, 2001) suggests that knowledge-intensive firms might be more usefully seen purely as 'systems of persuasion' – relying primarily on their persuasive strategies (esoteric skills) rather than expert knowledge or skills *per se* to convince clients of their superior ability and expertise to satisfy client expectations. This might be the case in some contemporary service-based knowledge-intensive firms, for example, some advertising agencies, but certainly not all knowledge-intensive firms. Whilst there is a lack of clarity and a degree of ambiguity around the term, it is a useful one with which to encapsulate a broad range of firms operating across sectors in a post-industrial economy. It is also a particularly useful term to adopt when considering the distinctive needs of knowledge workers. What is indisputable is that many types of knowledge-intensive firm emerged in the late twentieth century and now constitute important industry sectors within a post-industrial economy. The ways in which they organize and the drivers for particular modes of organizing need to be addressed.

The distinctive characteristics of knowledge work and knowledge workers

1. Autonomy

Generally knowledge workers expect to have considerable autonomy in their work. The nature of the work, often characterized by creativity and problem-solving, demands autonomy. It is the knowledge workers themselves who tend to be the most appropriate people to decide how to initiate, plan, organize and coordinate their major work tasks. Unlike other kinds of workers, knowledge workers 'own' the organization's primary means of production – that is, knowledge. They therefore expect and demand autonomy and management is not really in a position to deny them. In addition, it is not always the case that management in knowledge-intensive firms shares the same levels of skills and expertise as the expert workforce they are trying to manage. Therefore, knowledge workers' demand for autonomy, in combination with an insufficient understanding of the work in some instances, means that management is not in a position to directly control or even manage knowledge-work processes. Therefore, it is perhaps more appropriate within a knowledge-work setting to suggest that management's role is to provide conditions that will *facilitate* knowledge work.

2. Co-location

Another distinguishing factor of the type of work conducted by knowledge workers is that there is often the need to work remote from the employing firm, typically physically located at the client firm. This physical co-location of knowledge workers can be an important management issue to be addressed. For example, client firms may well be inclined to offer permanent employment to knowledge workers who produce good results and who might prove to be a lot less expensive if employed directly by the client rather than on a consultancy basis. The client firm might therefore be in direct competition with the employing firm for the services of knowledge workers. Not only is management therefore required to focus on strategies to aid retention in relation to direct competitors to the firm, they must also consider the development of retention strategies in relation to their client firms.

In addition, typically knowledge workers organize in teams with more or less interdependence depending on the nature of the task. Physical co-location can therefore also be problematic for teamworking even when sophisticated information and communication technologies are made available. The complexity of knowledge working often makes face-to-face modes of interaction the only viable medium for communication at critical points in the process. Here then, management again is required to develop strategies and mechanisms that will facilitate the coordination and integration of knowledge work processes across the team without directly intervening in those processes.

3. 'Gold collar' workers

These distinctive characteristics of knowledge workers and knowledge work processes have led to the term 'gold collar' worker being applied to knowledge workers (Kelley, 1990). This term implies that these workers need to be managed carefully, provided with excellent working conditions and generally afforded exceptional, or at least very good, terms and conditions of employment. Terms of employment and human resource practices are encompassed within the employment relationship and will be addressed in detail in Chapter 4.

In addition to terms and conditions of employment, modes of organizing need to be developed which will be conducive to knowledge work and found favourable by knowledge workers. Management must therefore pay careful attention to both the structural and cultural conditions that exist within the firm. Many knowledge-intensive firms do therefore need to organize along very different lines compared to more traditional firms in which, typically, workers are not considered to be the direct productive force of the organization and, in relative terms, are easy to replace. However, there is still a lack of in-depth empirical studies of the management of knowledge-intensive firms (though see Alvesson's 1995 account of the management of an IT consultancy – Enator). The following two sections therefore, draw predominantly on the organizational theory and strategy literature. The generic structural and cultural conditions which are considered to facilitate the management of knowledge-intensive firms are considered in conjunction with some of the structural or cultural barriers that might mitigate against successful outcomes from knowledge work processes.

Facilitating knowledge work – organizing as an adhocracy

The way in which knowledge-intensive firms structure and organize internally will be crucial where innovation and creativity are the basis on which the firm competes. Whilst it will be particularly important for management to offer good terms and conditions of employment to knowledge workers, the way in which the major work processes are controlled and coordinated will be equally significant. An approach to organizing needs to be developed that is synergistic with knowledge work.

The way in which many knowledge-intensive firms attempt to organize tends to reflect the more general trend towards flatter, less bureaucratized ways of organizing that are becoming more common across all sectors in the twenty-first century. In general terms, knowledge-intensive firms try to organize highly organically and flexibly, generally around teams. In 1979, Henry Mintzberg identified five archetypal structural forms that characterized the way firms organized. He suggested that where creativity and innovation were a conscious strategy, as often tends to be the case within knowledge-intensive firms, then an adhocracy was the most appropriate organizational configuration. The adhocracy is almost the complete opposite of the traditional bureaucracy. An adhocracy genuinely deemphasizes a hierarchical structure in preference to a dynamic organizational structure based on self-formed and self-managed project teams, decentralized decision-making and little formalization in terms of formal rules and procedures. Within an adhocracy, Mintzberg suggests, control tends to be based on professionalism and shared, organizational values – referred to as cultural or normative control – rather than on more typical forms of direct control such as direct supervision and adherence to rules and procedures.

Raelin (1991) argues that in traditional professional service firms conflict can often arise between competing professional and organizational values. For example, professionals will naturally want to complete client work to the best of their professional abilities, applying discipline-based knowledge (legal, financial, scientific) to client problems. However, time is always considered to be a precious resource in these firms and strongly associated with the fee structure. There can therefore, on occasion, be conflict between the professional values of the lawyer or accountant, for example, to do a 'good job' and the needs of the firm to manage the firm's resources across the client base as efficiently as possible. According to Raelin, managing partners within these types of professional service firm are required to find ways of mediating these conflicting tensions.

This conflict of values however, is not necessarily so apparent in other types of knowledge-intensive firm as the notion of professionalism is more broad and tends to refer to general beliefs and expectations around high standards of performance and a dominant work ethic. This is explored further later in this chapter. Thus the informal, loosely coupled organizational environment characterized as an adhocracy is considered to provide the necessary autonomous working conditions in which individuals will feel free to spend time experimenting with ideas and more generally engage in creative and innovative behaviour. Table 2.2 highlights the distinctive characteristics of the adhocracy in comparison to the traditional bureaucracy.

Table 2.2   The bureaucracy and the adhocracy compared

Bureaucracy	Adhocracy
Multiple level hierarchy	Minimal hierarchy
Work processes organized around functional groups	Work processes self-organized around teams
Many formal rules, policies and procedures	Few or no formal rules, policies and procedures
Direct control characterized by supervision	Normative control characterized by self-management
Centralized decision-making	Decentralized decision-making
Coordination achieved through explicit rules and procedures	Coordination achieved though mutual adjustment
Highly mechanistic form	Highly organic form

Structural constraints on knowledge work

Development of organizational 'best practice'

Research has demonstrated that even when the structural conditions are generally supportive of knowledge work tasks, it is still very easy for creativity and innovation to be stifled (Starbuck, 1992). Firms are therefore cautioned to try and avoid the development of particular norms and practices that might constrain innovative behaviour. For example, informal routines that have developed over time can quickly start to become standardized ways of working embedded in physical capital, routines and even organizational culture. These informal routines can develop into knowledge that becomes codified into firm-specific 'best practice' templates, such as systematic auditing procedures and tools for project planning and development. As the usage of these tools spreads and comes to be seen as almost mandatory within the firm, then innovation can be constrained as consideration of new tools, concepts and ways of working tends to be precluded.

Monitoring of time

Starbuck also highlights that in many knowledge-intensive firms, such as consultancies and advertising agencies, time spent working on client projects is often monitored and rigorously accounted for, as it is billable time and needs to be carefully documented to the satisfaction of the client. This monitoring, however, can often inhibit innovative behaviour even when timescales have been mutually agreed between the project team and the client – as should be the case in a genuine operating adhocracy. Where this is common practice knowledge workers often reduce or ultimately fail to spend time searching for, creating or acquiring new knowledge and actively learning. This 'redundant' time (Nonaka, 1994) is considered to be particularly crucial for innovation and yet is simply not a resource that is made available within those knowledge-intensive firms that are intent upon monitoring and controlling billable time.

Growth

Starbuck also emphasizes that, over time, knowledge-intensive firms often have a tendency to attempt to diversify and grow and this is not always a sensible strategic decision. Increasing growth and diversification often lead to increasing formalization, layers of hierarchy and increasing numbers of support staff which can all ultimately lead to the firm experiencing problems. As Starbuck states, 'when support staff come to outnumber experts greatly, or when knowledge intensive firms (KIFs) claim expertise in too many domains, KIFs lose their halos of expertise and their credibility' (1992, p. 737). Mintzberg in fact suggests that the adhocracy is a typical organizational form only in young, start-up, entrepreneurial firms. He argues that over time adhocracies evolve into other archetypes – in the case of knowledge-intensive firms they often evolve into professional bureaucracies. The firm necessarily becomes more formalized, introducing, for example, levels of professional management in an attempt to manage basic requirements such as efficiency criteria.

This shift in structure and organizing may however be counterproductive where innovation is the basis on which the firm competes. Research conducted by Lowendahl (1997) demonstrated that a strategy of growth can be counterproductive, particularly to those firms that compete on the basis of their ability to solve complex problems for clients. This more recent research therefore supports the earlier predictions made by Mintzberg and Starbuck. A compromise however might be achieved by creating new, autonomous business units as soon as the firm reaches a particular size. These new business units should ideally be led by those who recognize the importance and significance of low levels of formalization and decentralized decision-making for knowledge work processes. Several high-tech firms operating in the Cambridge area of the UK (often referred to as 'Silicon Fen') have adopted this strategy. 'Spinning out' new firms as opposed to organizational growth is the approach these firms have adopted in order to manage the exploitation of new innovations developed in-house. These firms are therefore consciously attempting to continue to operate as adhocracies by avoiding organizational growth.

Cultural conditions in support of knowledge work

Many knowledge-intensive firms do attempt to structure and organize along the lines of an adhocracy, recognizing that this approach is likely to facilitate knowledge work processes. However, as discussed in the previous section, this highly informal approach to organizing can often be problematic to sustain in the long run. In order for any for-profit organization to survive in the long term, it must be able to achieve and sustain a competitive level of profitability. When firms organize predominantly around self-formed and self-managed knowledge-based teams, it can be very difficult for leaders of such firms to both develop and manage efficiency criteria even when the firm remains small.

The nature of much of the work that is carried out can be both ambiguous and intangible and is therefore difficult to measure, control or even quantify. For example, advertising agencies develop 'ideas' for clients and specialist consultancy firms develop bespoke solutions to client problems. In these cases, it is often extremely difficult for managers or even knowledge workers themselves to estimate the resources required in terms of time, expertise and skills to successfully complete client projects. Often successful outcomes cannot be guaranteed. In many instances 'success' can only be measured by the degree to which the client is satisfied with the outcome. Rational, qualified judgements that highlight means–ends relationships are difficult or impossible to make.

Furthermore, it has already been emphasized that knowledge workers will, to a greater or lesser extent, resent any attempt to directly monitor and control their work, demanding and requiring as they do high levels of autonomy in order to carry out their major work tasks. The leaders of knowledge-intensive firms are therefore always seeking ways to manage the fundamental underlying tension that exists between efficiency and autonomy. Whilst structural conditions which emphasize flexibility and self-managed teamworking are important preconditions facilitating knowledge work tasks, the cultural conditions within the firm will be at least as important in ultimately facilitating knowledge work processes that are largely conducted autonomously. It is the cultural conditions within a knowledge-intensive firm that primarily promote responsible autonomy (Friedman, 1977) and a workforce that can be trusted to work in the interests of the firm, that is, working autonomously but working very hard and to the best of their abilities.

Cultural (normative) control

Whilst leaders of knowledge-intensive firms will be keen to employ individuals with particular skills and expertise, their general requirements will be rather broad, recognizing that diversity across the workforce is considered to be a significant facilitator of innovation (see for example, Grant, 1996; Lowendahl, 1997). In Chapter 1, it was highlighted that the nature of knowledge production is changing and increasingly knowledge production relies on the combination of knowledge from a variety of fields and disciplines. The leaders of innovative and creative knowledge-intensive firms are therefore often faced with a requirement to employ and manage a highly diverse workforce (in terms of race, age, gender, skills and expertise) in a very loosely organized environment. This is obviously quite a management challenge. As mentioned previously in this chapter, researchers (Mintzberg, 1979; Lowendahl, 1997) have suggested that a form of management grounded in cultural or normative control is the most appropriate approach to adopt within these organizational environments. The suggestion is that leaders of these types of firm are in a position to create and develop a corporate culture which workers will want and choose to identify with. By identifying with the organization workers then internalize the dominant organizational ideology – values, beliefs and norms – and behave in the interests of the firm.

The importance of a strong organizational culture

Writers such as Peters and Waterman (1982), Deal and Kennedy (1982) and Kanter (1984), reflecting the 'business excellence' literature of the early 1980s, and much of Edgar Schein's work (Schein, 1983, 1992), have promoted the idea that it is the primary task of leaders of organizations to develop and actively reinforce *strong* organizational cultures. 'Improvements in productivity and quality, it is argued, flow from corporate cultures that *systematically* recognize and reward individuals, symbolically and materially, for identifying their sense of purpose with the values that are designed into the organization' (Willmott, 1993, pp. 515–16; italics author's own). Naturally this 'leader-led' organizational culture will be characterized by an organizational (core) value system that represents the long-term interests of the firm.

Importantly, in this literature strong organizational cultures are those that are shared across the firm, strengthening the firm through integration and enhanced productivity. This integration perspective on organizational culture (Martin, 1992) sees culture as an organizational variable that can be directly shaped by the behaviour and core values of the leaders of the firm. These core beliefs permeate the whole organization over time and serve to influence the values and norms of behaviour of the rest of the workforce. There is an emphasis on homogeneity, consensus and, importantly, within the context of a knowledge-intensive firm, predictable behaviour which is shaped by shared values and attitudes. What tends to be overlooked here, however, is that whilst from this perspective predictable behaviour is sought with regard to knowledge workers displaying responsible autonomy, in other respects predictable behaviour may not necessarily lead to innovation and creativity.

The way in which leaders of firms can actively create and shape organizational culture is explained in detail in Schein's work. He suggests that leaders of firms are responsible for implementing primary embedding mechanisms and secondary reinforcement or articulation mechanisms, which will symbolically reflect and are consistent with the dominant, core values held by the leaders. Specific employment policies and practices such as the criteria used for recruitment and selection, performance management and reward are examples of what Schein refers to as primary embedding mechanisms. Organizational design and structure together with formal statements of organizational philosophy typically found in firms' mission statements are examples of secondary reinforcement mechanisms. Schein suggests that if leaders of firms implement all twelve mechanisms in a consistent and coherent manner then, over time, core organizational values will become shared values across the workforce leading to performance and productivity improvements.

From this perspective, if the leader of a knowledge-intensive firm wished to emphasize the importance of knowledge-sharing – as might be expected in knowledge-intensive firms – then mechanisms that directly or indirectly rewarded knowledge-sharing would need to be introduced. For example, knowledge workers might be financially or symbolically rewarded for contributing to projects they were not directly employed to work on. In this way, by implementing this embedding mechanism in conjunction with other mutually reinforcing mechanisms, Schein suggests that knowledge-sharing behaviour in the firm can be encouraged and promoted as knowledge workers begin to recognize that knowledge-sharing is a core value within the firm.

Multiple perspectives on organizational culture

There is an overriding assumption in Schein's work and all of the business excellence literature that it is in fact feasible for leaders of firms to actively create and shape an organizational culture which promotes integration and consensus around dominant organizational values. An expert, highly skilled and often highly educated workforce which displays considerable diversity might, however, quite naturally hold a wide range of beliefs and values, particularly when diversity extends to national culture. Therefore it should not simply be assumed or taken for granted that knowledge workers in knowledge-intensive firms will necessarily be willing to subsume their identity and own personal value systems to those of the firm. The integration perspective on culture, which this literature reflects, assumes certain structural preconditions such as a well-defined hierarchy and highly centralized decision-making. These however are often not apparent within knowledge-intensive firms – particularly those that organize as adhocracies. It may therefore be highly problematic to operationalize this approach to 'culture management' in a knowledge-intensive setting. To what extent the leaders of such firms are in a position to shape beliefs, particularly in such an informal organizational environment, is in fact highly questionable.

Leaders of knowledge-intensive firms may therefore have to acknowledge that knowledge workers will naturally hold a variety of beliefs, which cannot necessarily be altered or subsumed within a competing organizational value system. This is referred to in Martin's work as the fragmentation perspective on culture. The fragmentation perspective suggests that culture is better viewed as a metaphor rather than a variable – something an organization *is* rather than something an organization *has*. From this perspective culture is only loosely structured and partially shared, emerging dynamically as organizational members experience each other, events and the organizational context over time (Martin, 1992).

The fragmentation perspective importantly legitimates differentiation – that is, competing and contradictory value systems held by individuals across the firm, which is often the case in knowledge-intensive firms populated by a highly skilled, diverse workforce. This perspective acknowledges ambiguity, recognizing that within organizations individuals might experience a lack of clarity or simultaneously hold multiple meanings and beliefs. Lack of clarity can result from unclear structures, organizational boundaries or precise goals. These are likely to be apparent within a knowledge-intensive firm organized broadly as an adhocracy. It may well be the case, then, that knowledge-intensive firms display cultural characteristics more reminiscent of the fragmentation perspective rather than the integration perspective.

Leaders of such firms need to acknowledge and accept that differentiation and fragmentation rather than integration might predominate, and recognize that they are only in a position to loosely manage organizational culture, for example, by promoting values that knowledge workers will naturally wish to identify with. By promoting an organizational ethos that is more or less generally accepted and shared, rather than attempting to instil and reinforce a dominant core value system, there is a greater likelihood that knowledge workers will start to see the firm as a 'good' place to work. As far as is possible in such a diverse, loosely structured environment, this approach is more likely to aid retention and promote responsible autonomy within the firm. Timothy Koogle, the founder of Yahoo!, a leading web portal, argues that his organization became successful largely because he promoted the idea that employees should communicate freely with one another and join in whatever decisions needed to be made (Greenberg and Baron, 2000). This was considered to be essential in the fast-paced world of the Internet and at the same time intuitively appealed to the knowledge workers employed.

Conclusions

This chapter has highlighted the structural and cultural conditions that can facilitate or constrain knowledge work processes characterized by creativity and innovation. It needs to be emphasized, however, that the limited research that has been conducted in such firms highlights that there is no single 'best management practice' here. Many knowledge-intensive firms operate in niche markets – offering very specialized services – and the way in which many of these firms choose to organize is often quite unique and highly context-sensitive. Generally attempts will be made to only loosely structure and organize, characteristic of the adhocracy. Whilst the adhocracy might appear to be a somewhat chaotic, relatively unmanaged environment, it is perhaps useful to consider the way in which this configuration has been operationalized in a scientific consultancy firm based in the UK. The way in which structural and cultural conditions interact to facilitate knowledge work processes is explained in the following case study and illustrates the complex conditions actively promoted over time which have ultimately mediated the tensions around efficiency and autonomy within a knowledge-intensive setting. First the case is described and then two questions are posed.

In Chapter 3 we focus our attention on the actual process of knowledge creation or knowledge generation and adopt a micro-level of analysis. We move from a firm-level analysis of the way in which modes of organizing and organizational conditions can develop in support of knowledge work processes to an analysis of the dynamics of knowledge creation processes within a project team setting. Chapter 3 focuses attention on the importance of trust and power in project teams as both enablers and barriers to knowledge creation.

Case Study 2.1   ScienceCo managing an expert workforce

ScienceCo was founded in 1980. It is a medium-sized, technology-based consultancy company, located on the outskirts of London. It operates today on a global basis. At the time of its inception, the founder wished to create a consultancy environment that would not only develop solutions in response to client problems, but also stimulate invention and innovation more generally. Eighty-five per cent of the workforce are highly educated scientists and technologists, who rely primarily on their expertise and knowledge rather than equipment or systems to provide inventions and innovative solutions for manufacturing, engineering and pharmaceutical companies around the world.

Since 1980, the firm has grown from a small entrepreneurial business employing a handful of scientific consultants specializing in engineering and communications to a medium-sized company employing about 200 people and incorporating other scientific disciplines such as biotechnology, applied sciences and information systems. The workforce is truly international, incorporating 19 different nationalities. In defining the type of projects that ScienceCo conducted for their clients, it is important to understand the difference between invention and innovation. Consultants working in interdisciplinary project teams develop completely new concepts and products that are marketed as intellectual property rights (IPR) to clients and project teams. They also develop innovative solutions to client problems using existing concepts, ideas and technologies in new ways. The firm has been responsible for the invention of major scientific and technological developments that are recognized and used throughout the world. One such item is the electronic security tag, which since its invention has been manufactured and marketed by the Swedish firm Esselte. ScienceCo is primarily in the business of creating new knowledge and applying existing knowledge in new ways.

Case Study 2.1 continued

A crucial issue for management at ScienceCo has always been attracting and retaining a highly skilled, expert workforce of international standing in order for the firm to grow and successfully compete on a global basis. Thus developing an appropriate organizational environment in which expert consultants are keen to work has been of paramount importance. The following sections outline the organizational structure, human resource practices, patterns of IT usage and organizational culture that have developed within the firm over time.

Organizational structure

Attempts have been made to maintain a fairly flat organizational structure throughout the firm's development. Even today, there is fundamentally only one level of management, consisting of the founder (now Executive Chairman), Chairman and Managing Director. Decision-making within the firm has typically involved significant numbers of consultants as well as management. A worker committee, the Board of Management, which consists primarily of consultants and one or two support staff, make recommendations to management regarding day-to-day operations and organization. Management communicates constantly with the whole of the firm (generally using e-mail) regarding new projects and potential future projects. Turnover and profitability are also communicated to everyone on a monthly basis. Consultants are encouraged to innovate outside of client project work, and they can request financial resources for this through the Innovation Exploitation Board. This forum includes consultants from across the firm, as well as the management team, who meet regularly to discuss the feasibility of new ideas proposed by consultants. All members of the management team are also active consultants, contributing to project teamworking within the firm.

Consultants are organized across three divisions within the firm according to their particular scientific expertise. These are Business Innovation (BI), Technology, Internet, Media and Entertainment (TIME), and Engineering (ENG). While divisional managers head up divisions, there are actually no hierarchical levels either within or across divisions. Divisional managers tend to be those individuals who are prepared to take on some minimal administrative responsibilities such as recording revenue generation and monitoring the projects that are being managed by consultants within their own division. In many cases, divisional managers are actually remunerated less than other consultants within their division (see section on 'Performance management') and they also actively contribute to project working across the firm.

Divisions have emerged, merged and disbanded in a reactive manner over time, based on the client project work in hand. In 1980, there were only two skill groups, Engineering and Communications. However, in 1990, a divisional structure was introduced in order to provide improved financial accountability. By 1996, seven divisions existed including two business consulting divisions, Information Systems and Applied Sciences. The Life Sciences division emerged at this time from the Applied Sciences division when enough biotechnology

Case Study 2.1 continued

projects had been secured to ensure the divisions' sustainability in the medium term. By 2000, however, Life Sciences had again merged with the Engineering division together with Applied Sciences. Business Innovation by this time incorporated both business divisions and the Information Systems division. Despite the existence of divisions, consultants tend to work in an interdisciplinary manner across divisions within small project teams. This occurs because the nature of client requirements generally requires cross-disciplinary skills and expertise. These project teams are self-forming and self-managed. Project teamworking is discussed in more detail within the section on 'Performance management'.

Recruitment and selection

For many years, the firm did not employ a Human Resources (HR) manager. However, in 1995, based on predicted and expected project work, the firm was faced with a requirement to increase the expert workforce by 15 per cent (and this was projected to continue annually, compounded). The firm recruited a Human Resources manager to develop a more formal recruitment and selection process, and to develop ways of maintaining high retention rates across the firm.

In the past, consultants had typically been recruited informally by word of mouth, drawing upon consultants' global personal networks of colleagues and contacts. In order to make the recruitment process more effective, the HR manager developed good relationships with two international recruitment agencies that had offices throughout the world. Once provided with a person specification and a brief that described very broadly the type of work carried out by the firm, they provided shortlists of candidates on an ongoing basis. In terms of the selection process, the founder had always insisted that candidates take an AH6 intelligence test and Cattell's 16PF personality test. Given that the majority of candidates shortlisted by the agencies generally had a PhD in a scientific discipline, it was virtually impossible for any candidate to fail the AH6 test. It was also difficult to 'fail' the 16PF because the firm did not look for an 'ideal' profile other than 'openness' and a 'willingness to experiment'. Consultants were simply keen to see what sort of personality profile candidates had. Thus, almost all candidates who had been shortlisted proceeded to an initial short interview with the HR manager and the relevant divisional manager.

During this preliminary interview, the HR manager stated that candidates were expected to demonstrate a strong understanding of their own and, more importantly, other disciplines, because of the need to work in interdisciplinary teams sharing knowledge. They were also expected to be 'almost naturally innovative' and have a strong commercial awareness. The HR manager stated:

> It's quite a unique mix we are looking for. All the way through the selection process, we give out big indicators to say the sort of organization we are. It's quite aggressive maybe, and I'm sure interviewees will pick up quite a lot of arrogance on the part of the company. But the messages we are giving out are more about confidence in what we do and how we do it rather than us thinking we are better than anyone else.

Case Study 2.1 continued

The majority of candidates tend to be rejected at this initial interview stage and only approximately 25 per cent, which typically equates to four candidates, progress to a second interview. The firm was not overly concerned about the high numbers of candidates rejected. Management is only interested in individuals with either a PhD or particular expertise within a scientific discipline, who are fluent in English, have some commercial/industrial experience, and who are prepared to adopt the role of a consultant. This role involves marketing their own and, more generally, the firm's abilities and expertise. It is therefore a relatively unique set of characteristics which is sought in candidates.

The second interview focuses on assessing the candidate's ability to market to clients, their overall level of expertise, and their ability to work within interdisciplinary project teams. This second interview is a panel interview involving a number of consultants from several divisions, who 'quiz' the applicant in some depth on their knowledge of their own and other science- or technology-based fields. Panel members are randomly drawn from across the firm, based on availability at the time of the interview. If the panel agrees on a candidate, then the candidate will be recommended for appointment to the MD.

In 1996, typically, 16 candidates were interviewed for each post, and for each of those interviewed, approximately ten CVs would have been received from the recruitment agencies. The selection process is described as 'rigorous' by the HR manager. He emphasized that the interviews focus primarily on the candidates' ability to 'fit in' to the ScienceCo way of working. This involves willingness and ability to collaboratively share knowledge across different science- and technology-based fields, both within project teams and more generally. The HR manager commented:

> You get a CV, and the person has a PhD, and they've worked for a pretty high-powered research agency, and that's brilliant. You've got to see them, but you know that there is a pretty strong chance that the moment you meet them you're going to know what they're not – they're not one of us.

Performance management

Only one formal system exists at ScienceCo, and this is the performance management system that was introduced in 1990. This system was introduced at the same time as consultants were allocated to divisions. Before this, individual consultants' performance had not been managed. The system focuses on divisional revenue targets (DRTs) and personal revenue targets (PRTs). Management establishes these targets at the beginning of each financial year, and they are monitored monthly. The same monthly PRT applies to all consultants, regardless of age, experience and so on. Hence, DRTs are the accumulation of PRTs, premised on the number of consultants within the divisions. By default, then, the larger divisions had to generate more revenue.

Revenue is generated through project work that is generally priced at a flat rate rather than a fee rate. A lead consultant emerges on client projects. Typically, this is the consultant who has the most contact with a particular client. The 'lead' consultant is responsible for negotiating the value of the project with the client, after careful consideration of the resources that will be required in terms of breadth of expertise and time. Lead consultants will use e-mail to inform consultants throughout the firm about potential new projects and the skills and expertise that will be required. Once the value of a project has been determined with the client, it is the responsibility of individual consultants who want to work on the project to negotiate with the lead consultant regarding the amount of project revenue they will be allocated. As there are no formal systems to record these negotiations, e-mail messages serve as a record of any negotiations that take place. The allocation of project revenue contributes to the individual consultants' PRT and the DRT to which they are assigned.

Management described PRTs as a scheme for making people sell their skills to other people in an effective manner:

> It is a micro economy. It is a free market for expertise. Over the years it has been the subject of much controversy as it puts a lot of pressure on people, and it is in this way that we try to maintain a competitive (some would say combative) environment. It does create tension, but at the same time, it enhances innovation given by the rate at which new ideas come out of the organization.

In order to achieve PRTs, consultants generally work on a small number of projects at any one time, commanding a percentage of the overall revenue from each one. Achievement of PRTs consistently over time is expected of everyone, other than the most inexperienced consultants and recent recruits. The majority of consultants usually achieve their PRT. However, consistency across whole divisions is problematic and occasionally divisional managers find it difficult to achieve their DRT. At the end of each financial year, divisional managers performance-rank those within their division, based on achievement of PRTs and contribution to overall sales. This is a transparent process and individual consultants are free to discuss, and in some instances dispute, their overall ranking position. When divisional managers have agreed on their rankings within their division, they meet with the management team to agree on overall ranking across the firm. Individual consultants are then awarded percentage increments according to their ranking. Underperformers are tolerated in the medium term. Consultants who do not achieve PRTs over time will not receive a salary increment, but they are actively encouraged and helped by management to improve performance the following year. Management has never introduced salary scales within the firm, and no formal career structure exists because there is a no formal hierarchy. Individual consultants are therefore awarded a percentage increase based on the salary they have personally negotiated with the MD on their appointment to the firm.

It is also important to recognize that consultants manage their own time both within and outside of project working. Consultants are free to choose their hours of work and length of vacations. This means that some consultants work continuously, occasionally for months at a time and then take extended

Case Study 2.1 continued

vacations, up to two to three months at any one time. Other consultants choose to work regular hours and take shorter breaks. Divisional managers only expect to be made aware of vacations (time and length) and consultants are trusted to manage their time effectively.

Training and development

Professional development is particularly important to all consultants at ScienceCo. In order to stay at the top of their professional fields, consultants must be aware of any developments in their field, and they need to participate in activities that offer the opportunity for further professional development. Again, consultants are responsible for identifying their own requirements in terms of courses, conferences and workshops. Management simply provides the necessary financial resources, which in some cases are considerable. It is assumed that consultants will organize their workloads accordingly, in order to participate in professional development without any significant disruption of project work occurring.

Training for consultants has never been considered an issue within the firm. Management has always believed that the quality of the people employed negates any need for systematic training. It is assumed that if dedicated training is required, for example, in the use of particular software application for project work, then consultants are sufficiently skilled to train themselves at times that suit them.

IT usage

Significant resources have always been made available for investment in any technology that might facilitate project working. An e-mail system was introduced in 1990 to facilitate communication between consultants. By this time, the firm had grown to around 100 consultants, and the opportunities for regular face-to-face contact with everyone were rapidly diminishing. The e-mail system began to be used extensively almost immediately, as there were very few formal systems or procedures in use for communication, and on any one day, significant numbers of consultants would be working remotely at client firms. By 1996, consultants were receiving between 100 and 150 e-mails each day, and despite attempts to curtail the use of e-mail for trivial matters, consultants today still receive about this number. This is because no protocols are used to classify mail sent, other than to attach a prefix of SOC for 'social' communication and INNOV for an e-mail where the sender is searching for information.

It is the e-mail system that is generally used to broadcast requests for information when putting together proposals for clients. Anyone who wants to be involved in a potential project initially communicates in outline their potential contribution, in terms of skills and expertise, via e-mail. The system works well in this respect as the medium is good for communicating low-level information, quickly and across the whole firm. However, the level of e-mail communication consultants are exposed to on a daily basis is recognized

Case Study 2.1 continued

generally as a significant burden. Norms have developed, such as sending replies to everyone in the firm and failing to edit the title of e-mails to ensure that it relates to the content of the e-mail. These norms, while making the use of e-mail relatively thoughtless, informal and simple, have generated a somewhat chaotic and haphazard system of communication. For example, some consultants, when faced with ever-increasing numbers of e-mail, choose not to bother reading the majority, and only use the system when absolutely necessary.

Other technologies such as groupware technologies are occasionally used and intranets have been set up in and across divisions. Consultants are aware that packages such as Lotus Notes can provide useful project documentation. However, the majority of projects continue to be documented in a highly idiosyncratic manner because project leaders are free to provide documentation in whatever way they deem appropriate. Client requirements need to be fulfilled in this respect. However, if the client is satisfied with the documentation produced, no further effort is directed at producing, recording and classifying project documentation in a consistent manner across the firm. Again, consultants are trusted to produce high-quality project documentation, without recourse to formal standards, systems or procedures.

The use of both groupware and intranets tends therefore to be spasmodic and piecemeal. For example, groupware, such as Lotus Notes, only tends to be used when geographical constraints impose a need to work in this fashion. Consultants prefer project teamworking to be face to face, rather than via Lotus Notes discussion threads. Groupware technology is not generally considered rich enough to adequately convey some types of information and knowledge required during project work. In many instances, when significant decisions or results need to be shared across a project team, the technology is simply used to schedule a telephone conference call.

Culture

As stated in the introduction, from the outset the founder wanted to promote an innovative environment and one that would stimulate creativity. With this in mind, he attempted to develop and perpetuate an environment characterized by an absence of hierarchy, rules and formal procedures. An emphasis was placed on maintaining an egalitarian environment, one in which everyone was in principle free to contribute to decision-making, and one that allowed individuals relative freedom to be creative. While the founder was keen to promote a corporate culture around a small set of core values specifically regarding the importance and value of creativity and innovation, both to the firm and society more generally, he respected individuals as individuals. He did not, therefore, attempt to develop a strong culture that encompassed particular norms of behaviour. The ScienceCo way of working is therefore characterized by a lack of prescription, informality and idiosyncrasy.

Case Study 2.1 continued

The heterogeneity and diversity of the workforce exemplify the importance placed on individuality within the firm. Not only are 19 different nationalities represented, there are also significant differences across the firm with regard to age, experience and general attitudes and behaviour. Individuality often tends to be manifest symbolically in dress, ranging from the bizarre (for example, running shorts and vest in the depths of winter!) to the more traditional conformist dark suit and tie. During project working, however, diverse groups of individuals with differing expertise are expected to work together jointly, developing solutions to client requirements or problems. While conflict inevitably arises across such a range of diverse individuals, the environment is one in which individuals feel free to speak out without recrimination. Consultants are trusted to resolve any differences that might arise without recourse to the management team, so that ultimately client requirements are satisfied.

While everyone agrees that the environment is highly informal and this is considered to be one of the major attractions of working in the firm, consultants do have different perceptions of what constitutes organizational reality. For example, while everyone agrees that the organization is almost flat, it is widely recognized and acknowledged that a dynamic, informal hierarchy exists based on expertise. However consultants do differ (in some cases quite considerably) in their opinions as to the hierarchical ordering based on their own personal experience of working with others in the firm. As one consultant stated:

> Nobody in theory has a job title. Single status applies but obviously some people are seen as more powerful, more influential, higher status than others – based purely on what they are seen to contribute to the organization in terms of big projects or particularly innovative ideas.

Individuals across the firm can therefore command powerful positions within the informal hierarchy. Their position will be based on their ability to both acquire new business and command large proportions of project revenue that contribute to their PRT. Positions within this informal hierarchy, however, are transient and relatively ephemeral, as new clients and new projects requiring different skills and expertise are acquired over time.

Questions

1. Define and explain six critical organizational factors that have contributed to ScienceCo's growth and ability to retain an expert workforce.

2. What are the potential problems that might arise over time in this organizational environment?

Summary of key learning points

■ Knowledge-intensive firms rely on their human capital – specifically intellectual capital – for their competitive advantage. Therefore retention is a crucial strategic issue within these types of firm.

■ 'Knowledge-intensive firm' is a generic term that encapsulates a broad range of firms operating across sectors in a post-industrial economy.

■ Knowledge-intensive firms can be classified as client-based, problem-solving or output-based.

■ Knowledge workers are often referred to as 'gold collar' workers, acknowledging the autonomy and exceptional working conditions they are generally afforded.

■ The adhocracy, characterized by a dynamic organizational structure based on self-formed and self-managed teams, is considered to be an appropriate configuration where innovation is the basis on which a firm competes.

■ Structural constraints on knowledge work include the development of organizational 'best practice' templates, monitoring of knowledge workers' time and organizational growth.

■ Responsible autonomy is more likely to be achieved if management acknowledges that organizational culture is likely to be characterized by differentiation and fragmentation rather than consensus and integration. Hence management should only attempt to loosely manage culture, aiming to promote an organizational ethos rather than a dominant core value system.

References

Alvesson, M. (1993) Organizations as rhetoric: knowledge-intensive firms and the struggle with ambiguity. *Journal of Management Studies*, **30**(6): 997–1015.

Alvesson, M. (1995) *Management of Knowledge-intensive Companies*. Berlin/New York: De Gruyter.

Alvesson, M. (2001) Knowledge work: ambiguity, image and identity. *Human Relations*, **54**(7): 863–86.

Anderson-Gough, F., Grey, C. and Robson, K. (2000) In the name of the client: the service ethic in two professional services firms. *Human Relations*, **53**(9): 1151–74.

Deal, T. and Kennedy, A. (1982) *Corporate Cultures: The Rites and Rituals of Corporate Life*, Reading, Mass., Addison-Wesley.

Friedman, A. (1977) *Industry and Labour*. London: Macmillan – now Palgrave.

Gibbons, M., Limoges, C., Nowotny, H., Schwartzman, S., Scott, P. and Trow, M. (1994) *The New Production of Knowledge: The Dynamics of Science and Research in Contemporary Societies*. London: Sage.

Grant, R. (1996) Prospering in dynamically competitive environments: organizational capability as knowledge integration. *Organization Science*, 7(4): 375–87.

Greenberg, J. and Baron, R. (2000) *Behavior in Organizations*, 7th edn. Englewood Cliffs, NJ: Prentice-Hall.

Greenwood, R., Hinings, C.R. and Brown, J. (1990) 'P2-Form' strategic management: corporate practices in professional partnerships. *Academy of Management Journal*, **33**(4): 725–55.

Kanter, R. (1984) *The Change Masters*. London: Allen & Unwin.

Kelley, R. (1990) *The Gold Collar Worker – Harnessing the Brainpower of the New Workforce*. Reading, Mass.: Addison-Wesley.

Lowendahl, B. (1997) *Strategic Management of Professional Service Firms*. Copenhagen: Copenhagen Business School Press.

Luker, W. and Lyons, D. (1997) Employment shift in high-technology industries, 1988–96. *Monthly Labor Review*, June: 12–25.

Martin, J. (1992) *Cultures in Organizations*. New York, Oxford University Press.

Mintzberg, H. (1979) *Structures in Fives, Designing Effective Organizations*. Englewood Cliffs, NJ: Prentice-Hall.

Nonaka, I. (1994) A dynamic theory of organizational knowledge creation. *Organization Science*, **5**(1): 14–37.

Peters, T. and Waterman, R. (1982) *In Search of Excellence: Lessons from America's Best-run Companies*. New York: Harper & Row.

Raelin, J.A. (1991) *The Clash of Cultures: Managers Managing Professionals*. Boston, Mass.: Harvard Business School Press.

Schein, E. (1983) The role of the founder in creating organizational culture. *Organizational Dynamics*, Summer; 13–28.

Schein, E. (1992) *Organizational Culture and Leadership*, 2nd edn. San Francisco: Jossey-Bass.

Smircich, L. (1983) Concepts of culture and organizational analysis, *Administrative Science Quaterly*, **28**: 339–59.

Sproull, L., Weiner, S. and Wolf, D. (1978) *Organizing an Anarchy*. Chicago, Ill: University of Chicago Press.

Starbuck, W. (1992) Learning by knowledge-intensive firms. *Journal of Management Studies*, **29**(6): 713–40.

Weick, K. (1985) Sources of order in underorganized systems: themes in recent organizational theory. In Y. Lincoln (ed.) *Organizational Theory and Inquiry: The Paradigm Revolution*. Beverly Hills, Calif: Sage, pp. 106–36.

Willmott, H. (1993) Strength is ignorance; slavery is freedom: managing culture in modern organisations. *Journal of Management Studies*, **30**: 515–52.

3 Knowledge creation and teamworking

Learning outcomes

At the end of this chapter students will be able to:

- Understand the dynamics of knowledge creation as it takes place within project teams.
- Appreciate the critical role of trust and power in processes of knowledge creation.
- Identify the role of integration mechanisms in facilitating the development of trust.

Introduction

Chapter 2 focused on knowledge-intensive firms, in particular looking at a consultancy firm as an example of a knowledge-intensive organization. This highlighted the growing importance of knowledge as an organizational asset and considered the organizational – level factors, especially different organizational cultures, which influence the management of knowledge-intensive firms. In this chapter we look more at the micro processes and practices involved in knowledge work, focusing on team dynamics. We do this because knowledge creation or knowledge generation is typically an activity that is accomplished by a team of people rather than by individuals working alone. Understanding not only why teams are typically used but also the problems surrounding teamworking is therefore important. Moreover, concentrating on knowledge creation by teams is significant because, as Grant (2000) observes, most management principles and most 'Knowledge Management' effort within organizations has focused on improving the use of existing knowledge in order to enhance efficiency and has ignored the processes and practices necessary for the exploration or creation of new knowledge.

The importance of teams in the knowledge creation process

Whether the objective is to develop a new product or service or to design and implement a new organizational technology, such as a new ICT (information and communication technology) system, the key resource that is required is knowledge – knowledge of the markets and customers, knowledge of the available technologies, knowledge of materials, knowledge of distribution processes, and so on. These different types of knowledge must be brought together so that new knowledge is created which leads to the development of the new product, service or organizational process. Typically, this diversity of knowledge will not be known by a single individual, but rather will be dispersed both within the organization (for example, across functional groups) and across organizations (for example, with consultants or suppliers). Thus, knowledge creation, at least within the context of an organization, is typically not something that is done by a single person. Rather, knowledge creation is typically the outcome of an interactive process that will involve a number of individuals who are brought together in a project team or some other collaborative arrangement.

The project team will have a specific objective, for example, to design and implement an ICT system to support information-sharing across geographically dispersed business units, or to develop a new type of breakfast cereal that will be attractive to teenagers. The successful completion of these tasks will depend on selecting project team members with appropriate knowledge, skills and expertise, so teams ideally will be chosen so that their members have a mix of knowledge and capabilities. We can refer to this as the intellectual capital of the team – the 'knowledge and knowing capability of a social collectivity' (Nahapiet and Ghoshal, 1998, p. 245). Intellectual capital, and its mix across the team, is important. It is unlikely, however, that team members will have all the relevant knowledge and expertise necessary, either to design the system, product or service *per se* or to ensure that it is accepted and implemented by all those for whom it is intended. Rather, team members will need to network with a range of other individuals in order to appropriate the necessary knowledge. In doing this they will be drawing upon their collective social capital. Nahapiet and Ghoshal define social capital as 'the sum of actual and potential resources within, available through, and derived from the network of relationships possessed by an individual or social unit' (1998 p. 243).

Knowledge creation, then, needs to be seen as an *interactive* teamworking process – one which involves a diverse range of actors with different backgrounds, cutting across organizational boundaries, and combining skills, artefacts, knowledge and experiences in new ways. It is typically assumed that teamworking leads to more creative solutions than would arise if individuals worked alone or in sequence on a particular project. However, in this chapter we explore in more detail these teamworking processes and illustrate that simply putting a diverse group of individuals together will not necessarily result in a productive and creative output. Indeed effective teamworking is difficult to achieve, especially when the team members come from different backgrounds and have different disciplinary knowledge bases. Later in this chapter we illustrate this using the case example of a team of academics who were involved in a joint knowledge creation project. Before we look at the case, however, we need to consider research which explores the dynamics of teamworking. This literature highlights both advantages and problems of teamworking. In particular, we will focus on the importance, but also the difficulty involved, in establishing trust between team members. Trust is seen to be perhaps *the* most critical issue for effective teamworking and knowledge sharing. Yet trust is, as we will see, particularly difficult to establish where team members come from different backgrounds and have different perspectives and knowledge.

Creating synergy within teams

Cross-functional teamworking within organizations is often portrayed as the key to creativity and success for firms today and there is a long tradition in psychological research on teamworking of demonstrating how 'the whole *may be* more than the sum of the parts', in other words, how a diverse range of individuals can create, through synergy, ideas which go beyond what any single individual could have produced on their own. Similarly in the 'Knowledge Management' literature, where there is an emphasis on knowledge creation, collaboration, interaction and teamworking are seen to be crucial. For example, the knowledge creation model developed by Nonaka and Takeuchi (1995) puts heavy emphasis on social processes of dialogue and interaction. The two key processes in their SECI model (socialization, externalization, combination and internalization) that emphasize the creation of knowledge are socialization and externalization. In particular, these two processes depend on dialogue and interaction over a prolonged period. Occasional contact between members of different departments, customers or clients is not enough, they argue, because this does not allow for the sharing of tacit knowledge that is essential for knowledge creation. Instead, interactions must occur over a prolonged period within what they describe as an enabling context. Nonaka and Konno (1998) call this enabling context 'ba'. Ba may well involve a physical space where face-to-face interaction can occur, but can also involve virtual space (for example, using e-mails, intranets, video conferencing) and most importantly it involves developing a shared mental space (shared experiences, emotions, ideas).

The central idea here, then, is that creativity develops from the interaction of different knowledge sets. Differences in knowledge will tend to generate a conflict of ideas, but this conflict – that Leonard-Barton (1995) has termed 'creative abrasion' – can positively influence performance. This positive influence will occur if the individuals involved can sustain a meaningful and synergistic conversation with the others. This depends on more than simply social skills, which enable team members to 'get along' with each other. It also depends on those involved having cognitive skills which allow them to appreciate and understand the technical knowledge of others. Iansiti (1993) refers to this as having T-shaped skills – depth in a particular discipline but combined with a breadth of understanding of other disciplines. This cognitive skill allows those involved to go beyond merely tolerating the ideas of others to interacting meaningfully at a cognitive level to create 'creative abrasion'.

In addition, shared mental models among team members allow the team to construct a shared understanding of their situation. This is dependent on the team members working closely together over a prolonged period, since with prolonged interaction individuals can share information over and above that required for each individual to do their particular job. This has also been referred to as knowledge redundancy. Knowledge redundancy affects a team's absorptive capacity (Cohen and Levinthal, 1990). Absorptive capacity refers to the capability to recognize the value of new and external information, absorb it, and apply it productively. Absorptive capacity in relation to the capability of synthesizing the knowledge of other team members is unlikely unless some knowledge redundancy or a T-shaped skill profile exists.

Teamworking is, then, a key mechanism that can provide the enabling context for knowledge creation where mutual understanding of deep tacit knowledge can be achieved based on shared experiences over a prolonged period. Rich personal interaction is necessary in order for those involved to get sufficient opportunity for the sharing of tacit knowledge (a fuller discussion of tacit knowledge is provided in Chapter 5).

Problems of teamworking

The literature on teamworking, however, also emphasizes some of the problems of developing and sustaining collaborative working – problems which are frequently overlooked in prescriptive accounts of the benefits of teamworking for knowledge creation. There is now an extensive literature on the problems that can occur when people work jointly in teams. This dates back to very early work by Ringlemann (1913), who found that for some tasks (for example, tug-of-war games) there was a reduction in individual effort as the number of people engaged in a collaborative task increased. So in a tug-of-war situation, the more people there are on each side the less effort does each individual actually exert. This is sometimes referred to as the social-loafing phenomenon and has been found to be more common where individual contribution to the team effort cannot be easily identified (Latene *et al.*, 1979). At the present time there is a whole list of teamworking problems or phenomena that can be cited from the literature. We can consider a few here that are pertinent to knowledge creation in teams.

1. Conformity

The famous experiments on conformity by Stanley Milgram (1964) demonstrated the extent to which individuals obey the instructions of an authority figure even when they are asked to behave in a callous way towards an innocent other. In these experiments a naive subject was asked to give progressively higher levels of electric shock to a supposed 'learner' (actually a confederate of the experimenter who therefore never actually received any shocks) every time this learner made a mistake in remembering a list of paired words. The subjects in this experiment did not enjoy doing this, and indeed the majority of those who conformed (about 65 per cent of those participating) protested strongly and urged Milgram to stop the experiment and check that the learner was not suffering unduly (the learner was located in another room so that there was only an audio connection between the teacher and the learner). Despite these protestations, however, Milgram's command – 'you must continue' – was enough to persuade the majority of participants to progressively increase the level of shock given to the learner to a massive 450 volts. Essentially these participants were conforming to the demands of an authority figure – in this case a university professor in a prestigious US university, Yale.

In a group situation, the problems of conformity can be particularly acute, as evidenced by the phenomenon of 'groupthink', considered next.

2. Groupthink

Perhaps the most well-known teamworking problem is the problem of groupthink identified by Irving Janis. Janis (1982) studied high-level strategy teams in the USA who had made some seemingly non-rational decisions in relation to crisis situations. He found that this was related to excessive conformity pressures that built up within these teams. He labelled this phenomenon 'groupthink' and identified a number of symptoms associated with it:

1. *Illusion of invulnerability*: members believe that past successes guarantee future successes and so take extreme risks.

2. *Collective rationalization*: members collectively rationalize away information that contradicts their assumptions.

3. *Illusion of morality*: members believe that they are all moral and so could not make a bad decision.

4. *Shared stereotypes*: members dismiss evidence that is contradictory by discrediting the source of that information.

5. *Direct pressure*: sanctions are placed on members who do dissent from the majority opinion, for example, using assertive language to enforce compliance.

6. *Self-censorship*: members keep quiet about any misgivings they have so that they do not voice concerns.

7. *Mind-guards*: members screen out information from outsiders where this might disconfirm the group's assumptions and beliefs.

8. *Illusion of unanimity*: given these other symptoms it appears that there is consensus within the group, even though there are many of those involved who do not agree with the group decision.

Groupthink has been found to develop where there is a strong drive to reach consensus because of pressures of time, which means that a decision needs to be reached quickly. Groupthink is also likely to occur where there is a powerful team leader who makes known his or her preferences at an early stage. In this situation, conformity to this leader's preference is likely to occur. The tragic launching and subsequent explosion of the Challenger Space Shuttle has been analysed as an example of groupthink (Moorhead *et al.*, 1991).

3. Group polarization

Another problem that we can identify from the literature on teamworking is that teams tend to make more extreme decisions than individuals working alone. Originally research suggested that teams tend to make more risky decisions (Stoner, 1968). The experimental design to study this was as follows: an individual is provided with a brief scenario which describes a situation in which a decision has to be made; the individual is given a series of decision options, ranging from a very safe decision but with a low pay-off to a very risky decision but with a high pay-off; the individual is asked to say which level of risk they would be prepared to take; individuals are then put together in groups to discuss the scenario; once this group discussion has finished the individual is then asked to say whether they would like to change their original risk-taking decision option. In general, research using this type of study design found that, following the group discussion, individuals tended to increase the level of risk they saw as appropriate.

Subsequent research has demonstrated that you can also get a cautious shift following group discussion. The important point, however, is that research suggests that groups tend to make more extreme decisions, sometimes with a fatal outcome as with the Challenger Space Shuttle disaster. One explanation of this suggests that this group polarization occurs through a process of social comparison. During the group discussion we compare our decision with the decision of the others in the group. At the outset we tend to think of ourselves as being fairly risk-taking, because this tends to be a valued personal attribute, at least in many societies and in relation to many situations. When, during the group discussion, we discover that we are not particularly risky compared to others, we then increase the level of risk of our decision when asked to remake the decision. The cautious shift occurs in situations where caution rather than risk is the socially valued option.

Many of these problems of teamworking are related to issues of power and control. This is addressed in the next section. An essential feature, especially of knowledge-creating teams, is that of self-management and an equal sharing of ideas. After all, that is the rationale for bringing together the particular individuals – the notion that all can contribute their knowledge or their intellectual and social capital. However, in most knowledge-creating teams in organizations, there are power differentials between those participating. In particular, there is often a team leader who may have power to reward and punish team members, for example, by being able to influence their appraisal or promotion outcomes. In such situations, where there is personal risk involved in disobeying the authority figure, conformity, groupthink or group polarization may be even more likely to occur than in the experiments described above, where there was nothing 'at risk' for the subjects. In the next section, then, we address more specifically this issue of power and control in teams.

Teams and power and control

Teams are often presented as *the* organizational panacea that will tackle all the problems of organizational life, including as here knowledge creation. Teams, it is claimed, can satisfy both individual needs (for example, for sociability and self-actualization) and organizational needs (for example, for productivity and innovation). We might say, therefore, that there is a dominant prevailing ideology that espouses the benefits of teams in relation to virtually any organizational problem, including knowledge creation. Of course, as seen, problems of working in teams have been acknowledged. However, for the most part these problems are seen as the outcome of ineffective team processes that can be overcome in order to achieve effective teamwork. So, for example, through facilitating the development of trust within a team (see below), conflicts can be worked through to enhance creativity, as in the idea of 'creative abrasion', rather than lead to destructive outcomes.

However, there are scholars who question this simplistic account and recognize that teamwork is often much less effective than many of those advocating the benefits of teamwork would suggest. For example, Nadler, Hackman and Lawler (1979) note that the quality of interpersonal relationships among group members often leaves much to be desired. They conclude that people fall too readily into patterns of competitiveness, conflict and hostility, and that only rarely do group members support and help one another.

The problem is that, as Sinclair (1992) points out, the ideological assumptions of the prevailing team paradigm are naive. In particular, Sinclair points to the ways in which, within groups, power has been treated as 'a regrettable and regressive tendency exercised by individuals who fail to identify with the collective task' (Sinclair, 1992, pp. 618–19). Thus, while there is a clear recognition that political pressures exist within groups, the dominant response to this is to seek to minimize this impact 'through training and containing or banishing power-seekers or by creating an organizational environment in which a spirit of egalitarianism renders power and conflict irrelevant' (Sinclair, 1992, p. 619).

In contrast to this view, Sinclair (1992) advocates treating individual power-seeking within groups as endemic. Group behaviour from this view would be seen as essentially conflict between individuals seeking to exercise power in different ways in order to advance their own individual ends. The outcome of teamwork is, then, the result of the successful assertion of some individuals' power-seeking efforts over others'. Where consensus is achieved this simply conceals conflicts and power discrepancies. This implies that groups with a clear and accepted distribution of power are most likely to be *judged* as productive because the output of the group conforms to expectations, even though the actual teamworking effort may be very limited, judged in terms of the level of information exchanged, the quality of group interactions, the level of creativity and so on. Indeed, from this perspective, effective group work, which involves substantial levels of information exchange, group interactions and creativity, actually depends on achieving some redistribution of power. Only with a redistribution of power will conflict be allowed to emerge so that the false consensus (as with groupthink) is eroded. In the ResearchTeam case discussed below, this issue of false consensus and the attempt to ignore conflict were very apparent.

Ironically perhaps, while the redistribution of power is central to the team working philosophy, in reality power becomes quickly formalized within teamworking situations and leads to high levels of team control and coercion over individual members. Power is passed from the hierarchy to the team members themselves, so that they become self-managing teams. This power is used by the team members to police and control each other's behaviours. Barker (1993) demonstrated very vividly how a team comes to use its power to increase control of individual team members. Barker describes a manufacturing organization that changed from a system of bureaucratic control to a system of self-managed teams. Senior management at this organization set out a vision for these teams, which the teams accepted. This vision enshrined values such as team autonomy, responsibility and achieving objectives. These shared values led the teams to develop a set of norms to guide their behaviour (for example, we need to be at work on time). Over time, these simple norms were turned into highly formalized and objective rules (for example, if you are more than five minutes late, you will lose a day's pay). Other team members censored individuals who failed to abide by these rules.

The Barker (1993) case demonstrates very clearly how a new form of control emerges very quickly within the context of self-managed teams. He refers to this new form of control as 'concertive' control. Concertive control shifts power from management to the workers themselves. The individual team members collaborate to develop their own ideas, norms and rules that enable them to act in ways that are functional for the organization. Essentially, teams can create a system of control that is more powerful and repressive than traditional bur-eaucratic systems of control. In the Barker case the team control was far more powerful than had been the traditional hierarchical managerial control since other team members could constantly monitor the behaviour of each other. In effect, the other team members had become peer managers. This can be stressful for individuals but can also detract from the creativity potential of the team; following team rules can become more important than finding the creative solution to problems or exploiting opportunities.

Thus, while working in teams can potentially create synergies so that the team shares knowledge and expertise which allows it to produce an output which is better than could have been achieved by any individual member working

Table 3.1 Summary of the advantages and disadvantages of team decision-making

Advantages	Disadvantages
Increased pool of knowledge to draw upon	Conformity can stifle creativity
Increased acceptance and commitment of the selected decision	Groupthink can override individual judgement
Wider range of perspectives taken into consideration	Group polarization can lead to overly risky decisions
Novice team members can learn from more experienced team members	Diffusion of responsibility leads individuals to avoid feeling responsible
Greater understanding of the rationale of the selected decision	Satisficing so that the decision is acceptable rather than optimum

alone, teams can also produce outputs which are worse than could have been produced by the most competent team members (Hackman, 1990), as demonstrated by the groupthink phenomenon. West *et al.* (1998) provide a useful review of the advantages and disadvantages of teamworking. Drawing on this work, Table 3.1 provides a summary of some of the most important advantages and disadvantages of teamworking.

Teamworking and integration mechanisms

Grandori and Soda (1995), recognizing this problem of achieving collaboration, identify a number of what they describe as integration mechanisms that, they argue, can encourage cooperation. They list ten such mechanisms and suggest that in teams or networks where the objective is the joint production of knowledge, all ten mechanisms need to be employed. These mechanisms include access to communication channels, social coordination through agreed norms, providing individuals with particular role responsibilities for linking individuals together, assigning authority and control to particular individuals, careful selection of individuals to ensure an appropriate mix of skills and expertise, and utilizing incentive systems.

Dodgson (1994), focusing more on the social problems of collaboration, argues that it is crucial to create and sustain personal relationships between the team members. He goes on to claim that for the exchange of knowledge and resources to be effective, a high-trust relationship needs to be developed. Partners need to trust one another to be 'honest, capable and committed to joint aims' (p. 291). In a similar way, Von Krogh *et al.* (2000) delineate five aspects of an enabling context for knowledge creation – mutual trust, active empathy, access to help, leniency in judgement and courage. Trust, they suggest, is the fundamental basis of effective interaction for knowledge-sharing. The aspect of trust, therefore, seems to be central to understanding knowledge-sharing and knowledge creation within the context of a project team. We need therefore to look at what is meant by trust and consider how trust can be developed and sustained.

The importance of trust in teamworking

It is argued, then, that trust can lead to, and is a necessary condition for, cooperative behaviour among individuals, groups or organizations. High levels of trust are considered necessary in order to facilitate the levels of communication that are needed for people to share tacit knowledge and generate learning and knowledge creation. In many articles on the management of knowledge work the importance of trust for knowledge-sharing and knowledge creation is indeed recognized. For example, Von Krogh *et al.* (2000) argue that an effective enabling context, allowing for a network of interactions, must be characterized by care and trust among the participants, if it is going to encourage knowledge-sharing and knowledge creation. In such a context, knowledge can be created spontaneously as conceptual insight and practice are merged in action. However, in most cases there is little more than a simple statement that 'trust is necessary'. In this section we consider the issue of trust in much more detail and illustrate that while trust is indeed important for knowledge creation, it is also difficult to establish – individuals will not necessarily 'grow to trust each other' simply because they are told to work together in a project team. Understanding the different types of trust that exist and the processes influencing trust development is crucial for considering the people management practices (see Chapter 4) that are likely to be effective for stimulating the effective management of knowledge work and knowledge workers.

Definitions of trust

Trust is defined in different ways in the literature, although two issues seem central: first, that trust is about dealing with risk and uncertainty; and second, that trust is about accepting vulnerability. Luhmann (1988), for example, sees trust as an attitudinal mechanism that allows individuals to subjectively assess whether or not to expose themselves to situations where the possible damage may outweigh the advantage. This attitude develops where individuals choose to accept vulnerability to others. In other words, to trust someone there must be a situation of uncertainty in which there is an element of perceived risk on the trustee's part: 'the willingness of a party to be vulnerable to the actions of another party based on the expectation that the other will perform a particular action important to the trustor, irrespective of the ability to monitor or control that other party' (Mayer *et al.*, 1995, p. 712). There are many sources of vulnerability that may be 'at risk' in collaborative situations, for example, reputation, financial resources, self-esteem, conversations. Where tasks are interdependent and there are goods or things that one values, vulnerability and the need for trust are higher. This will be precisely the situation in a knowledge-creating project team within an organization.

While we can have a generally agreed broad definition of trust, the literature also makes it clear that there are different types of trust, based either on different sources of trust or on different processes of trust development. For example, Sako (1992) considers three different reasons for being able to develop trust, that is, different reasons for being able to predict that another will behave in a 'mutually acceptable manner': first, because of a contractual agreement that binds the parties in the relationship; second, because of a belief in the competencies of those involved; and third, because of a belief in the goodwill of those involved. This is very similar to the typology developed by Shapiro *et al.* (1992), which distinguishes between deterrence-based trust, knowledge-based trust and identification-based trust.

Other writers have concentrated on understanding how trust is developed and maintained. In terms of development, Zucker (1986) depicts three central mechanisms of trust production – process-based (that is, based on reciprocal, recurring exchange), characteristic-based (that is, based on social similarity), and institutional-based (that is, based on expectations embedded in societal norms and structures). In terms of maintenance, Ring and Van de Ven (1994) distinguish between fragile (easily developed but easily broken) and resilient (hard-won and less likely to break) trust. Similarly, Jones and George (1998) distinguish between conditional and unconditional trust. Conditional trust is established at the beginning of a social encounter as long as there are no obvious indications that the other has different values and so should not be trusted. This is because it is easier to assume trust than distrust. Over time, as one becomes more confident that the other person shares one's values, this trust will be converted into unconditional trust. Unconditional trust, they argue, is more enduring and is the basis for the development of synergistic team relationships, which can lead to increased knowledge creation and superior performance. In other words, Jones and George (1998) argue that unconditional trust leads to more effective cooperative behaviour than does conditional trust.

Other research has focused on trust-building when there is a time pressure. Meyerson *et al.* (1996), for example, argue that in temporary groups working on short-lived complex tasks that require the specialist skills of relative strangers, trust needs to form very quickly if the group is to make any progress at all. They suggest that this 'swift trust' has unusual properties in that its development is driven more by contextual cues than by personalities or interpersonal relations. Thus swift trust is a pragmatic strategy for getting on with the job at hand involving 'artful making do with a modest set of general cues from which inferences are drawn about how people might care for what we entrust to them' (p. 191), The concept of swift trust is particularly useful in relation to knowledge-creating teams. In many cases those involved in the project teams, put together in order to share knowledge and develop new products or processes, have never worked together before. At the same time they often have very tight deadlines – just the situation where 'wading in on trust' may be more likely and indeed necessary.

Drawing these different ideas about trust together, a threefold typology is presented below. This typology pulls together the typologies that already exist in the literature.

Companion trust: This refers to trust that is based on judgements of goodwill or personal friendships. The trust rests on a moral foundation that others will behave in a way that does not harm other members of the network. The parties will expect each other to be open and honest. Such trust will be process-based in that it will develop over time as people get to know each other personally (and possibly become friends) through continuing, reciprocal exchange. This trust should be slow-forming and resilient. It has a strong emotional component and is important for the maintenance of social networks. Partners should be relatively tolerant of others' (well-intentioned) mistakes. However, if eventually broken, this trust is also likely to cause the greatest rift between the parties involved.

Competence trust: This trust is based on perceptions of the others' competence to carry out the tasks that need to be performed and will be important where the skills needed to perform a task are not able to be found within one person. In other words competence trust is based on an attitude of respect for the abilities of the trustee to complete their share of the job at hand. The truster feels that they can rely on the trustee. The development of this form of trust thus relies on perceiving the competences of the other partners. This may not necessarily need to occur through interpersonal exchange – competence judgements can also be driven by contextual cues such as the reputation of the institution that the person works for or the status of the professional group to which they belong. This type of trust can therefore develop much more swiftly but it is also likely to be more fragile since if the trustee does not quickly demonstrate the competences which were expected, the trust breaks down.

Commitment trust: This trust stems from the contractual agreements between the parties. In this case, the trust is developed on an institutional basis. Each party is expected to gain mutual benefit out of the relationship, and so can be relied on to be committed to deliver according to the details of the contract. While the contract itself embodies formal obligations on the part of the signatories, the important element as regards risk and uncertainty is that it allows those involved to believe that those others with whom they are working will demonstrate commitment trust, that is, that others can be trusted to put in the effort necessary to complete the joint work. This commitment trust means that only rarely will the contract itself be used to settle conflicts between the parties. Indeed, resorting to 'the contract' would be a sign that the commitment trust had broken down. This type of trust probably falls in between the first two in terms of how resilient it is. It is more resilient than competence-based trust because the contractual agreement underpinning commitment trust will still encourage a continuation of the alliance even if those involved stop respecting each other's abilities (they know they can resort to 'the contract' if all else fails). However, it is not likely to be as resilient as goodwill or companion trust. Partners that fail to demonstrate their commitment by delivering their share of the work on one contract are likely to be dropped from any future joint collaboration.

These different types of trust are all likely to be related to the ability of a project team to create knowledge. Thus, having identified the importance of teamworking for knowledge-sharing and knowledge creation and the centrality of trust in these processes, we can now look at a case example to further illustrate these points. The project team in the case example (ResearchTeam) essentially failed to share knowledge effectively and this was largely because of problems in developing and sustaining trust between the individuals concerned. In addition, issues of power and conflict were also very apparent in explaining the failure to create knowledge in the team.

Conclusions

In conclusion, this chapter has demonstrated the centrality of teamworking for knowledge creation. However, it has also illustrated that putting individuals with different backgrounds together will not automatically and inevitably generate the synergy that will result in knowledge creation. In certain situations power differentials and group conformity pressures will impede the team so that a false consensus is generated which is certainly not the result of the collaborative involvement of the different knowledge sets represented. In order to overcome these problems of collaborative teamworking, this chapter has emphasized the importance of developing trust between the various parties involved.

Different types of trust have been identified that help us to consider in more depth the relationship between trust and knowledge creation. This will be unpacked in more detail as we consider the ResearchTeam case next. This case also demonstrates the difficulty of actually creating trust within a team, which is very heterogeneous. Where those involved have very different backgrounds and perspectives, considerable time needs to be devoted to providing shared experiences so that some mutual understanding (knowledge redundancy) and trust can be developed. As we shall see in the ResearchTeam case, the failure to give teams enough time to develop trust and to consider obstacles to knowledge-sharing is likely to result in reduced rather than enhanced creativity. This chapter has focused on the micro processes of knowledge creation. In the next chapter we explore more generally the Human Resource Management (HRM) practices that can support the human processes involved in knowledge creation that have been considered in this chapter.

Case Study 3.1   ResearchTeam

The case to be considered in this chapter is that of a university research team, working on a project to develop new knowledge in a particular subject area. The team consisted of four principal investigators (PIs), who wrote the original proposal, four research officers (ROs), and one full-time administrator. These individuals worked at three universities (with two PIs and two ROs and the administrator working at one university and one PI and RO at each of the other two universities), which were geographically separated, although all in the UK. The PIs and ROs also had different disciplinary backgrounds and experience to offer to the project (including, for example, experience in engineering, operations management, marketing and organizational behaviour). The project was supported by a research grant from a government Research Council together with funding from a major industrial partner.

The case is described in relation to three phases of the project: Phase 1, where the PIs worked together to submit a project proposal to the potential funding body; Phase 2, where the ROs and administrator had been appointed and were working together with the PIs on the project; and Phase 3 which considers the outputs from the project.

Phase 1:   submitting the proposal

Initially the project team consisted of the four PIs who came together as a result of a complex set of interrelated contacts; in particular through their joint membership of an expert panel, but also because of contacts made at conferences and other academic networking. In addition, two of the PIs were professors who had been friends since their university days together. The team decided to work together when they learnt that the Research Council was prepared to sponsor a large project in the research area they were all involved in, albeit from different disciplinary perspectives. The four PIs thus identified a potential mutual benefit from winning the research contract and started to work together collaboratively to put together a proposal.

While two of the four PIs knew each other well, the other two PIs had no prior 'history' other than casual acquaintance. Yet trust had to be established quickly if this group was to meet the deadline for the proposal specified by the funding body. This was achieved since competence could be inferred from the fact that each of the four PIs had published in credible journals and each belonged to a reputable university. There were no grounds for expecting harmful behaviour from others. The only cues available signalled expectations of high levels of competence that would allow them to put together, and subsequently deliver on, a creative research project.

The outcome of this phase was a proposal for a research project which included a list of 'deliverables' that the research team would produce jointly. This proposal then became the contract, which bound the team of four together and against which they would be judged by the funding body once the project was completed. While there were no real sanctions that would apply if the team failed to deliver, there was a potential that their reputations

Case Study 3.1 continued

could be tarnished, especially with the funding Research Council. This was clearly significant since this body was a major source of research income for all of them. Unfortunately, the proposal was subsequently interpreted differently by the PIs, and so became a source of continuous tension and conflict (see below). This occurred largely because, in the rush to meet the deadline, the detail in the proposal, in terms of the stated objectives and how they would be achieved, had not been clearly negotiated and defined at the outset.

Once the research contract had been awarded, the PIs started working on the project. This involved several meetings to work out how they would operate as a team (for example, establishing who would be responsible for what) and also to flesh out more precisely the nature of the research problem (for example, which theoretical perspectives and empirical approaches would inform the research). Once the team actually started to work together, however, the swiftly made assumptions of competence trust started to break down. It became apparent that at least some of the PIs had in reality known very little about the academic work of some of the others. Indeed, one of the PIs eventually commented in exasperation that she would in future always read at least three articles by anyone she was considering working with; implying that if she had done so in this case she would not have gone ahead. This deterioration in perceptions of competence trust occurred because the PIs had fundamentally different theoretical and epistemological positions, which meant that the possibility of ever reaching a consensus on how the research should be done was remote, despite their genuine attempts to do so. The written contract (that is, the research proposal) also became a problem during this phase. In retrospect at least some of the PIs felt they had committed themselves to a proposal that had not been mapped out well in the first place.

Phase 2: enlarging the team

Once the proposal had been accepted and the grant awarded, the research team was enlarged with the recruitment of four ROs and one project administrator. The four individuals initially recruited as ROs were total strangers to each other. They were geographically dispersed across the three universities but were told that they needed to collaborate in order to undertake the research. They were encouraged by the PIs to work together, and several coordination mechanisms were introduced by the PIs to encourage this integration. For example, the project was divided into a series of work packages, which essentially laid down a formal project plan. At first these work packages were each led by one of the ROs. However, this did not work very effectively as the ROs found it difficult to demand action from their more senior PIs. Moreover, the work packages proved too inflexible for the inevitable complexities of a large-scale research project. Deadlines for the different work packages were never adhered to and the planning framework was therefore largely redundant. Meetings were spent revisiting the plans and making new plans that were then never followed.

Case Study 3.1 continued

In terms of more general and informal social integration mechanisms, the ROs were largely left to 'make sense' of their role and their relationships with each other by themselves. On the first day on the project they telephoned each other to 'say hello' and subsequently met at a meeting of the whole research network that had been arranged by the PIs. Thereafter, they were expected to coordinate between themselves.

One of the first problems to emerge among the ROs occurred very quickly and related to the process of recruitment. Three of the ROs recruited were young (under 30), having just finished, or being in the process of completing, either Master's or doctoral degrees. They applied for the particular job because they wanted to pursue an academic career and were selected through a conventional process where they had to apply and be interviewed for the job in competition with other applicants. The fourth RO selected (we shall call him Pat) was older and was appointed without any competition on the basis of a single PI's personal opinion. Pat did not have a conventional academic background and had also failed to complete a postgraduate qualification. However the PI who recruited him had decided that Pat would be better able to take over more of the work than would typically be expected of an RO. This was despite the fact that Pat already had a consultancy business which put considerable demands on his time. While the other ROs tried to be accommodating, Pat himself felt uncomfortable with the situation. He was also action-oriented and frustrated with what he felt was 'overtheorizing' by the others. Pat therefore soon tired of his new post, becoming irritated with the convoluted nature of much academic debate, together with the emphasis on rigorous process rather than on the generation of results. Within months he had left, an event which had significant effects in the context of a three-year project.

After Pat had left the project, no one was recruited to replace him for six months, so the three remaining ROs worked as a smaller team, dispersed at the three different universities. The work was divided up between them. Initially, the ROs recognized the need to coordinate their different tasks and they agreed to meet regularly. However, over time their meetings became less and less frequent. Thus, from weekly or at least fortnightly contact among this group, there was a period when they did not meet for almost six months. The reason for this increased estrangement was that trust did not develop between two of this group of three. The repeated contact actually led to a distrust based on a belief in the other's *in*competence. Again, as was the case with the PIs, these two individuals came from very different disciplinary backgrounds and each was simply not able to respect the other's contributions to the project. The two individuals were also quite different in terms of their personalities and interests. Their only common ground was the research project so that companion trust was difficult to develop in the absence of competence trust. This situation was uncomfortable for all the ROs, particularly these two. The outcome was that one of the pair left the project.

Much later, once the two departing ROs had been replaced, meetings between the new set of four ROs were once again instigated. These meetings were

Case Study 3.1 continued

more successful and would run on into an evening meal and became a valuable integrative event, at least among the ROs. However, despite this early success the ROs eventually became discouraged from holding such gatherings, in part because the conceptual frameworks they developed during these meetings were heavily criticized by the PIs at whole team meetings (although the ROs claimed that their work surfaced again later in PI analyses). The low importance attached to RO contributions was reinforced at the whole team meetings, in which their involvement was limited to presenting some previously prepared findings from their local universities. They took little part in discussion and when they attempted to join in their contributions were generally disregarded. The low point in their marginalization from these meetings occurred when the PIs decided to split the whole team meetings into two parallel streams, holding a separate PI meeting in an adjoining room.

An important tension for the ROs, then, was that the espoused consensual approach to the research – we are all equal and the contributions from PIs and ROs are of equal importance – cut across the more hierarchical department structures, which were particularly apparent at one of the universities. Here the autocratic leadership style of the PI was reinforced by the layout of the building, in which all the professors, including this PI, were housed separately in a luxurious suite of rooms at the top of the building, commonly referred to as 'Prof. Corridor'. This PI preserved a remoteness from most aspects of the project, not taking part in the research and minimizing contact with the ROs. At full team meetings, to which he travelled first-class, he regularly employed a mocking and dismissive approach to the younger male RO working at his university. He clearly placed his departmental needs above those of the project, insisting that the project coordinator spend one day a week working for the department and 'not just the project'. However such role expectations (of a superior, distant and 'figurehead' status) were not shared by the PI from one of the other universities, whose approach was to get considerably more involved in the project and to work closely with her RO.

Phase 3: outcomes

The emergent solution to the tensions and frustrations that were being experienced by both the PI and the RO groups within the project was a division of the project into three fairly autonomous 'bits', which therefore reduced the interdependencies between the project team, so that conflict could be more easily avoided. Essentially the project was run as three separate projects, broken down along disciplinary lines (which happened to also coincide with the geographical dispersion of the project team). This move to a federated approach completely undermined the initial explicit intention to ensure a synthesis across the team; indeed such an integration of the three disciplinary areas had been a major part of the academic rationale for the project. However, throughout the life cycle of the project two of the PIs continued to argue for the need to fulfil this early commitment to an integrated project. They tenaciously opposed the emerging tendency for the project to develop into three 'federated'

Case Study 3.1 continued

sub-projects; arguing, for example, that all four ROs should carry out research fieldwork together. However, in reality the low synthesis across the team emerged very rapidly and quickly became strongly embedded so that a return to a synthesized approach became impossible.

The team did continue to have fairly regular face-to-face meetings where those working on the now independent projects came together to share experiences and analyses. However, these were never as frequent as originally intended because of the difficulties of actually finding dates when all the PIs could attend. There were, in the event, few meetings where all the PIs were present. This fluctuating membership was a problem because a lot of time had to be spent in bringing those absent from meetings up to date. More problematical still was the lack of follow-through and building on what was agreed at these meetings. One PI described it as 'the syndrome of hitting reset at the end of the meeting'. They tried to resolve this problem by having one of the PIs summarize the key points from the meetings and then circulate this to the others using e-mail. However, there were frequently problems in this process as individuals had interpreted the same meeting very differently.

Between meetings the team relied on e-mail communication to share experiences across the three federated projects. This created problems because some of those involved were lax in responding to their e-mails. Moreover, this mode of communication was found to be ineffective where conceptual and methodological issues needed to be resolved. The team then moved to using telephone conferencing to try and resolve differences between the various subgroups. Observing these conferences at any particular institution revealed how those at one site would ridicule those taking part from other sites. Mocking gestures and written comments, invisible to those on the other end of the telephone line, were clearly well-practised by the local group. This disdain towards team members from other departments was similarly seen in the distinction between e-mails circulated around a university group and those disseminated throughout the whole team.

The main formal outputs from this project were publications. The first publication from the project caused considerable conflict because one of the PIs decided to publish some of the research outputs without consulting, or crediting, team members from the other departments. The other PIs argued that they should all be jointly involved in publications, since this would provide the opportunity to synthesize across the different disciplines. Following this first publication, therefore, there was a standing item on the agenda of every project team meeting so that they could discuss this as a group. Thus, at every meeting they talked about writing papers jointly, albeit the ROs were typically excluded from this discussion. However, the reality was that virtually all output was written by team members from only one of the universities, in other words by individuals from the same disciplinary background. The only real output that was jointly produced was the final report that was written for the sponsoring Research Council. This had to be written jointly and present an integrated conceptual framework and analysis, in line with the initial project

Case Study 3.1 continued

proposal. However, those involved were relatively dissatisfied with this output, feeling that it did not do justice to the richness of the independent parts of the research conducted at the separate university departments. While it is difficult to clearly evaluate the creativeness of such research, the grading of this final report, given by independent peer reviewers, did not rate this research project highly.

Questions

1. How did interaction affect the development of trust in this project team? Was this different among the PI and RO groups?
2. What impact did integration mechanisms have on the development of trust?
3. How did power affect knowledge creation within this project team?
4. What does the ResearchTeam case teach us about knowledge creation in multidisciplinary contexts?

Summary of key learning points

- Knowledge creation within organizations, leading to the development of new products, services or processes, typically occurs within teams.
- Both the intellectual and social capital of team members is important.
- The process of knowledge creation within teams depends on achieving a synergy between team members so that, through 'creative abrasion', something new and useful will emerge.
- Knowledge-sharing within a team will only be successful if there is some shared understanding or knowledge redundancy among team members such that the team develops an absorptive capacity for new ideas.
- Teams should not, however, be seen as a panacea for all organizational problems; nor should the problems of enabling effective teamworking be underestimated.
- Teams essentially consist of individuals, each of whom has his or her own agenda, and individuals may use their power to attempt to satisfy personal goals. Some individuals, however, have more power than others and so can more easily persuade the team to work in a way that satisfies their agendas.
- Teams thus suffer from many potential problems, including a propensity to conformity, groupthink, social loafing and group polarization effects.
- To overcome some of these problems there is a need to consider implementing integration mechanisms and in particular encouraging the development of trust between team members.

> **Summary of key learning points continued**
>
> ■ There are different types of trust that are important, including companion, competence and commitment trust. These three types of trust do not develop through the same mechanisms nor do they necessarily develop simultaneously.
>
> ■ Trust is not easy to develop, especially where team members come from very different backgrounds and so have different knowledge and understanding. In such situations, prolonged interaction and common experiences are necessary to develop the shared understanding necessary for trust to develop and knowledge-sharing to be possible.

References

Barker, J. (1993) Tightening the iron cage: concertive control in self-managing teams. *Administrative Science Quarterly*, **38**(3): 408–33.

Burgoyne, J. (1994) Managing by learning. *Management Learning*, **25**(1): 1–29.

Burgoyne, J., Brown, D., Hindle, A. and Mumford, M. (1997) A multi-disciplinary identification of issues associated with 'contracting' in market-oriented Health Service reforms. *British Journal of Management*, **8**: 39–49.

Cohen, M. and Levinthal, D. (1990) Absorptive capacity: a new perspective on learning and innovation. *Administrative Science Quarterly*, **35**(1): 128–52.

Dodgson, M. (1993) Learning, trust and technological collaboration. *Human Relations*, **46**(1): 77–95.

Dodgson, M. (1994) Technological collaboration and innovation. In M. Dodgson and R. Rothwell (eds) *The Handbook of Industrial Innovation*. Aldershot, UK: Edward Elgar.

Grandori, A. and Soda, G. (1995) Inter-firm networks: antecedents, mechanisms and forms. *Organization Studies*, **16**: 183–214.

Grant, R. (2000) Prospering in dynamically-competitive environments: organizational capability as knowledge integration. *Organization Science*, 7(4): 375–87.

Hackman, R. (1990) *Groups That Work (and Those That Don't): Conditions for Effective Teamwork*. San Francisco: Jossey-Bass.

Hakansson, H. and Johanson, J. (1988) Formal and informal cooperation strategies. In F. Contractor and P. Lorange (eds) *Cooperative Strategies in International Business*. Lexington, Mass.: Lexington Books.

Iansiti, M. (1993) Real-world R & D: jumping the product generation gap. *Harvard Business Review*, **71**(3): 138–47.

Janis, I.L. (1982) *Groupthink*. Boston, Mass.: Houghton Mifflin.

Jones, G. and George, J. (1998) The experience and evolution of trust: implications for cooperation and teamwork. *Academy of Management Review*, **23**(3): 531–46.

Knights, D. and Willmott, H. (1997) The hype and hope of interdisciplinary management studies. *British Journal of Management*, **8**: 9–22.

Latene, B., Williams, K. and Harkins, S. (1979) Many hands make light work: the causes and consequences of social loafing. *Journal of Personality and Social Psychology*, **37**: 822–32.

Leonard-Barton, D. (1995) *Well-springs of Knowledge: Building and Sustaining the Sources of Innovation*. Boston, Mass.: Harvard Business School Press.

Luhmann, N. (1988) Familiarity, confidence, trust: problems and alternatives. In D. Gambetta (ed.) *Trust: Making and Breaking Cooperative Relations.* New York: Basil Blackwell, pp. 94–107.

McCune, J. (1998) Working together but apart. *Management Review,* **87**(8): 45–7.

Mayer, R., Davis, J. and Schoorman, F. (1995) An integration model of organizational trust. *Academy of Management Review,* **20**(3): 709–19.

Meyers, P. and Wilemon, D. (1989) Learning in new technology development teams. *Journal of Product Innovation Management,* **6**(2): 79–88.

Meyerson, D., Weick, K. and Kramer, R.M. (1996) Swift trust and temporary groups. In R.M. Kramer and T.R. Tyler (eds) *Trust in Organizations: Frontiers of Theory and Research.* New York: Sage.

Milgram, S. (1964) Behavioral study of obedience. *Journal of Abnormal and Social Psychology,* **67**: 371–8.

Moorhead, G., Ference, R. and Neck, C. (1991) Group decision fiascos continue: space shuttle Challenger and a revised groupthink framework. *Human Relations,* **44**(6): 539–51.

Nadler, D., Hackman, J. and Lawler, E. (1979) *Managing organizational behaviour.* Boston, Mass.: Little, Brown.

Nahapiet, J. and Ghoshal, S. (1998) Social capital, intellectual capital and the organizational advantage. *Academy of Management Review,* **23**(2): 242–66.

Nonaka, I. (1990) Redundant, overlapping organization: a Japanese approach to managing the innovation process. *California Management Review,* **32**(3): 27–38.

Nonaka, I. and Konno, N. (1998) The concept of 'ba': building a foundation for knowledge creation. *California Management Review,* **40**(3): 40–54.

Nonaka I. and Takeuchi, H. (1995) *The Knowledge-creating Company.* Oxford: Oxford University Press.

Ring, P.S. and Van de Ven, A.H. (1994) Developmental processes of cooperative interorganizational relationships. *Academy of Management Review,* **19**: 90–118.

Ringlemann, M. (1913) Recherches sur moteurs animés: travail de l'homme. *Annales de l'Institut National Agronomique,* 2e série, **XII**: 1–40.

Sako, M. (1992) *Prices, Quality and Trust: How Japanese and British Companies Manage Buyer–Supplier Relations.* Cambridge: Cambridge University Press.

Shapiro, D., Sheppard, B. and Cheraskin, L. (1992) Business on a handshake. *Negotiation Journal,* **8**: 365–77.

Sinclair, A. (1992) The tyranny of a team ideology. *Organization Studies,* **13**(14): 611–26.

Stoner, J. (1968) Risky and cautious shifts in group decision: the influence of widely held values. *Journal of Experimental Social Psychology,* **4**: 442–59.

Von Krogh, G., Ichijo, K. and Nonaka, I. (2000) *Enabling Knowledge Creation: How to Unlock the Mystery of Tacit Knowledge and Release the Power of Innovation.* Oxford: Oxford University Press.

West, M., Borrill, C. and Unsworth, K. (1998) Team effectiveness in organizations. In C. Cooper and I. Robertson (eds) *International Review of Industrial and Organizational Psychology,* Vol. 13. Chichester: Wiley, pp. 1–48.

Westbrook, R. (1991) *Why Don't we Work Together? Issues in Multi-disciplinary Teaching and Research.* Working paper. London Business School, September.

Zucker, L.G. (1986) Production of trust: institutional sources of economic structure, 1840–1920. In B.M. Staw and L.L. Cummings (eds) *Research in Organisational Behaviour,* Vol. 8. Greenwich, Cann.: JAI, pp. 53–111.

4 Human Resource Management and knowledge work

Learning outcomes

At the end of this chapter students will be able to:

- Identify the major Human Resource Management (HRM) issues relevant to the management of knowledge work.
- Evaluate the potential impact of HRM policies on the performance of knowledge worker groups.
- Analyse the linkages between HRM and Knowledge Management.
- Identify the appropriate HRM context for different Knowledge Management strategies.

The overall aim of this chapter is therefore to introduce students to the HRM challenges raised by knowledge work and the importance of HRM policies in effective Knowledge Management.

Introduction

The management of knowledge and knowledge workers involves a number of different tools and practices. As we describe in more detail in Chapter 5, knowledge may be exploited and applied in a variety of ways, including encoding it in ICT (information and communication technology) systems or embedding it in the rules and procedures of the organization itself. Many of the most important forms of knowledge, however, cannot be separated from the human work groups who create, communicate and apply them (Blackler, 1995). This means that the way these groups are managed has important implications for organizational performance. In the first instance, this involves addressing the distinctive characteristics of knowledge workers as an employee group. In Chapter 2 we highlighted many important aspects of the way knowledge workers interact. In this chapter, however, our concern is with the factors which make knowledge workers distinctive as an employee group. In particular, we are interested in identifying those characteristics which make them crucial to business strategy, yet at the same time difficult to manage. Some of these characteristics have been identified by Reich (1991) as follows:

- Knowledge workers are a directly productive force for the company.
- They represent an investment for the business – they are not just labour costs.
- They bring labour-saving benefits in their ability to reorganize production and design.
- Their knowledge represents a form of personal 'equity' – many knowledge workers are potential entrepreneurs.

Knowledge workers are frequently distinguished from more conventional professional groups such as lawyers, architects and doctors. Where these groups work *from* knowledge, drawing on a distinctive predefined body of expertise, knowledge workers work *with* knowledge. This includes not only their own expertise but also that of other knowledge workers as communicated through information systems, as well as the knowledge encoded in programmes, routines and managerial discourse (Scarbrough, 1999). In this respect, knowledge work can be defined as those activities which encompass the dual processes of 'transformation' and 'maintenance'. That is, knowledge workers transform the objects of their work into symbolic form – producing software, for example, or consultancy reports – while also maintaining the systems and tools which they employ (Whalley and Barley, 1997).

These characteristics have a number of possible implications for HRM in the employing organization. As we noted in Chapter 2, the selection process for knowledge workers is highly intensive with a great emphasis on finding the right fit between the individual and other members of the knowledge worker group. Also, training and development can be seen as an investment and not just a cost because the knowledge workers' expertise is producing direct benefits for the organization. Depending on the scarcity of their expertise, this can prompt energetic efforts to boost the retention of valued knowledge workers. This may involve high, performance-related salaries or even a direct stake in the organization through stock options (that is, a share in the ownership of the business).

But even if an organization is able to recruit and retain knowledge workers, this still begs the question of how to motivate them in their work. Where other employee groups may adopt an instrumental attitude to their work – that is, focusing on pay – knowledge workers are likely to have greater expectations. The nature of the work is itself of great interest; knowledge workers typically respond to interesting and challenging tasks. Moreover, they are also likely to see their current job as one rung on a longer-term career ladder. The pay they get from their current job may be less important than the career benefits of experience and development. Also, managers need to recognize that knowledge workers are interested in both the tangible and intangible rewards of their work. Intangible rewards may include status, reputation and recognition by one's peer group. These characteristics have been summarized by Tampoe (1993), whose study identified four key motivators for knowledge workers:

- *Personal growth*: the opportunity for individuals to fully realize their potential.

- *Operational autonomy*: a work environment in which knowledge workers can achieve the tasks assigned to them. This is more important than the strategic autonomy to actually determine such tasks (Bailyn, 1988).

- *Task achievement*: a sense of accomplishment from producing work which is of high quality and relevance to the organization.

- *Money rewards*: an income which is a just reward for their contribution to corporate success and which symbolizes their contribution to that success.

These motivational factors show how the HRM policies of reward, career development and work design can influence the *individual's* behaviour. But there is also a need to understand motivation and commitment in terms of the expectations and attitudes of knowledge workers as a group or community within the organization. Thus, other accounts of knowledge workers have stressed the importance of organizational culture and social identities in influencing their motivation and behaviour (Alvesson, 1993). Corporate culture, which we highlighted in Chapter 2, is seen as helping to socially integrate employees within the company, making employees whose work is often highly autonomous and individualistic feel like part of a bigger team (Kunda, 1992). Likewise, the social identities which knowledge workers develop through their work – the sense of being part of an elite group, for example – can also play a critical role in motivation and retention.

Overall, whatever view we take of the role of individual psychology or group identity, the implications of these distinctive characteristics of knowledge workers cut right across the management process in organizations. In this wider context, knowledge workers have traditionally enjoyed a good deal of autonomy and have not been managed as tightly as other groups. This reflects two major factors:

- *The work itself:* knowledge work cannot be so readily prescribed as operational or administrative work since there will always be an element of judgement involved and the creative application of expertise.

- *The expectations of knowledge workers:* the training and education of knowledge workers has led them to expect some autonomy in their work. They expect to be able to use their professional expertise, rather than simply follow a prescribed routine. (Davenport *et al.*, 1996)

These characteristics mean that conventional command-and-control forms of management which rely on managerial authority are unlikely to be successful because they simply inhibit the kind of autonomy which knowledge workers need to exercise in their work. Management needs to find ways of ensuring that the knowledge worker's autonomy is employed for the benefit of the firm, as well as being motivational for the individual. A recent study of Microsoft, outlined in Case Study 4.1, provides some insights into the management practices which can help to secure such an outcome (Cusumano and Selby, 1996).

Case Study 4.1   Microsoft

Microsoft's success is seen as reflecting the way in which the company has developed a distinctive culture and structure which avoid the usual clash of values and practices between management and knowledge workers. This

Case Study 4.1 continued

involves ensuring that management practice is grounded four-square on both knowledge of technology and knowledge of the business. The company is said to possess a CEO with a deep understanding of both the technology and the business and managers who are equally at home in creating the product and making the technical decisions. Indeed, Microsoft ensures that managers retain their technical expertise by continuing to work part-time as developers. Similarly, bureaucracy is avoided through process design and cultural features. For example, Microsoft has put in place a development process that allows large teams to work like small teams. The prevailing culture is also seen to play an important role. Shared values and high levels of employee commitment allow management to accept a high degree of employee autonomy and yet still achieve the necessary degree of control over product development.

Finally, individual needs are also addressed in the Microsoft organization. First, there is an intensive process of self-selection which ensures a good fit between the individual and the organization. Second, Microsoft reduces the conflict between individual self-interest and organizational goals by integrating individual expertise within a collective framework. This they do, for example, by ensuring that knowledge of product development details is possessed by more than one person, thus avoiding the creation of 'prima donnas'. Product development is controlled by program managers rather than individual 'superprogrammers' for the same reason. At the same time, high-performing employees are rewarded with stock options which give them a tangible stake in the company's future performance.

HRM and knowledge work

As we noted in Chapter 2, HRM policies can influence knowledge worker behaviour in a number of ways, including selection, appraisal and reward. If employees do not possess or develop the right competences and if they are not motivated to create and share knowledge, the organization will not be able to exploit its knowledge base effectively. Moreover, just as knowledge work has been interpreted in a variety of ways, it is important to recognize that there are many different views of HRM. Some writers have hailed HRM as a radical shift in the management of people, moving away from an emphasis on controlling employees towards gaining their commitment. Others, however, are sceptical about these claims and highlight the gaps between 'rhetoric' and 'reality' in the way people are managed. Thus, while the term 'knowledge work' needs to be viewed critically, we need to be equally alert to the double-edged nature of a term like 'human resources'. In a positive sense this may mean treating employees as a crucial resource for the organization, not just a cost. On the other hand, it could also mean treating people as a resource to be ever more intensively exploited.

This section will address these double-edged qualities in the application of HRM to knowledge work by drawing out three different perspectives that address this topic: best practice; best fit; and the human and social capital perspective.

Best-practice perspective

This is the most straightforward recipe for the application of HRM to knowledge work. Basically, it involves identifying a set of HRM practices which are universally applicable across a range of settings (Wood, 1995) and which result in high levels of performance from employees. The particular label attached to best practice varies from one writer to another. 'Business excellence' was the influential aspiration of Peters and Waterman (1982), but more recent candidates include Strategic Human Resource Management (Fombrun *et al.*, 1984) and 'high commitment management' (Wood, 1995). Depending on the version adopted, the policies associated with best practice will include factors such as empowerment for employees, flexibility and teamworking in work organization, performance-related pay, and a supportive, performance-oriented culture. These factors are seen as leading to high levels of commitment and effective individual performance.

Clearly, if the best-practice perspective is taken at face value, managers need hardly worry about tailoring their HRM practices to the specific demands of knowledge work. However, even if we accept this view, managers are left with the question of which best-practice model to follow, for, as the above labels indicate, there are many recipes available. Moreover, there is also a good deal of evidence to suggest that the effect of different HRM practices is context-specific – that the same practices may have different effects or be interpreted differently in one organization compared to another (Tyson and Fell, 1986; Collinson *et al.*, 1998). And even if the effects were uniform or predictable, the influence of the historical context and management capabilities may prevent the best practice being adopted (Mueller, 1994). This analysis suggests that creating an effective link between HRM practices and Knowledge Management may involve going beyond best practice to more customized approaches.

Best-fit perspective

Unlike the best practice perspective, this approach suggests that there is no 'one best way' to manage employees. The important thing is to find the right fit between management practices and the characteristics of the knowledge work process.

One of the most important contributions to this perspective comes from Hansen *et al.* (1999) who argue that there are basically two strategies for managing knowledge. These strategies they term 'codification' and 'personalization':

- *Codification*: 'Knowledge is carefully codified and stored in databases where it can be accessed and used readily by anyone in the company' (p. 107).

- *Personalization*: 'Knowledge is closely tied to the person who developed it and is shared mainly through direct person-to-person contacts' (p. 107).

These strategies help to frame the management practices of the organization as a whole as outlined in Table 4.1.

Although they do not claim that organizations pursue these strategies exclusively, Hansen *et al.* argue that competitive success involves pursuing one strategy predominantly. Attempting to 'straddle' both strategies leads to failure, they claim. The codification approach to knowledge demands well-trained people who are able to exploit ICT databases and communication systems. Andersen Consulting and Ernst & Young are good examples. On the other hand, with a personalization strategy knowledge is closely tied to the person who developed it, and it is shared informally through person-to-person contacts. Again a different kind of employee is required, one able to creatively develop and apply knowledge to unique business problems. The Bain and McKinsey consulting firms are cited as good examples of this different kind of consulting organization.

This study focused on consulting firms, of course, and, as Chapters 5 and 6 will make clear, it is possible to question whether their analysis emphasizes the role of individual experts at the expense of the role of groups and communities in creating and sharing knowledge. It may be relevant for consultancy firms employing talented individuals, but it is doubtful whether it applies to all organizations. As far as HRM is concerned, however, this study does make several useful contributions. First, it links both Knowledge Management and HRM to the competitive strategy of the organization: a useful corrective to the idea that the management of knowledge work is all about creating massive ICT databases – as if the sheer quantity of 'knowledge' communicated and

Table 4.1 Knowledge Management strategies

	Codification strategy	*Personalization strategy*
Use of ICT	Invest heavily in ICT – connect people with reusable knowledge	Invest moderately in ICT to facilitate conversations and exchange of tacit knowledge
Human Resources:		
Recruitment and selection	Hire new college graduates who are well-suited to the reuse of knowledge and the implementation of solutions	Hire MBAs who like problem-solving and can tolerate ambiguity
Training and development	Train people in groups and through computer-based distance learning	Train people through one-to-one mentoring
Reward systems	Reward people for using and contributing to document databases	Reward people for directly sharing knowledge with others

Source: Adapted from Hansen *et al.* (1999).

stored was the secret of business success. This analysis shows that it is not knowledge *per se* but the way it is applied to strategic objectives which is the critical ingredient of competitiveness. Second, this account highlights the need for 'best fit' between HRM practices such as reward systems and the organization's approach to managing knowledge work. The relevant fit is outlined as follows:

> The two Knowledge Management strategies call for different incentive systems. In the codification model, managers need to develop a system that encourages people to write down what they know and to get those documents into the electronic repository ... companies that are following the personalization approach ... need to reward people for sharing knowledge directly with other people. (Hansen *et al.*, 1999, p. 113)

This is one of the more persuasive arguments for developing both an internal and external 'fit' (Fombrun *et al.*, 1984) between management practices and the business environment. In this view HRM practices need to be tailored to factors such as the use of ICT, Knowledge Management practices and overall competitive strategy. In other words, HRM policies and practices need to be internally consistent – that is, they all need to be pulling in the same direction. At the same time they need to be aligned with the overall management system in the organization. The result should be mutually reinforcing management practices where the overall effect is greater than the sum of the parts.

Human and social capital perspective

The best-fit perspective on the role of HRM finds support from a number of quarters (for example, Tyson, 1995). However, other studies of the role of knowledge in organizational performance tend to suggest an alternative view which differs from the best-fit perspective on a number of counts. First, the best-fit perspective is essentially *managerial* in its focus. The rational adaptation of management practice is seen as the key to success. The behaviour and perceptions of those who are being managed is secondary. In contrast, other views of the role of knowledge emphasize the essentially *social* nature of organizations. Thus the firm is viewed as a social institution (Kogut and Zander, 1992) whose aims are achieved primarily through the social resources and relationships it creates in the pursuit of economic goals. In this view, the effectiveness of HRM practice is defined not by its short-term alignment with other management functions but by its long-term effects on the development of human resources and relationships. In other words, the primary contribution of HRM is the long-term development of skills, culture and capabilities within the organization (Stalk *et al.*, 1992).

Second, this view of HRM's influence draws attention to a different aspect of the management of knowledge work. The Hansen *et al.* account stresses

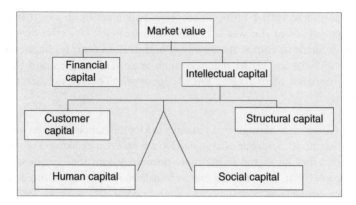

Figure 4.1   The formation of intellectual capital

the *flows* of knowledge within the organization – from people to people, or from people to ICT systems. However, as Starbuck (1992) points out, *stocks* of knowledge are equally important. Stocks take a number of forms including informal routines and individual and group expertise, together with the knowledge encoded in computer systems and organizational procedures. These stocks accumulate from what Starbuck terms the firm's input–output systems such as hiring, training and the purchase of capital goods. Stocks develop from the inflows of R&D and the development of culture. They are depleted through staff turnover, imitated routines and sales of capital goods.

Stocks of knowledge have been popularly represented as different contributions to the intellectual capital of the organization (Edvinsson and Malone, 1997; Stewart, 1997), as outlined in Figure 4.1. Applying the metaphor of 'capital' to these different aspects of organizational activity also raises the question of the ways in which these different resources can be accumulated and measured. The terms themselves are briefly defined in Box 4.1.

Box 4.1   Tangible and intangible assets of the organization

Financial capital

The financial assets of the organization. These have traditionally been measured through accountancy metrics focusing on assets and liabilities in the balance sheet or profits and losses in the profit and loss account. The limitations of these traditional measures when applied to knowledge-based business is one of the reasons why other forms of capital have received so much attention.

Box 4.1 continued

Customer capital

This represents the quality of the organization's relationship with its customers. This is more difficult to measure than financial capital but can be gauged from broad factors such as customer retention and satisfaction, as well as more specific indices including annual growth of new customers versus current customers, number of world-class products or services, and measures of the employees' knowledge of the customer.

Structural capital

Roughly speaking, this encompasses all the non-financial assets that remain when knowledge workers go home. This includes the physical assets that affect the organization's capability to effectively create and produce knowledge. Structural capital also includes areas such as: work environment, information systems, databases, workgroup tools for collaboration, organizational structures and business processes. Examples of structural capital performance measures include factors such as the percentage of world-class processes, and even the percentage of employees equipped with portable laptops and Internet access.

Human capital

This represents the value that employees bring to the organization, encompassing the wide range of human abilities and potential. Measures of this kind of capital are more difficult and context-specific but progress in accounting for 'intangible assets' is beginning to make their contribution more visible.

Social capital

Social capital can be defined as 'networks of relationships [that] constitute a valuable resource for the conduct of social affairs' (Nahapiet and Ghoshal, 1998, p. 243). As such, social capital makes an important contribution to the development and exploitation of intellectual capital. This is because much of the knowledge created by individuals and teams is socially embedded – that is, it can only be accessed and exploited through participation in 'communities of practice' (Lave and Wenger, 1991). Development of social capital promotes trust and improved personal relationships leading to more effective knowledge-sharing and the more intensive exploitation of knowledge.

The metaphor of 'capital' draws our attention to the way human skills and relationships can theoretically represent assets for an organization. The metaphor of network, however, highlights the importance of developing the interconnections between such skills and relationships if they are to truly become assets for the organization. In particular, the role of social networks in knowledge work is increasingly recognized through research studies (for example,

Nohria and Eccles, 1992) which demonstrate that the configuration of such networks is important in influencing the kinds of knowledge which can be exchanged between groups and individuals. This is partly to do with the improved ease of access to knowledge, but also reflects the extent to which valuable knowledge is often controlled by specific groups or individuals – that is, who you know affects what you know. The benefits of social networks may also be transferable from one task to another and thus may facilitate the development of innovations and new activities.

Networks are composed of different types of ties between individuals:

• Strong ties – where there are close links among a relatively small number of individuals in regular contact who have common interests.

• Weak ties – where there are loose links across a range of individuals who have occasional contact and diverse interests.

Hansen (1999) argues that strong ties are most effective in transferring tacit knowledge, while weak ties are most effective for accessing explicit knowledge. It is also argued in a noted paper on 'the strength of weak ties' that precisely because they provide links to information outside the usual interpersonal domain weak ties can be an important source of new ideas and innovation (Granovetter, 1973).

Because social capital and the networks underpinning it are an informal part of the organization, they do not appear on the organization chart and are often overlooked by management. Unlike financial or human capital, which can be possessed by a large number of people, social capital is unique. It resides in the structure of relationships between or among actors, making it a resource that does not lie with one individual, but instead is jointly owned (Putnam, 1995). Therefore, it is a potential source of competitive advantage. In this light, the human and social capital perspective draws attention to the impact of HRM on the organization's ability to exploit stocks and flows of knowledge for competitive advantage.

One further consequence of this view is to question the idea that 'best fit' alone – all parts of the business 'singing from the same hymn-sheet' – is the key to managing knowledge work. Taking the longer-term view shows how HRM practices from the past can continue to influence knowledge work in the present. Speaking positively, this influence may arise from the endowment of human and social capital which has developed over a number of years within the business. Negatively, it might mean coping with a chronic lack of trust or skills due to previous underinvestment in human resources.

All of this suggests that HRM practices need to be evaluated more precisely in relation to their impact on the sources of intellectual capital. Taking human capital in the first instance, this is obviously critical in this context as so much of the knowledge – especially tacit knowledge – which organizations seek to mobilize is embodied in individuals. On the other hand, human capital makes a rather precarious knowledge asset. This is because the job mobility of individual employees undermines the firm's ability to appropriate – that is, derive the benefits from – the skills they bring to the organization. Studies of professional service firms which depend heavily on individuals (for example, Alvesson, 1993) show how the acquisition of the firm itself may count for nothing if its major assets are able to leave and set up in business elsewhere.

This problem can be addressed to some extent by ensuring that human capital is absorbed over time into team skills, as in R&D teams, for example (Kamoche and Mueller, 1998), or into corporate routines and collective skills. This limits the mobility of human capital and gives management much greater control over the organization's knowledge assets (Grant, 1991).

As for HRM's impact on social capital, HRM policies often have both intended and unintended consequences for the quality of social relations within a business. Intended consequences might include cross-functional training programmes or teamworking projects. But unintended consequences would encompass things like the breakdown of trust due to job losses or the loss of personal networks that arise from the delayering of management or the restructuring of the business.

Three major ingredients are seen as especially critical for the development of social capital: social identity, trust and teamworking.

Social identity

The selection processes, career development and performance management systems of the organization exert an important influence on the identities forged by individuals. For example, as we noted in Chapter 2, highly rigorous selection may create a strong elite identity amongst particular groups, which is reinforced by performance-based reward systems. Such shared identities enhance employees' willingness to share knowledge.

Trust

A key element of social capital is the trust which emerges through interactions between individuals. As we noted in Chapter 3, trust can take a number of different forms. Repeated informal networking allows the development of both *goodwill trust* (that is, trust that the other person will not act against your interests) and *competence trust* (that is, trust that the other person has relevant skills and expertise). Both of these types of trust are important precursors to sharing best practice (Newell and Swan, 1999). A number of HRM practices may affect the development of trust. Reward systems which focus on individual performance, for example, are often seen as undermining interpersonal trust, though they may equally increase trust between managers and employees if they are reasonably transparent and open in the way they work.

Teamworking

Teamworking, as noted in Chapter 2, is not just about the organization of work. It also builds upon and creates social capital in organizations. Team-based knowledge may be exploitable through the development of strong team and interteam relationships. HRM practices again influence the development of teamworking through the design of work organization, reward systems and patterns of employee relations.

Because the unintended consequences of HRM policies are often as great or greater than the intended consequences, we need to look for the managerial influences on social capital at the level of overall HRM strategy or approach. Tyson (1995) usefully summarizes these broad strategic choices open to management in distinguishing between 'hard' and 'soft' contracting (see Table 4.2).

The hard contracting approach views the firm as an instrument for coordinating economic activities, but soft contracting basically views it as a social institution. The former tries to reproduce a kind of free market for labour through a hiring and firing regime. The latter, however, involves an internal labour market and a sophisticated HRM function. These different types of HRM policy have important effects on social capital. Thus, the soft contracting mode involves a long-term process of socialization through developed career paths. Here deep social affiliations and communities of practice are much more likely to flourish than in the harsh, short-term environment of hard contracting. The result is that not only is the organization potentially more flexible in dealing with the uncertainties of change and innovation, but – equally important – it is likely to enjoy greater capabilities in these areas because of its endowment of trust and socially embedded knowledge.

This is not to say that soft contracting is always the best option. Firms which are subject to extreme competitive pressures may find that hard contracting is the only feasible option available to them. It is also fair to note that the embeddedness (Granovetter, 1985) of social relations may sometimes prove to be an obstacle to change. Deeply embedded social groups, such as long-established professionals, may be highly resistant to change or innovation.

Table 4.2   Hard versus soft contracting in HRM policy

Hard contract	*Soft contract*
Management emphasizes the transaction costs of the employment relationship	Management emphasizes the vision and values of the organization
Departments within the firm are treated as contractors with specified service agreements	The organization aims to develop a high-trust culture
Dismissal is a visible sanction for non-performance	Long-term socialization is normal
A 'Taylorist' approach to pay	Rewards are linked to experience and length of service
People are employed in 'jobs', not careers	Longer-term careers are encouraged through appraisal and development policies

Source: Adapted from Tyson (1995).

Overall, the differences between hard and soft contracting help us to grasp some of the specific mechanisms through which HRM policies can help or hinder the development of social capital in organizations. HRM policies which view employees as a disposable commodity are basically hostile to developing and sustaining human and social capital. Policies which view the organization as a social institution, stressing socialization, integration and development, seem on current evidence more likely to generate the trust and social networks through which intellectual capital can be effectively accessed.

Impact of HRM policies

In this section, we move beyond the different ways of analysing the relevance of HRM to knowledge work to examine three key areas where HRM policies have a direct influence on such work: reward systems, corporate culture and organizational careers.

Reward systems

The greater the commitment required of the employee, the greater the need to address the incentives that help to create such commitment. The importance of incentives in knowledge work was underlined by a 1998 KPMG Web-site survey where 39 per cent of respondents said their organization did not reward knowledge-sharing. This was considered to be one of the most important barriers to storing and sharing knowledge.

Incentives range from tangible financial rewards to the intangible rewards of recognition and status. Knowledge-intensive environments may also permit a more innovative approach to rewarding commitment. Examples of innovative rewards being used to foster Knowledge Management include the example of Hewlett Packard where free Lotus Notes licences were distributed to encourage educators within the organization to submit comments and ideas to knowledge bases. Also, when a new knowledge base was established 2000 free air miles were offered to the first 50 readers and another 500 miles to anyone who posted a submission. Similarly, Rajan *et al.* (1998) suggest building a personal recognition system based on the number of 'hits' per site and using the system to influence decisions over promotion and reward.

Where knowledge-sharing is vital to a firm's strategy there may well be an argument for more formalized approaches to incentives. However, this may be easier to manage where knowledge work involves exploiting the expertise of individuals. For example, long-term achievement within a particular discipline may be rewarded by promoting individuals to senior expert positions within a 'dual career' system. This practice avoids siphoning off knowledge leaders into mainstream management positions. Conversely, Rajan *et al.* (1998) stress the importance of 'soft rewards': 'it is essential that employees can see that sharing means immediate gains such as less hassle, or easier tasks, reducing working hours or earlier closing' (p. 14).

When we move towards linking tangible financial rewards to Knowledge Management, however, we also have to recognize the problems. Rewards for some can create dissatisfaction for others, and they may lead to an over-emphasis on the rewarded behaviour rather than effectiveness. Individuals may put more effort into highlighting their personal contribution – bombarding an intranet with facile suggestions, for example – than in cooperating effectively with other employees. Another pitfall is the potential for the reward systems themselves (especially if salary-based) to make teamworking more difficult:

> Relationships among employees are often casualties of the scramble for rewards. As the leaders of the Total Quality Management movement have emphasized, incentive programmes, and performance appraisal systems that accompany them, reduce the possibilities for cooperation. (Kohn, 1993, p. 59)

There are ways of avoiding the problems of the past – for example, by developing a 'balanced scorecard' approach, involving team-based rewards and the development of appropriate metrics (Rajan *et al.*, 1998). But in some contexts it seems difficult to apply formal reward systems to Knowledge Management. These are situations where the value of knowledge is hard to measure and where it is the product of a team rather than an individual. In these situations we need to ask why individuals and groups are unwilling to share knowledge. It may be because they are afraid to lose power which is based on their knowledge, or because the hoarding of knowledge is seen as a legitimate tactic. These are answers which again point towards the cultural norms and values that underpin such behaviour.

Corporate culture

Knowledge work is difficult to manage and control. In most other areas of organizational life, control is exercised either directly over the work process itself, by specifying the standards, methods and pace of the way employees work (behavioural control), or by specifying and measuring the outputs of work (output control). But knowledge work is difficult for managers to observe, and its outputs are unpredictable and hard to specify. As a result, knowledge workers enjoy a good deal of autonomy. They may have to account for their time, but they do not have to account for their actions in the detailed way that other employees do.

Employee autonomy poses a problem for organizations. On the one hand, they want knowledge workers to behave autonomously and to be cooperative, team-oriented and self-managing. On the other, they want to ensure that this autonomy is employed for the benefit of the organization and not for slacking or pursuing the individual's own goals. Thus, organizations have to rely on more sophisticated means of seeking to influence knowledge worker behaviour. As we described in Chapter 2, this often focuses on developing the appropriate culture for the workplace – that is, influencing the values and norms which employees bring to their work. In management's ideal scenario, knowledge workers internalize the norms, values and broad goals of the organization. They identify with the organization, seeing themselves not as an engineer, ICT analyst or mathematician but as a member of the XYZ company team.

Sadly (for management), this ideal rarely translates into practice. Corporate culture cannot be engineered from the top down by managers, because to a large extent it emerges from the bottom up. Whatever the company policy, the actual values and norms adopted by employees arise out of their own shared experience and interactions with fellow employees. It follows that the organization's culture can exert both positive and negative influences on the management of knowledge work. In a positive sense, the culture of knowledge-sharing which developed at Buckman Labs (see Chapter 6) is a good example of values and norms becoming aligned with the demands of the business. But culture's constraining effects can also be seen in a number of cases. This applies not only in traditional, bureaucratic settings but also in dynamic knowledge-intensive organizations where a distinct professional subculture has emerged. For example, there were even problems in the introduction of Knowledge Management at Ernst & Young consulting:

> The E&Y consulting culture was traditionally based on pragmatism and experience rather than a conceptual orientation; while the culture was changing there were many consultants who had entered the firm and prospered under the old model and found it difficult to aggressively pursue structured knowledge in systems and documents. (Thomas Davenport website: www.bus.utexas.edu)

Organizational careers

Careers seem to represent one important way of integrating and sharing knowledge as individuals progress between jobs and departments. The impact of careers on the knowledge base of the organization has been discussed by a variety of authors. Sonnenfeld *et al.* (1988), for instance, analyse careers in terms of the 'supply flow' – movement in and out of the organization – and the 'assignment flow', the movement between jobs within the organization. They suggest that the choices available to firms are essentially two fold in each case: whether to promote from internal or external sources, and whether to assign jobs on the basis of individual or group contribution – the star performer versus the solid citizen.

This analysis suggests four major types of career system: internally recruiting, star-promoting firms are called *academies*, and are characterized by fast-track schemes and low turnover; firms that emphasize the internal recruitment and promotion of group contributors are termed *club* organizations; externally recruiting, star-promoting firms are labelled *baseball teams*, with on-the-job development and high turnover; finally, firms with an external recruitment policy, high turnover and little commitment to employees are labelled *fortress* firms because their major concern is survival.

The implications of the career system for the organization are clear. First, the career system is likely to reflect the strategy of the organization. To take the extremes of the range, baseball teams are likely to have a strategy based on the rapid pursuit of new products and opportunities. On the other hand, fortress organizations are likely to react to their threatening environment through successive waves of retrenchment and redundancy. Second, however, it is clear that the career system has implications for the kind of Knowledge Management which operates within the organization. In the baseball team company, for instance, Knowledge Management will focus on leveraging the knowledge of individual stars. There may be limited opportunity (or inclination) to translate the individual's expertise into a collective asset, and the aim may be one of servicing the requirements of high performers. Contrast this with club organizations where the emphasis on group contribution suggests great potential for systems centred on knowledge-sharing and codification.

Although the four types of career system presented here are not the only options open to organizations, they do point up the way in which knowledge and learning can be managed through recruitment and development programmes. In the consultancy sector, for example, it is instructive to compare the different approaches taken by Andersen Consulting (now 'Accenture') and Bain & Co. to this issue. Andersen Consulting can be seen as an academy. It recruits graduates from universities and seeks to socialize them in the Andersen Consulting knowledge base through its development programmes. Firms which employ Andersen Consulting consultants know that they will be getting the Andersen Consulting recipe. In contrast, Bain & Co. seems to operate more as a baseball team. It recruits individuals who have a proven

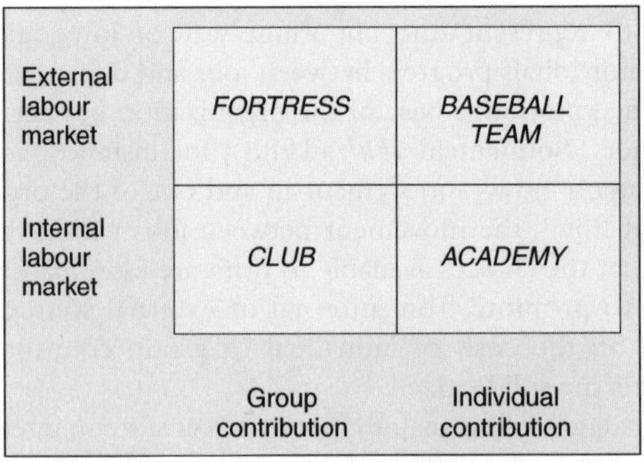

External labour market	*FORTRESS*	*BASEBALL TEAM*
Internal labour market	*CLUB*	*ACADEMY*
	Group contribution	Individual contribution

Figure 4.2 Organizational career systems
Source: Based on Sonnenfeld *et al.* (1988).

track record in top management, and seeks to apply their unique skills to consultancy assignments. Firms who employ Bain consultants expect a one-off, tailored solution to their problems.

These different career patterns clearly have implications for the way knowledge is managed in organizations.

Conclusions

In identifying the three major perspectives outlined above, this chapter has highlighted the different ways in which HRM policy and practice may impact on knowledge work. As outlined in Figure 4.3, the range of impacts is not only extensive but may potentially operate over a long time period.

Studies of HRM's impact have highlighted two major problems for management. One is the need to align HRM policies with the distinctive characteristics of knowledge workers, and the other is need to link HRM to Knowledge Management in order to enhance organizational performance. The first problem demands greater sensitivity to the motivational characteristics and career patterns of knowledge workers. It may not be easy to tailor HRM policies to the characteristics of a particular group because such policies are often standardized for the organization as a whole. It is certainly easier to do so when the organization is relatively small or is

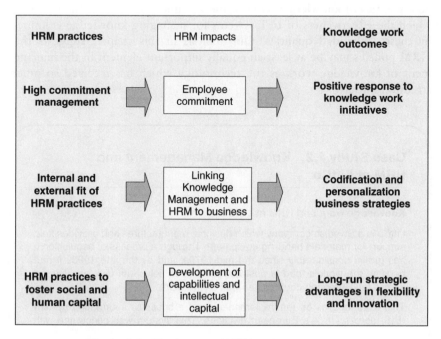

Figure 4.3 The impact of HRM on knowledge work

composed largely of knowledge workers itself – as in the ScienceCo case described in Chapter 2. Whatever the context, however, the importance of recruiting and retaining expert groups who are often in great demand poses significant challenges for HRM policy and practice. It highlights the need for greater flexibility in designing and applying such policies, and, by implication, greater awareness on the part of HRM specialists themselves.

As for the second problem, existing perspectives have tended to focus on getting the right HRM policies, or at least of aligning those policies with business strategy. This emphasizes management's ability to design and implement policy as the critical factor in exploiting human resources. However, the growing realization of the contribution of intellectual capital to competitive advantage (Grant, 1996) has begun to question this emphasis on management's decision-making powers. By drawing our attention to the intangible ingredients which make up intellectual capital – human and social capital, in particular – this perspective has stressed the long-term evolution of the firm's strategy as a major influence on its core capabilities. Put simply, business strategy is important primarily for the way it shapes the firm as a social institution. Changes in strategy mean shifts in social networks, levels of trust and the relevance of particular skills which all have long-term repercussions for the organization's future ability to create and exploit its intellectual capital. As we will describe in Chapter 5, the focus on tools and systems for manipulating knowledge which we find in much of the Knowledge Management literature often neglects the socially embedded qualities of knowledge. One of the key questions here is the extent to which the effectiveness of ICT systems for managing knowledge is limited by these embedded qualities. Our analysis in this chapter suggests that HRM policies may be at least an equally important element in the management of knowledge work as the technology which has received so much attention hitherto.

Case Study 4.2   Knowledge Management and HRM at LiftCo

Knowledge work and HRM at LiftCo

LiftCo is a Swedish company which designs, manufactures and provides field support for materials handling equipment. Through a process of acquisition it has grown considerably since the mid-1970s, and by the late 1990s it had become the world's third largest company in its field, with divisions spread across ten European countries as well as the USA.

This case focuses on the implementation of a business information system (BIS) across LiftCo's European divisions. This system was concerned with

Case Study 4.2 continued

managing both external information such as customer orders, as well as internal information such as inventory levels. The development of the system was aimed at improving the efficiency of LiftCo's response to customers, as well as improving stock control systems. The project involved collaboration with the BIS supplier – a firm called Consense – to customize the system to the specific requirements of LiftCo's different divisions. LiftCo and Consense agreed on a long-term partnering agreement, as both companies could derive a number of benefits from working together. For LiftCo the benefit was that Consense would dedicate the amount of time they required to undertake the desired modifications, while Consense benefited from being able to improve BIS and use LiftCo as one of their key reference sites.

Overall responsibility for the BIS project lay with the corporate IS (Information Systems) function, which was based at LiftCo corporate headquarters in Sweden. The leader of the BIS project, the director of the corporate IS/ function, regarded it as necessary to the success of the project that attention was given to both Knowledge Management and HRM issues. This involved special attention to recruitment and selection to ensure the creation of a project team with the necessary ICT skills and expertise. The close attention given to these issues was based on an evaluation of the reasons for the failure of a previous ICT implementation. In the early 1990s, LiftCo had made previous attempts to implement a common business information system, but all these attempts had been unsuccessful. When this experience was evaluated, LiftCo's senior management concluded that insufficient attention had been paid to HRM issues.

The participation of the HRM function was achieved through directly involving HRM staff in designing the project management procedures to be used on the BIS project, which was done before work formally began on the project itself. This involvement was channelled through a formal HRM team which included both the BIS project leader, the corporate HRM director, and a number of other relevant corporate management staff from a range of functional areas. This team examined a wide range of HRM issues, including selection, recruitment, training, development, communication (awareness-raising) and motivation (getting 'buy-in' from divisional management). Following this early involvement the HRM function was less formally involved during the actual development and implementation phases, but the BIS project leader continued to turn to the HRM director for advice.

Recruitment and selection

The BIS project required both local knowledge of each division's management practices and a detailed knowledge of BIS itself so that the system could be customized to the circumstances and needs of each division. Two main selection methods sought to address this requirement. One of these involved temporary secondments of divisional ICT staff to work on the project. This provided the BIS project with personnel who had knowledge of the business requirements and existing operating procedures of LiftCo's European divisions.

Case Study 4.2 continued

Historically each of the European divisions had implemented their own ICT systems in isolation from each other, which had resulted in a diverse range of different systems being used across the company. To develop a common ICT system which was compatible with these existing legacy systems therefore meant involving divisional staff with knowledge of these different systems in the BIS project. Thus project members were selected carefully in order to bring together a team of divisional staff who possessed an adequate in-depth knowledge of the range of different operating and business demands of LiftCo's various operating divisions and the existing ICT systems used within them. This was achieved by the BIS project leader talking to senior management in each division, who suggested relevant divisional staff with a detailed level of understanding of the particular ICT systems that they used.

A second selection method was to obtain the full-time use of a number of Consense graduate trainees, who provided the project with knowledge of Consense's BIS system. This not only addressed the staff resource shortage, but also provided LiftCo with project staff who had the necessary knowledge of Consense's BIS system to be able to programme in the necessary modifications. One of the particular benefits, in terms of Knowledge Management and development, from having these Consense staff working on the project was that through working closely with the other LiftCo staff on the project they were able to develop a good knowledge of LiftCo's business requirements. This, combined with their existing technical knowledge of Consense's BIS system, meant that over time they developed a good understanding of both the knowledge domains relevant to the BIS project and were thus able to play key roles in the BIS project.

In recruiting these trainees, LiftCo were also looking to the longer-term benefits of acquiring staff who would be developing expertise uniquely relevant to the company. For this reason, LiftCo agreed with Consense that it would be possible to offer permanent jobs at LiftCo to the Consense trainees once the BIS project had been completed. This commitment by Consense of a number of staff to work exclusively with LiftCo during their BIS project was only possible due to the long-term partnering arrangement they had agreed at the start of the project.

Equally close attention was paid during the development phase to creating an environment conducive to creating effective knowledge-sharing. For the leader of the BIS project, the development phase, which involved modifying BIS to the specific business requirements of LiftCo's operating divisions, required a mutual sensitivity between, and to some extent the integration of, the two knowledge domains outlined. This knowledge-sharing was facilitated through the physical co-location of the different project team members in their own specific, dedicated work area. This made it relatively straightforward for them to work together intensively during the development phase. As well as allowing the necessary level of knowledge-sharing to occur, this work environment also resulted in the creation of a good sense of team spirit amongst the BIS project staff.

Case Study 4.2 continued

Training and development

The BIS implementation methodology adopted by LiftCo involved making local, divisional staff responsible for their own implementation. This meant that there was a need for substantial amounts of development and training to be provided to divisional staff before they could effectively begin their local implementations. Each local implementation involved taking the basic BIS system that had been designed during the development phase and configuring it to the needs of the individual business. This meant that the local staff involved in these projects needed to possess a high-level knowledge not only of their local business needs and operating procedures, but also of the BIS system they were implementing. Thus the focus in BIS training was on endowing local staff with an adequate knowledge of the system to undertake this kind of configuration work. The provision of virtually all the training and support to the ten European divisions was the responsibility of three support teams made up of the personnel who had worked on the development phase of the project. This meant that each support team was responsible for a number of local implementations, and had to divide their time accordingly.

The training provided to local staff occurred in two main phases. First there was an early period of conventional classroom-based learning, when the support team spent two to three weeks providing basic orientation training with BIS. Much of this training was provided communally, with all of the local implementation team learning together in a single room. One of the benefits this produced was to create a sense of identity, of team spirit, amongst the local implementation team members, which had the benefit of facilitating communication and knowledge-sharing amongst them, during both phases of their implementation.

This outline training provided the local project staff with enough basic knowledge of BIS to start the second phase of their implementation. This involved the local implementation team then continuing to learn about BIS on their own, while simultaneously undertaking their own, specific, departmental configuration work. The shortness of the implementation timescale adopted resulted in each of the three support teams being involved in simultaneous and parallel implementations with a number of divisions. This therefore meant that they were not able to remain on-site at each division while this further self-directed learning and configuration work were taking place. Instead, they had to commute between the different divisions they were supporting. Thus, during the second phase of their implementations, the support teams were only able to visit each division on an occasional, but regular basis.

Between visits, when the local project staff ran into problems they were able to utilize the social networks they had developed with the other implementation team members during the communal training phase. Further, through the use of both e-mail and telephone they were able to communicate with their designated support team whenever necessary. However, these communication media proved to be adequate to answer the queries of the local implementation teams, and there were few cases where problems were experienced due

Case Study 4.2 continued

to the need to use distant communication. Thus the sharing of knowledge during the second phase of this implementation was facilitated by the utilization of both social and virtual networks.

The local implementation teams' understanding of BIS was further improved by the sensitivity of the support teams to the importance of motivation when teaching new skills and knowledge. This was because as well as learning new skills and knowledge, the importance of some of the skills already possessed by the local project teams was simultaneously being reduced. Therefore, particularly during the early phases of the implementation, when the local implementation staff had only started to learn about BIS, it was found to be important to motivate them and reassure them about their ability to learn the necessary capabilities to use and develop BIS.

Finally, in terms of outcomes, it is worth noting that the BIS implementations in all of LiftCo's local divisions were relatively successful. This can be attributed in large part to the careful attention that was paid to linking HRM to Knowledge Management issues.

Questions

1. Identify at least three major ways in which HR factors contributed to the management of knowledge for the BIS project.

2. Evaluate, using the LiftCo case as an example, the role of HR specialists in managing knowledge-based projects.

This case is based an a project funded by the Economic and Social Research Council (ESRC) and conducted by Hislop, Swan, Scarbrough and Newell. We gratefully acknowledge Donald Hislop's authorship of the original version of this case.

Summary of key learning points

- Much of the knowledge within organizations is embodied in groups of knowledge workers.
- Knowledge workers are a group with distinctive motivational needs.
- There are a variety of perspectives on the way HRM policies can influence knowledge: a best-practice perspective; a best-fit perspective; and the human and social capital perspective.
- The best-practice perspective suggests that there is a specific set of HRM policies which are effective for knowledge workers in all types of organizations.

Summary of key learning points continued

■ The best-fit perspective suggests that HRM policies are only effective in managing knowledge work when they are customized to fit the strategy and context of the individual organization.

■ Two major strategies for managing knowledge work are *personalization*, which emphasizes the acquisition and sharing of experience between individuals, and *codification*, which seeks to make explicit knowledge available throughout the organization.

■ The human and social capital perspective argues that managerial policy *per se* is less important than the long-term development of skills, trust and personal relationships within the organization. These intangible assets which accumulate over time are the key to achieving competitive advantage.

■ Social capital is based on informal networks composed of both weak and strong ties. Different types of network are appropriate for sharing different kinds of knowledge.

■ There are three major ingredients in social capital: social identity, trust and teamworking.

■ HRM policies have an impact in three key areas which influence knowledge work directly: rewards, corporate culture and organization careers. They can have both positive and negative effects in each of these areas.

References

Alvesson, M. (1993) Organizations as rhetoric: knowledge-intensive firms and the struggle with ambiguity. *Journal of Management Studies*, **30**(6): 997–1015.

Bailyn, L. (1988) Autonomy in the industrial R&D lab. In R. Katz (ed.) *Managing Professionals in Innovative Organizations*. New York: Ballinger, pp. 223–36.

Blackler, F. (1995) Knowledge, knowledge work and organizations: an overview and interpretation. *Organization Studies*, **16**(6): 1021–46.

Collinson, M., Hutchinson, S., Kinnie, N., Purcell, J., Scarbrough, H. and Terry M. (1998) Employment relations in SMEs: customer-driven or market-shaped? *Employee Relations*, **21**(3): 218–35.

Cusumano, M.A. and Selby, R.W. (1996) *Microsoft Secrets*. London: HarperCollins.

Davenport, T.H., Jarvenpaa, S.L. and Beers, M.C. (1996) Improving knowledge work processes. *Sloan Management Review*, Summer: 53–65.

Edvinsson, L. and Malone, M. (1997) *Intellectual Capital*. New York: Harper.

Fombrun, C., Tichy, N.M. and Devanna, M.A. (1984) *Strategic Human Resource Management*. Chichester: Wiley.

Granovetter, M.S. (1973) The strength of weak ties. *American Journal of Sociology*, **78**, 1360–80.

Granovetter, M.S. (1985) Economic action and social structure: the problem of embeddedness. *American Journal of Sociology*, **91**(3): 481–510.

Grant, R.M. (1991) The resource-based theory of competitive advantage: implications for strategy formulation. *California Management Review*, **34** (Spring): 114–35.

Grant, R. (1996) Prospering in dynamically competitive environments: organizational capability as knowledge integration. *Organization Science*, 7(4): 375–87.

Hansen, M.T. (1999) The search transfer problem: the role of weak ties in sharing knowledge across organizational sub-units. *Administrative Science Quarterly*, **44**: 82–111.

Hansen, M.T., Nohria, N. and Tierney, T. (1999) What's your strategy for managing knowledge? *Harvard Business Review*, March–April: 106–16.

Kamoche, K. and Mueller, F. (1998) Human Resource Management and the appropriation-learning perspective. *Human Relations*, **51**(8): 1033–60.

Kogut, B. and Zander, U. (1992) Knowledge of the firm, combinative capabilities and the replication of technology. *Organization Science*, **3**(3): 383–97.

Kohn, A. (1993) Why incentive plans cannot work. *Harvard Business Review*, September–October: 54–63.

Kunda, G. (1992) *Engineering Culture: Control and Commitment in a High-Tech Corporation*. Philadelphia: Temple University Press.

Lave, J. and Wenger, E. (1991) *Situated Learning: Legitimate Peripheral Participation*. Cambridge: Cambridge University Press.

Mueller, F. (1994) Teams between hierarchy and commitment: change strategies and the 'internal environment'. *Journal of Management Studies*, **31**(3): 383–403.

Nahapiet, J. and Ghoshal, S. (1998) Social capital, intellectual capital and the organizational advantage. *Academy of Management Review*, **23**(2): 242–66.

Newell, S. and Swan, J. (1999) Trust and interorganizational networking. *Human Relations*, **53**(10): 1287–1328.

Nohria, N. and Eccles, R.G. (1992) *Networks and Organizations: Structure, Form and Action*. Cambridge, Mass.: Harvard Business School Press.

Peters, T. and Waterman, R.H. (1982) *In Search of Excellence*. New York: Random House.

Putnam, R.D. (1995) Bowling alone: America's declining social capital. *Journal of Democracy*, **6**: 65–78.

Rajan, A., Lank, E. and Chapple, K. (1998) *Good Practices in Knowledge Creation and Exchange*. Tunbridge Wells: Create.

Reich, R. (1991) *The Wealth of Nations: Preparing Ourselves for 21st Century Capitalism*. London: Simon & Schuster.

Scarbrough, H. (1999) Knowledge as work: a conflict-based analysis of the management of knowledge workers. *Technology Analysis and Strategic Management*, **11**(1): 5–16.

Sonnenfeld, J.A., Peiperl, M.A. and Kotter, J.P (1988) Strategic determinants of managerial labour markets: a career systems view. *Human Resource Management*, **27**(4): 369–88.

Stalk, G., Evans, P. and Shulman, L.E. (1992) Competing on capabilities: the new rules of corporate strategy. *Harvard Business Review*, **92**: 57–69.

Starbuck, W. (1992) Learning by knowledge-intensive firms. *Journal of Management Studies*, **29**(6): 713–40.

Stewart, T. (1997) *Intellectual Capital: The New Wealth of Organizations*. New York: Doubleday.

Tampoe, M. (1993) Motivating knowledge workers: the challenge for the 1990's. *Long Range Planning*, **26**(3): 49–55.

Tyson, S. (1995) *Human Resource Strategy: Towards a General Theory of HRM*. London: Pitman.

Tyson, S. and Fell, A. (1986) *Evaluating the Personnel Function*. London: Hutchinson.

Weick, K.E. (1979) *The Social Psychology of Organizing*. Reading, Mass.: Addison-Wesley.

Whalley, P. and Barley, S.R. (1997) Technical work in the division of labour. In S.R. Barley and J.E. Orr (eds) *Between Craft and Science: Technical Work in US Settings*. London: ILR Press, pp. 23–52.

Wood, S. (1995) The four pillars of HRM: are they connected? *Human Resource Management Journal*, **5**(5): 48–58.

5 Knowledge work and information and communication technologies

---

Learning outcomes

At the end of this chapter students will be able to:

■ Understand the complex relationships between ICTs and organizations generally.

■ Develop a critical appreciation of the role of ICTs in the management of knowledge specifically.

■ Understand the differences between the 'cognitive' and 'community' approaches to the management of knowledge.

Introduction

In the last chapter we considered the Human Resource Management (HRM) practices that can effectively support the sharing and creation of knowledge, particularly where the work is knowledge-intensive. Unfortunately, as we will see, most organizations do not focus on such practices in their bid to improve knowledge-sharing. Rather, a more common response among organizations interested in facilitating improved knowledge-sharing is to implement information and communication technologies (ICTs), assuming that the mere presence of a potential communication channel will encourage this. We critically review the impact of such a strategy, in particular through exploring the case of BankCo. In BankCo, ICTs were used as *the* Knowledge Management strategy to facilitate knowledge-sharing across its globally distributed operation. The outcome, as we shall see, was not as intended!

Before considering this more specific impact of ICTs on Knowledge Management, however, we step back and consider the broader impact of the rapid and far-reaching changes in ICTs on organizational forms in general and on knowledge work in particular. In relation to the general impact of ICTs on organization and work, simplistic accounts suggest that technology *per se* will 'revolutionize' the nature and, perhaps more importantly, the location of work. So, the advent of the Internet, the World Wide Web, the mobile phone, teleconferencing, groupware and so on will automatically mean that people will start to work virtually (many from home), and that geographical distance will no longer be relevant. In this chapter we will demonstrate that technology *per se* cannot affect change. Rather, new technologies provide constraints and opportunities for human action. Moreover, this human action is embedded in a particular institutional context, which both constrains and facilitates action. Thus, political, economic, cultural and societal institutions exist in any given context and influence behaviour by constituting rules, defining key players, and framing situations (Scott, 1995, p. 137). This institutional context simultaneously empowers and controls behaviour since it legitimizes some forms of behaviour while simultaneously prohibiting other forms.

In relation to the more specific impact of ICTs on the management of knowledge, we will consider the differences between data, information and knowledge. Considering these differences leads us to conclude that, in the majority of situations, ICTs *per se* cannot actually 'manage knowledge'. Rather, they can provide access to data and information, which will be interpreted by someone based on their existing knowledge. We develop two models of managing knowledge work, which depict the difference between those who argue that ICTs can automatically facilitate 'Knowledge Management' and those who view knowledge as socially constructed and based on interaction. From this latter perspective, ICTs plays a more limited (although still potentially important) role in the process of managing knowledge work and knowledge workers. We illustrate both the general point about the impact of ICTs on organization and the more specific point about its impact on managing knowledge through exploring the BankCo case. This bank had introduced intranets in order to facilitate knowledge-sharing between people geographically distributed across its global network. However, rather than encourage knowledge-sharing, the impact was actually to reinforce existing boundaries with 'electronic fences'.

The relationship between technology and organization

Early research into the relation between technology and organization developed contingency accounts. For example, in one of the earliest studies Woodward (1965) argued that different types of technology were associated with different forms of organization. Others followed suit, considering different attributes of technologies and their relationship to organizing and organizational structures (for example, Perrow, 1967). In these accounts, technology was depicted as a determinant of an organization's structure and/or processes. For example, it was suggested that the more complex and unpredictable the production system technology, the more likely were organizations to adopt organic rather than mechanistic structures (Burns and Stalker, 1961). Such deterministic accounts, however, ignore the agency of human actors in influencing choices both about the technology and the organization (Child, 1972). More recently social constructionist accounts of the relation between technology and organization have been developed. Such accounts view technologies as fundamentally social objects. Individuals and groups shape both the design and the adoption of technologies depending on their interests and perspectives (Bijker *et al.*, 1987).

The social construction of technology, however, does not occur in a vacuum. Rather, this process will be influenced by the institutional context. Institutional research considers the ways in which broad social and historical forces shape the actions of organizations (DiMaggio and Powell, 1983). Organizations are embedded in 'a web of values, norms, rules, beliefs, and taken-for-granted assumptions' (Barley and Tolbert, 1997, p. 93). These institutional influences both enable and constrain action. Institutional perspectives then alert us to the ways in which technologies are embedded in complex social, economic and political networks. This directs attention to the exploration of ways in which these broader institutional influences shape technologies.

While both the social constructionist perspective and the institutional perspective have been extremely valuable in highlighting the importance of human agency in the design and appropriation (adoption and use) of technologies, including ICTs, there has been a tendency to ignore the material properties of the physical artefacts. What is becoming increasingly clear is that technologies are simultaneously social and physical artefacts (Orlikowski and Barley, 2001). In terms of agency, all technologies represent the particular set of choices that designers have made. So, for example, designers make assumptions about users and how they will use the technology, and this influences the way they design the technology. Furthermore, users shape the way technologies are actually used in everyday practice because most technologies can be used in multiple ways – they are 'open-ended' (Orlikowski, 2000). Weick (1995) refers to this as the 'interpretative flexibility' of technologies. At the same time the physical properties of technologies influence the ways they can be used. In other words, every technology both constrains and affords use. For example, the traditional design of the telephone system constrained use to set physical locations because of the need for land-line connections. Today, mobile phone technology frees up the use of the phone so that people's communication becomes much less geographically restricted. Such a difference reflects the material properties of the technology, which therefore constrain the options available to designers (Barley, 1990).

This suggests that in order to understand the impact of technology on organizations we need to integrate the influences of human agency, the physical properties of specific technologies and the context within which the technology is used. We can illustrate this by considering the phenomenon of teleworking.

Teleworking

ICTs potentially allow many workers to work remotely from 'the office'. It is no longer necessary to be physically present to have access to most organizational information and indeed to be in contact with others. E-mails can be sent to anyone from almost anywhere in the world and files and other information can be downloaded to be worked on, again almost anywhere. So, a software engineer, working on a project to design a new software package, can be working with a team that is geographically distributed across all continents, communicating with them using e-mail, videoconferencing and other groupware. Indeed, each member of the team could possibly be working from their own home, or even from the beach if they found this a conducive place in which to write software! While not all jobs can be done virtually, and most jobs demand some physical presence some of the time, it is the case now that many employees could work, at least part of the time, from their home or some other remote location of their choice. We will refer to this as teleworking (others call it virtual homeworking or telecommuting) to distinguish it from virtual working, which implies a person is working with others when they are not physically co-located but this may still be in an on-site work environment. The basic point, then, is that teleworking contravenes the separation of work and home that has characterized employment since the Industrial Revolution.

ICTs are an enabler of such altered work arrangements. True, some people have continued to work from home throughout the industrial era, for example, women working from home in cottage industries where work, such as garment-making, is taken to individuals' homes for completion. However, developments in ICTs open up this option to a much greater range of workers through the kinds of technologies listed in the introduction to this chapter. Nevertheless, the development of ICTs *per se* does not drive such change. Indeed, research has tended to show that, despite the fact that developments in ICTs make it potentially possible for many people to work at home, at least some of the time, the evidence suggests that the numbers who actually do this are very small. For example, Korte and Wynne (1996), examining the penetration of teleworking in Germany, France, Britain, Italy and Spain, found that only around 5 per cent of workers (1.1 million workers) did any work from home. Similarly in the USA, O'Mahony and Barley (1999) estimated that only 6.7 per cent of all permanent employees worked from home, even some of the time.

So, while ICTs provide the opportunity for many people to work from home at least some of the time, the evidence suggests that in fact very few make use of this opportunity. Moreover, this is the case despite the fact that the balance of evidence shows that teleworking has benefits for the individual, for the organization and for society. From the perspective of the individual, research shows that most people like teleworking, finding that it allows them to better balance the demands of a family and a job. Teleworking has also been shown in general to result in better feelings of well-being (compared to having to go to the office, shop or factory) (Newell, 2002). From the perspective of the organization, there are also benefits associated with teleworking. For example, it has been suggested that teleworking allows firms to tap the expertise and skills of workers in high demand who do not wish to be tied to permanent employment and of workers who cannot be physically present during the normal working day because of other demands on their time, especially childcare. Teleworking is also advocated as a way of reducing the cost of building overheads (because fewer offices will be needed if people are working from home). Finally, from the perspective of society teleworking is seen to be beneficial because it reduces commuting and all the associated costs, especially costs in relation to the pollution of the environment.

So we are left with a question – why has the proportion of people engaged in teleworking remained small, despite the opportunities afforded by advancements in ICTs and despite the obvious benefits for individuals, organizations and societies? To address this question we need to consider the institutional-level perspective. From this perspective, teleworking has not become more widespread because it challenges existing norms and practices. In particular, teleworking challenges existing norms about control that are central within the context of employment relations. These mechanisms of control vary by the type of work. For clerical and factory workers, their output is tangible and so easily measurable. This measurable output means that workers can be readily monitored and controlled. However, managerial, professional and knowledge work is primarily mental and interpersonal, and so is difficult to monitor. In this situation, physical presence has been used as a proxy for productivity. You are assumed to be working hard if you work long hours. This helps to account for the long-hours culture that has become ubiquitous, especially in Japan, the UK and the USA. Moreover, workers have come to believe that they will only be promoted if they are visibly present in order to be noticed. Staying late and arriving early can be particularly important in this respect. So much so, that in some cases workers 'fiddle the system' by going home but leaving their work station open and their jacket on their chair, to suggest that they are still around and working! Given this 'game', what would be the point of working long hours from home where no one could see the effort that was put in?

In this context, managers will resist allowing their workers to work from home because they fear that they will exert less effort. In other words, managers do not trust their employees to work at home where they are not visible. At the same time, workers will also be reluctant to work from home, because they may feel that this will reduce their visibility and therefore their potential for promotion. From the institutional perspective, then, teleworking, at least as a substitute for working 'at the office', will only become more widespread when these deep-seated attitudes and cultural traditions change, regardless of advances in ICTs which can support teleworking, and the obvious benefits of such an arrangement.

New organizational forms

While developments in ICTs provide opportunities for teleworking, they also open up new possibilities for organizational designs more generally. In particular, ICTs enable the creation of organizational designs that provide more supportive environments for work that is knowledge-intensive. As has already been suggested in Chapter 2, knowledge work is best conducted in 'organic' and informal settings, with egalitarian cultures and where horizontal, as opposed to vertical, communication dominates. Such work settings are very different to the traditional bureaucratic forms of organization advocated by Scientific Management that were considered in Chapter 1. Bureaucratic organizational forms continue to exist, but it is evident that new forms of organizing are emerging which are much more fluid and dynamic than these traditional structures. These new forms of organizing have looser structures which allow them to be more flexible (Volberda, 1998). This is achieved by breaking down the large bureaucratic structure into subsystems or modules. These smaller units can adapt more quickly to changing circumstances. In other words, even in a complex system, there is the potential for rapid evolution, if that system is broken down into a set of stable subsystems. These subsystems can then each operate nearly independently of the processes going on within other subsystems, so that rapid change can be accomplished. Decomposability or modularity is thus seen as the solution to managing increasing complexity, with networks supported by ICTs linking together the different parts, whether internally or externally (Nohria and Eccles, 1992). These new forms of organizing have a number of characteristics including:

1. *Decentralization through the creation of semi-autonomous business units (BU)*: This allows each BU to focus on a particular market niche and so respond more flexibly and adaptively to the needs of the particular market niche.

2. *Flatter, less hierarchical structures*: This has been achieved through removing layers of middle managers. With fewer managers, close supervision and control are less possible, so that power is devolved down the hierarchy, giving individuals more autonomy (or empowerment) in their work.

3. *Cross-functional project teams*: Rather than have each function work relatively independently and pass things 'over the wall' to the next function in the process, people are brought together to work in cross-functional teams. The objective is to encourage a faster response rate so that lead times, for example on new product developments, are considerably reduced.

4. *Interorganizational networking*: Rather than attempt to integrate new required skills and competencies into the organizational hierarchy, organizations are increasingly working in collaborative alliances and partnerships with other organizations or using outsourcing arrangements to service particular internal requirements. This enables organizations to innovate much more quickly since they can access knowledge and expertise that are not held internally.

5. *Globalization of business*: Organizations are increasingly geographically distributed, working on a global rather than a national basis. This has been achieved either through the acquisition of businesses in other countries (as in the BankCo case presented at the end of this chapter), through partnership arrangements, or through internal international growth. This allows them to capitalize on global market opportunities and so grow in size and profitability.

While developments in ICTs have not driven these changes, they have made these options more feasible. In the next section we consider this in more detail by considering the example of globalization.

Globalization

The ability to coordinate globally is dramatically increased through advances in ICTs. Earl and Fenny (1996) consider this in relation to what they describe as the three imperatives for successful global business – global efficiency, local responsiveness and transfer of learning. Global efficiency implies that an organization coordinates and consolidates its various activities so that it achieves economies of scale. This requires, for example, the collection of comparative performance information from its operations around the globe. Global ICTs such as enterprise resource planning (ERP) systems allow this information to be collected in a common form so that these global efficiency decisions can be made. The case example in Chapter 6 provides an illustration of the design and adoption of an ERP system.

Local responsiveness implies that BUs must respond to the requirements and idiosyncrasies of local markets – so the 'global car' is actually modified to suit each of the particular local conditions where it is sold. Production system ICTs which support high variety are helpful here. This philosophy is obviously very different from the earlier mass production era, where single products were produced with few options and variants. So, for example, Henry Ford was reported to have once said, 'My customers can have any colour car, as long as it is black'!

Finally, in relation to the transfer of learning, a global business needs to ensure that it shares learning so that expensive reinvention is prevented. ICTs such as e-mail and teleconferencing can help to facilitate dialogue among professionals so that learning is shared. This was the aim of the Knowledge Management initiative at BankCo, described later in this chapter. Of course, this is not to say that globalization, and especially attempts at globalization, did not occur before developments in the Internet and the World Wide Web. History is replete with examples of nations, if not corporations, attempting to expand their global empire. Nevertheless, it is clear that advances in ICTs have facilitated globalization along with the other features of the new organizational forms discussed above.

New organizational forms and the management of knowledge

While these new organizational forms are more conducive to knowledge-intensive work, paradoxically they also make it more difficult to manage knowledge. In bureaucratic organizations, job descriptions, rules, procedures and so on were clearly defined and the hierarchy of command provided a clear pathway for communication. In the newer organizational forms discussed in the last section, there are potentially more opportunities for knowledge to be lost or reinvented in new contexts. So, knowledge is lost between BUs, between companies involved in interorganizational alliances, across projects, and across geographical locations. And, since hierarchies have been flattened, there is no middle management to try and coordinate and provide a communication link across these boundaries.

In traditional bureaucratic structures, control and information exchange were achieved by having each manager in the hierarchy only responsible for a small number of subordinates. Managers thus had a relatively narrow span of control and were able to closely supervise and control their subordinates. They would then pass on information about their section to the manager above, who also had a narrow span of control. With the flattening of organizational structures, the span of control of each manager in the organizational hierarchy is much greater. So while in the past a manager may have supervised only seven to ten subordinates, today they may be supervising fifty to sixty. In this situation it is not possible to know what each subordinate is actually doing and to closely control and monitor their activities. The subordinates must therefore control their own activities to a much larger extent. They are empowered to make their own decisions. This is entirely appropriate for knowledge work and knowledge workers, which as we have seen cannot be tightly controlled and organized. However, it does mean that middle managers are no longer able to act as the communication conduits within an organization – they do not know in much detail what is happening within their particular sphere of responsibility nor do they necessarily have time to engage in such activities.

Organizations have, in essence, become too stretched and virtual, so that important opportunities for face-to-face social interaction have been lost. So, in a situation where knowledge is seen as perhaps *the* most valuable resource of a company, organizational forms have been developed to nurture knowledge creation. However, these very same organizational forms that help to nurture knowledge creation also provide more opportunity for knowledge loss. 'Knowledge Management' initiatives can be seen as an attempt to resolve this paradox (although it should also be noted that the spread or diffusion of Knowledge Management initiatives has also been promoted by a 'bandwagon' effect; see, for example, Abrahamson and Rosenkopf, 1993)

ICTs and Knowledge Management

Schemes described as 'Knowledge Management initiatives' are a relatively recent phenomenon (Scarbrough *et al.*, 1999). Surveys of firms introducing what they describe as 'Knowledge Management initiatives' show that these are dominated by ICT implementations – now sometimes referred to as Knowledge Management Systems. For example, Ruggles (1998) reports on a survey of 431 organizations and describes what firms are actually doing to 'manage knowledge'. The four initiatives that were the most popular were all related to

ICT developments – creating an intranet, data warehousing, decision-support tools and groupware. Similar findings were reported by Alavi and Leidner (1999).

These organizational responses suggest that decision-makers believe that sophisticated ICT tools (such as intranets, e-mail, groupware, data warehousing) can help in the capture, storage and sharing of knowledge. Many commentators, however, are more sceptical about the utility of new ICTs for delivering organizational performance improvements: 'There is increasing hype about the wonders delivered by the newest information technologies in an era characterized by knowledge as the critical resource for business activity' (Malhotra, 1998, p. 58). Moreover, the link between ICT investment and business performance is not strong (Strassmann, 1998). In the next section we consider the limitations of an ICT-based approach to managing knowledge. In particular, a key reason for the lack of success in using ICTs to support the management of knowledge is that such an approach focuses only on the management of knowledge that can be made explicit. In understanding the limitations of ICTs in supporting the management of knowledge, we therefore need to consider the differences between data, information and knowledge and the distinction between explicit and tacit knowledge.

Data, information and knowledge

Data, information and knowledge are inextricably linked. Data provide a record of signs and observations collected from a variety of sources. These data are presented in a particular way in relation to a particular context of action and so become information. Information is thus data endowed with relevance and purpose (Drucker, 1980). Data and information are selectively collected and presented – they do not provide an objective account of the 'real world'. More importantly, data and information are meaningless to someone without relevant knowledge. Knowledge provides the means by which these data and information can be interpreted. People with different knowledge will interpret the same data and information differently. In this sense knowledge is the basis for the sharing of data and information. Only with common knowledge can data and information be shared such that common understanding is derived from this sharing.

A popular definition of knowledge is that it is 'justified true belief' (see Nonaka, 1994). So, we say we 'have knowledge' when we understand, or at least believe that we understand, the causal or interacting relations involved in a particular situation and believe this understanding is justified. 'Having knowledge' allows us to act with confidence because we assume that we can predict the outcome of our actions. Thus, a firm's 'knowledge' about its customers (based on data and information about buying habits and market trends, made sense of in the light of other experience) allows it to develop new products or services that it predicts it will be able to market and sell at a profit. However, belief refers to an individual's or group's idea about what is 'truth'. While the individual or group may believe that this 'truth' is justified, 'truth' is always problematic. In the social sciences there is increasing acceptance that the search for 'truth' and 'laws' of behaviour is a redundant exercise because what is truth is socially constructed (Gergen, 1999). So 'truth' is always contestable. Given that truth, and so knowledge, is contestable, knowledge cannot be transferred between people through ICTs in any straightforward way. A particular version of 'truth' can be transferred but, were this to be understood by the intended recipients (and this in itself is problematic), it may not be accepted given alternative 'justified true beliefs'.

Knowledge and action are coupled through a process of sense-making (Weick, 1995). I do 'this' rather than 'that' because I 'know' that 'this' will lead to a preferable outcome to 'that'. Of course, at times we (the individual or the organization) might act without full knowledge or in apparently less than rational ways, for example, because we are influenced by others and follow 'fashions'. We also take risks. Typically, however, even these risks are based on hunches or intuitions, which are themselves based on knowledge, albeit knowledge which is perhaps only partial and difficult to justify. This limited knowledge nevertheless provides some degree of expectancy that the risk will 'pay off'. Even if the accepted knowledge turns out to be wrong (for example, customers do not buy the new product or service in the numbers expected), without the assumption of knowledge an organization's (or an individual's) ability to act would be stifled. It should be noted, however, that in many cases the knowledge base of action is not conscious, but is rather embedded in organizational routines (Nelson and Winter, 1982) or in taken-for-granted assumptions.

Knowledge, or rather knowing, cannot therefore be disassociated from the beliefs and experiences of those people that have and use the knowledge. ICTs marketed as 'Knowledge Management Systems' obscure and deny the socially constructed nature of knowledge and truth. Instead, those promoting such systems imply that, by introducing standard processes and ICT-supported communication channels which link people and groups, 'best practice' knowledge can be shared throughout a global organization. Unlike data, knowledge cannot be simply transferred from a sender to a receiver. Knowledge (that is, justified true belief) is located in practice (embodied knowledge) as well as thought (embrained knowledge), and it must be recreated or reconstructed in each new situation, even when people are following routines (embedded knowledge). As such, while knowledge can be actively *shared* or constructed, through the interaction between people or groups, it cannot be passively transferred. Data or information can be directly transferred but their interpretation, which involves the process of 'knowing', may be highly variable.

Some of the differences between data, information and knowledge are summarized in Table 5.1.

Table 5.1 Key characteristics of data, information and knowledge

Data	Information	Knowledge
Explicit	Interpreted	Tacit/embedded
Exploit	Explore	Create
Use	Build/construct	Rebuild/reconstruct
Accept	Confirm	Disconfirm
Follow old recipes	Amend old recipes	Develop new recipes
No learning	Single-loop learning	Double-loop learning
Direction	Communication	Sense-making
Prescriptive	Adaptive	Seminal
Efficiency	Effectiveness	Innovation/redundancy
Predetermined	Constrained	Flexible
Technical systems/networks	Socio-technical systems/networks	Social networks
Context-free	Outer context	Inner context

Source: Adapted from Galliers and Newell (2001).

Explicit and tacit knowledge

In taking this further and thinking about what can be shared between people, it is helpful to consider the widely accepted view that knowledge can be either explicit or tacit (Polanyi, 1958), a distinction already briefly introduced in chapter 1. Explicit knowledge is that knowledge which has been expressed either verbally or in text form. A recipe book is an example of explicit knowledge since it takes an individual's knowledge about how to make something – the particular ingredients and their relative quantities and the process of combining these to produce the finished product – and reproduces it so that someone else (without this knowledge) can nevertheless make the product. Implicit knowledge, on the other hand, is that knowledge which is not easily or clearly articulated. Rather it resides 'in our heads' and in our practical skills and actions.

While this distinction is useful it is also oversimplistic because tacit and explicit knowledge cannot be this easily differentiated. For example, the explicit recipe that has been written down can only be followed if the reader of the recipe has the implicit or tacit knowledge that underpins the interpretation and understanding of the explicit knowledge. Most obviously, if the recipe is written in Dutch, an English speaker would not be able to follow it (presuming of course that they could not speak Dutch). But the reader also needs to know, for example, how to 'measure 50 g of sugar'; how to 'switch the oven on to 300 degrees centigrade'; how to 'fold in' flour; and how to 'beat' an egg. So, to 'beat' an egg does not mean to place it on the table and smash it with a hammer! The instructions in the recipe have to assume this tacit knowledge or else they would become so detailed, long and complex that they would overload the reader and/or be impossible to follow. This is why Tsoukas (1996) argues that implicit (tacit) and explicit knowledge are 'mutually constituted'.

In other words, to be able to use explicit knowledge codified by someone else, there has to be a common implicit structure for understanding, or, as Trompenaars (1996) calls it, 'a shared system of meaning'. This means that even if 'knowledge' is made available more widely in the organization via its embodiment through ICT-based tools, this explicit knowledge cannot necessarily be effectively used. This is because the potential users are not necessarily able to interpret or understand what has been codified by others if those others have a different system of meaning. Yet, a common system of meaning or understanding is unlikely when the knowledge-sharing involves individuals from different cultures or different functional backgrounds, as seen in the ResearchTeam case in Chapter 3.

Another issue in understanding the problems with ICT-based approaches to the management of knowledge involves considering why some tacit knowledge may not readily lend itself to capture and codification. There are a number of reasons for this, including:

1. *Difficulty*: Some knowledge may just be too difficult to express in written form and so may be more effectively communicated through face-to-face interaction or learning by doing. For example, it may be far easier to simply show a person how to set up, log on and use a computer than to ask them to follow a set of detailed written instructions on how to do this. The complexity of computer manuals and the continued attempts by designers to create 'user-friendly' help services attests to this. The telephone helpline where knowledge can be communicated through two-way interaction is often preferred to the text-form help databases available on the computer itself.

2. *Uncertainty*: Some knowledge may be too uncertain. For example, I may feel that I 'know' that the best way to design a training course is to include humour and anecdotes. However, this is based on personal experience and intuition, and so I am uncertain of its accuracy. I am therefore not likely to write it down (in case it is wrong), although I may well share this 'knowledge' informally.

3. *Dynamism*: Some knowledge may be subject to continuous change. For example, 'process mapping' attempts to articulate and represent in written form the underlying processes involved in work tasks. However, organizational routines are subject to almost continuous change such that by the time the processes are mapped they are almost immediately out of date or wrong in some detail.

4. *Context-dependency*: Some knowledge may be highly context-dependent. For example, knowledge about how customers react to a particular new

humorous marketing campaign is likely to be unique to a particular country, given what we know about national predispositions in humour. Reusing the same campaign in a different country, ignoring the importance of context, is likely to prove ineffective and may even produce the opposite effects to those expected.

5. *Cost*: Some knowledge may cost more to codify than to learn by trial and error. For example, writing down in detail instructions about how to use a simple mechanical device, like a stapler in an office environment, is not likely to prove very useful. This may sound like a trivial example, but it does not take much imagination to realize that there is an awful lot of material 'written down' in an organization, which is rarely if ever referred to.

6. *Politics*: Some knowledge may be politically too sensitive to codify. For example, very important knowledge when managing a project relates to who is a good team player and who is likely to be obstructive and difficult. It is very unlikely that someone will formally share this knowledge with others, stating on a database that 'Sue is a pain to work with!' (and in any case it might well be considered libellous if it were formally codified).

All these issues mean that what is actually codified on the organizational 'Knowledge Management System' (for example, an intranet or database – 'encoded' knowledge in Blackler's terms) may be trivial and unhelpful while the really important knowledge continues to reside in people's heads – 'embrained' knowledge (Blackler, 1995). Moreover, not only are there problems in actually codifying some tacit knowledge, but also it must be recognized that people may be reluctant to 'brain dump' what they know on to a database because knowledge is also a key source of personal power within organizations. Ironically, in cases where an individual has knowledge that really needs to be shared – that is, where it is both in short supply and central to the organization – there may be a particular reluctance to share it with others. This is because knowledge confers personal advantages and so is secreted by the 'knower'. Why share your knowledge if that knowledge is precisely what enables you to gain rewards and to climb the career ladder in your company?

Given these problems of codifying and transferring knowledge, we can look at an alternative approach to the management of knowledge work and knowledge workers. This is considered in the next section.

Two different approaches to the management of knowledge work and knowledge workers

The ICT-based approach to the management of knowledge adopts a cognitive, information-processing view of the firm where valuable knowledge located

Table 5.2 Two contrasting views of the Knowledge Management process

Cognitive model	Community model
Knowledge is equal to objectively defined concepts and facts	Knowledge is socially constructed and based on experience
Knowledge can be codified and transferred through text: information systems have a crucial role	Knowledge can be tacit and is transferred through participation in social networks including occupational groups and teams
Gains from Knowledge Management include exploitation through the recycling of existing knowledge	Gains from Knowledge Management include exploration through the sharing and synthesis of knowledge among different social groups and communities
The primary function of Knowledge Management is to codify and capture knowledge	The primary function of Knowledge Management is to encourage knowledge-sharing through networking
The critical success factor is technology	The critical success factor is trust and collaboration
The dominant metaphors are the human memory and the jigsaw (fitting pieces of knowledge together to produce a bigger picture in predictable ways)	The dominant metaphors are the human community and the kaleidoscope (creative interactions producing new knowledge in sometimes unpredictable ways)

inside people's heads or in successful organizational practices (that is, the input) is identified, captured and processed via the use of ICT tools so that it can be applied in new contexts (that is, the output). The aim, then, is to make the knowledge inside people's heads or knowledge embedded in successful routines widely available. Indeed the practice of 'Knowledge Management', as seen, is frequently reduced to the implementation of new ICTs for knowledge transfer: 'the idea behind Knowledge Management is to stockpile workers' knowledge and make it accessible to others via a searchable application' (Cole-Gomolski, 1997, p. 6).

A core assumption behind this ICT approach to the management of knowledge work and knowledge workers is that technology enables effective knowledge-sharing. However, this privileges an information-processing view where knowledge is seen as cognitive abilities (inputs), which can be processed using technology to produce certain outputs. This equates knowledge to the skills and cognitive abilities of individuals. In contrast, organizational theorists highlight the need to understand knowledge as also embedded in and constructed from and through social relationships and interactions (Nonaka and Takeuchi, 1995; Blackler, 1995). According to this view, knowledge (unlike data) cannot simply be processed; rather it is continuously recreated and reconstituted through dynamic, interactive and social networking activity. The core differences between the cognitive and community approaches to the management of knowledge work and knowledge workers are shown in Table 5.2.

The community model highlights the importance of relationships, shared understandings and attitudes to knowledge formation and knowledge-sharing

(Kofman and Senge, 1993). It is important to acknowledge these issues since they help to define the likely success or failure of attempts to implement ICT-based 'Knowledge Management' initiatives. The community model suggests that it is likely to be fairly easy to share knowledge between individuals who are relatively homogeneous, because they share a common understanding and belief system. So globally distributed software engineers, with a similar training and understanding, may be able to work collaboratively without much difficulty. However, it is extremely difficult for such globally distributed collaboration where the individuals have heterogeneous beliefs and understandings, as in the ResearchTeam case in Chapter 3. Yet, the sharing of knowledge across functional or national boundaries is precisely the goal of most initiatives that focus on the management of knowledge.

In sum, ICT-led approaches to the management of knowledge work typically fail to take into account the preexisting organizational structures, norms and cultural values that lead different groups to have divergent, possibly even irreconcilable, interpretations or beliefs of what needs to be done and how best to do it. In other words, ICT-led approaches ignore the very different tacit knowledge and understanding of individuals. The community model thus stresses that knowledge has to be continuously negotiated through interactive social networking processes. This model emphasizes dialogue occurring through networks rather than linear information flows. Various ICTs may facilitate or enable such dialogue, but the passive codification, storing, mining and transfer of information, will not necessarily lead to knowledge-sharing, especially when individuals come from different functional and/or cultural backgrounds.

Conclusions

In this chapter we have considered the ways in which advancements in ICTs are opening up new possibilities for the design of organizations which are more supportive for knowledge-intensive work. However, we have also seen that these advancements in ICTs will not automatically or deterministically lead to the adoption of new organizational forms or new arrangements for organizing, as is sometimes naively assumed. Rather, the way the new ICTs are used, and their effectiveness, will depend on complex interactions between technology, organization and context. More specifically, we have considered the fallacy of assuming that the adoption of ICTs such as intranets will allow an organization to painlessly improve knowledge-sharing across its globally distributed operation. Instead, we have presented a community approach to the management of knowledge work and knowledge workers which sees knowledge as socially constructed and shared and developed through interactions. ICTs can play a role in the creation and maintenance of such communities but this role is rather different to that promoted by many suppliers of 'Knowledge Management

Systems'. In the next chapter we consider the development and maintenance of these communities in more detail.

In order to illustrate the problems of assuming that technology determines behaviour in organizations generally and the problems of assuming that implementing ICTs will encourage knowledge-sharing specifically, a case is described next. This illustrates the limitations of both the general and specific assumptions. First the case is described and three questions are posed.

Case Study 5.1 BankCo

BankCo is a large European bank which was created in the early 1990s by merging two separate banks. It is located across 70 different countries. It has grown via acquisitions of existing banks across these countries. Its structure and function are highly decentralized, with resources allocated to the independent divisions and with very few resources retained at the centre. It consists of a number of different product divisions including domestic, international and investment banking.

In 1995 a major global client left the bank because it did not feel that it was getting an integrated service across countries. Thus, despite BankCo calling itself a 'global bank', the reality was very different. It was disintegrated, with each country and department operating relatively independently and having their own systems and processes. There was little knowledge-sharing across these internal boundaries. The vision from the top was to create a truly global networked bank. A paper was written by members of the corporate business strategy committee in 1996, recommending that BankCo develop a worldwide communications network (infrastructure) connecting all of its businesses with intranet technology. Moreover, it was recognized that the true competitive advantage for the bank was not simply in financial transactions, but also in providing knowledge to customers. Thus, the bank takes information from external sources, processes this using its own internal knowledge of financial markets, competitive forces and so on, and then sells this knowledge to its customers.

As an example of this, a bank may be able to advise one of its clients (say a large European supermarket chain) to buy a particular small supermarket chain in China. The bank would make this recommendation based on its knowledge of the client and its knowledge of developments in China and this particular Chinese supermarket chain. However, in order to be able to develop such innovative service provision and offer such advice, the knowledge from a range of different departments, divisions and geographical locations would need to be integrated. At the time this was not possible within BankCo because knowledge-sharing across such internal boundaries simply did not occur.

So the vision was to develop a global network in order to integrate the knowledge existing within the bank to support innovation and prevent reinvention. Basically this was a 'Knowledge Management' vision, and within BankCo this

Case Study 5.1 continued

was referred to as the Knowledge Management project. Intranet technology was seen as central to the achievement of this vision.

An intranet pilot project was started almost immediately. This was a very technically focused project to test out the infrastructure. It was centrally coordinated and funded, bringing together individuals from a number of different divisions. The evaluation of this pilot project occurred after about 18 months. One of the main conclusions from the pilot was that there was a need for greater overall coordination in the development of ICTs. Ironically, the outcome was that many independent intranet projects began almost spontaneously, supported by departmental funding. There were an estimated 150 independent intranet sites within BankCo, although the actual number was not known. The pilot had highlighted the perceived benefits of the intranet for knowledge-sharing. So each division (and even each function within a division) then opted to develop their own intranet, using local resources of both money and people.

The fact that each department/group was 'doing its own thing', but within the context of the broader Knowledge Management vision and within one particular company, is especially useful for understanding the opportunities and problems associated with the management of knowledge work and knowledge workers in practice. Interviews with individuals representing different intranet projects were carried out. A selection of the different intranet Knowledge Management projects are described in the next section.

iWeb

Following the initial pilot, the IT division recognised the potential of the intranet and started its own project to develop an intranet, 'iWeb'. This was an intranet specifically designed for sharing knowledge within the IT function, although what precisely would be shared was not clearly defined at the outset. As originally they did not have their own internal expertise, they bought in two external consultants from CG Consulting. These external consultants worked with the Information Management (IM) department within IT, which consisted of six people. This was the project team, and with the help of the external consultants they quickly acquired the technical expertise needed to develop an intranet. Moreover, expertise soon developed more widely within the IT function because there were a lot of 'hobbyists' who learned and played with HTML in their spare time.

The CG involvement stemmed from the fact that this consultant company was one of the few national organizations, at that time, that had developed their own intranet for knowledge-sharing. However, their involvement only lasted three months because the project leader of iWeb was not satisfied with the expertise they were offering. The crux of this was the recognition that an intranet is not simply about techniques. They could deal with these largely in-house, but an intranet is really about cultural change within the organization. They would have to get people to use the information on the intranet.

Case Study 5.1 continued

CG offered the solution to this organizational problem that they had used themselves, which was to force all their employees to buy a PC and equipment (at a reduced cost) that would allow them to use the intranet via remote access. Then after six months, they simply stopped sending mail physically and everything went via the intranet. However, it was felt that this solution was not appropriate for the IT function of BankCo.

The iWeb intranet was soon operative and rules and procedures were established for inputting information on to the system and keeping it up to date. The iWeb project team within IM took on the responsibility for editing, and at times helped to create web pages. In addition to this central editorial group, within every department of the IT division a decentralized editorial group with responsibility for keeping things up to date and putting on new pages was created.

At the time of writing this case study, the iWeb intranet was being used to centrally store information that was previously available in other forms, often as written documents. Many potential users continued to use the original sources, although overall iWeb was seen as a useful tool. When asked to give an example of the kind of knowledge that users were finding useful on iWeb, the best example that could be found was that of the corporate bus timetable! This gives information on when the company bus will be at the different city sites of the bank. The bus travels between the different sites, and so is at any one site about once every 20 minutes. This information was now located on iWeb.

GTSNet

Global Transaction Services (GTS) is a new division of BankCo set up to provide an integrated service for global customers. The business case for setting up this separate division was made by CG Consulting, and it was finally approved in 1997. There were about 40 CG consultants involved in defining the business case. CG also involved some consultants from a company called Renaissance, a UK/USA company which specializes in Knowledge Management, so that Knowledge Management requirements were specified by Renaissance within the business case. The idea was that the basic services offered to clients are commodity services like cash management, which are selected based on lowest cost with little to differentiate between the banks. However, it is possible to differentiate in terms of also offering advisory and information services (for example, how best to make your payments in a certain country or at a certain time of year).

As soon as the approval was granted, they started talking to two vendors who would develop the information system for this new division. CG were involved in evaluating the bids from the two potential vendors, and then selecting Orc as the consortium leader with other companies, including Renaissance, involved in developing various aspects of the new system. Initially Orc had 140 people working within GTS, with very few internal BankCo employees.

Case Study 5.1 continued

To give an indication of the size, the GTS project was bigger than the yearly national turnover of Orc.

Given the composition of the project team, there were communication problems: 'Whatever obvious problems you can think of with such an arrangement, we had them,' said the project leader. Orc came in and divided the large project into lots of sub-projects, and problems of communication and integration surfaced. The main problem was in terms of the business focus as Orc had the technical expertise but not the business expertise. The problem was that there were few 'spare' BankCo employees to be assigned to the project team because so many of them were involved in other big projects like the introduction of the euro for 1999.

The GTS project team relied almost exclusively on external expertise and did very little internal networking. It was argued that this was because GTS needed to develop its intranet very quickly and so was time-constrained. It was also argued that the requirements of each intranet project will be different, so that cooperation would not work anyway. Nevertheless, those interviewed recounted the fact that recently they had become aware of projects in Belgium, Chicago and Singapore that had all independently created very similar browser-based systems to the one developed in GTS.

Renaissance had pushed the idea that Knowledge Management was not about building an ICT system, but about changing the culture so that people were willing to work together and share knowledge. It was acknowledged that this conflicted with current practices that rewarded individuals for their personal knowledge, not for sharing. However, the main thrust of the project focused on developing the technology.

GTSNet was developed. It was a simple, HTML, browser-based system with information on countries, trade, cash management, people in the network, general BankCo information and GTS-specific information. None of the information was new. People could simply now obtain their information from one integrated source and have the possibility to feed back and set up discussion groups. GTSNet had been rolled out to GTS employees in 17 countries.

However, there were complaints from users that the information on the intranet was not up to date. In response, the GTSNet project team was introducing a system to monitor content. Each item of information on GTSNet was given a rating of 1–3 so that users could assess the credibility of the knowledge they were accessing. The rating scale was as follows: (1) fully-approved content, the accuracy of which the Knowledge Management team would guarantee; (2) content monitored by the Knowledge Management team; and (3) content for which the Knowledge Management team takes no responsibility. However, they continued to allow the level 3 information to be input on to GTSNet because otherwise, it was argued, they would have been constraining personal creativity. This meant that there continued to be problems of both the supply and demand of information on GTSNet.

Case Study 5.1 continued

The future vision within GTS was one of integrating external sources of information with internal knowledge. The vision was of a technological system with a knowledge-mining capability which automatically searched and categorized documents. Then there would be a profiling system where individuals indicated what sort of information they were interested in. When any information on these topics was mined, it would be automatically directed to those interested.

OfficeWeb

OfficeWeb was designed for the domestic division of BankCo – the national branch network. At the time, the level of ICTs in the branches was very low, with the vast majority of internal communication via fax and internal mail. A 'vision engineering' workshop was hosted by IT, to help identify the ICT needs of the branches and consider the options available. The workshop was led by CG Consulting. During this workshop, the domestic division became aware of the possibilities of the intranet and a six-week pilot (a Quickscan project) was implemented in 1997. The project leader from the domestic division wanted to introduce a simple stand-alone notes system, but the IT representatives on the project wanted to develop an integrated network solution, that is, an intranet. This solution won, and the project was carried forward – OfficeWeb. The idea was that an intranet would support the more decentralized approach that was being sought within this division, making the branches more entrepreneurial and innovative so that they could respond to their own regional conditions and rely less on the corporate centre.

The OfficeWeb project team recognized the importance of involving the users, and talked to branch account managers about the content they wanted on the system. These managers had been very enthusiastic and could see the potential of an intranet for managing their businesses. However, the domestic division had no technical expertise to draw upon as, following the completion of the Quickscan project, the representatives from the IT division ceased involvement. Moreover, resources were tight so that the project team could not afford to buy expertise.

OfficeWeb was developed and contained both internal information (previously available in paper form) and external information (general information on the industries and companies relevant to the bank). OfficeWeb was taken for a pilot trial to a bank branch. However, this pilot demonstrated severe infrastructure problems. The bandwidth of the infrastructure was too small for the traffic they were trying to send through OfficeWeb. It took 20 seconds to change pages, which users found too slow.

Even though they had anticipated some problems, the OfficeWeb project team had been 'shocked' by the scale of the difficulties uncovered by the pilot. Those in the IT division were not shocked and the OfficeWeb team felt some bitterness about this. The OfficeWeb team had not anticipated the amount of bandwidth the system would require given the amount of information they

Case Study 5.1 continued

wanted to send. The infrastructure problems, which the domestic division came across, had not been faced by those in the IT function who had a much more highly developed infrastructure. Perhaps because of this, IT personnel did not alert the OfficeWeb team to the constraints of the infrastructure.

The OfficeWeb project team tried to overcome the constraints. Instead of trying to roll it out to branches, they tried to roll it out to the twelve regions, even though the regions were supposed to be losing importance as the branches assumed more autonomy under the decentralization initiative. However, this did not work either, and the project was effectively abandoned, despite the fact that considerable resources (both in people's time and equipment costs) had already been spent on developing OfficeWeb.

Questions

1. What has been achieved as a result of BankCo's Knowledge Management vision?

2. Why was the intranet solution to BankCo's problem of managing knowledge work and knowledge workers not successful?

3. What might BankCo do more successfully to realize its Knowledge Management vision?

Summary of key learning points

- The impact of ICTs on an organization is influenced by human agency, the physical properties of particular ICTs, and the context in which the technology is used.

- ICTs enable, but do not determine, more distributed working, including teleworking. Teleworking can be beneficial for the individual, the organization and society. However, it is not widely used because it challenges existing norms about the control of workers (workers cannot be trusted) and about what constitutes measurable performance (visible presence).

- More generally ICTs afford opportunities for, but do not deterministically create, new organizational forms that are supportive of work that is knowledge-intensive. This includes organizational forms, which are more decentralized, less hierarchical, based on teamworking, use interorganizational networks and are globalized.

- There are three imperatives for successful global business – global efficiency, local responsiveness and transfer of learning. ICTs can facilitate these activities, although they can also be facilitated by other means.

Summary of key learning points continued

■ Paradoxically, while new organizational forms are conducive to the support of knowledge-intensive work, they also make it more difficult to manage knowledge since they open up more opportunities for knowledge loss. Knowledge Management initiatives can be seen as an attempt to resolve this paradox.

■ The most prevalent Knowledge Management initiative involves the introduction of ICTs, for example, intranets, databases, groupware. Such Knowledge Management Systems are limited in their impact.

■ Relying on Knowledge Management Systems to encourage knowledge-sharing ignores differences between data, information and knowledge. In fact, ICTs can really only transfer data.

■ Relying on Knowledge Management Systems to encourage knowledge-sharing ignores the fact that explicit and tacit knowledge are mutually constituted and that much important knowledge cannot be readily codified.

■ Two different approaches to the management of knowledge work can be articulated – the cognitive and the community models. The cognitive model underpins much current Knowledge Management practice in organizations, while the community model is more realistic in relation to an understanding of the characteristics of knowledge work and knowledge workers.

References

Abrahamson, E. and Rosenkopf, L. (1993) Institutional and competitive bandwagons. *Academy of Management Review*, **18**(3): 487–518.

Alavi, M. and Leidner, D. (1999) Knowledge Management systems: issues, challenges and benefits. *Communications of the AIS*, **1**(5): 1–35.

Barley, S. (1990) The alignment of technology and structure through roles and networks. *Administrative Science Quarterly*, **35**(1): 61–104.

Barley, S. and Tolbert, P.S. (1997) Institutionalization and structuration: studying the links between action and institution. *Organisation Studies*, **18**(1): 93–117.

Bijker, W.E., Hughes, T. and Pinch, T.J. (eds) (1987) *The Social Construction of Technological Systems*. London: MIT Press.

Blackler, F. (1995) Knowledge, knowledge work and organizations: an overview and interpretation. *Organization Studies*, **16**(6): 1021–46.

Boland, R.J. and Tenkasi, R.V. (1995) Perspective making and perspective taking in communities of knowing. *Organization Science*, **6**(4): 350–63.

Burns, T. and Stalker, G.M. (1961) *The Management of Innovation*. London: Tavistock.

Child, J. (1972) Organizational structure, environment and performance: the role of strategic choice. *Sociology*, **6**: 1–22.

Ciborra, C. and Jelassi, T. (1994) *Strategic Information Systems: A European Perspective*. Chichester: John Wiley.

Ciborra, C. and Patriotta, G. (1996) Groupware and teamwork in R & D: limits to learning and innovation. *R&D Management*, **28**(1): 1–10.

Cole-Gomolski, B. (1997) Users loathe to share their know-how. *Computerworld*, 31(46): 6.

DiMaggio, P.J. and Powell, W.W. (1983) The iron cage revisited: institutional isomorphism and collective rationality in organizational fields. *American Sociological Review*, 48: 147–60.

Drucker, P. (1980) *Managing in Turbulent Times*. Oxford: Butterworth-Heinemann.

Earl, M.J. and Fenny, D.F. (1996) Information systems in global business: evidence from european multinationals. In: M. Earl (ed.), *Information Management. The Organisational Dimension*. Oxford: Oxford University Press.

Galliers, R. and Newell, S. (2001) Back to the future: from Knowledge Management to data management. European Conference on Information Systems, Bled, June.

Gergen, K.J. (1999) *An Invitation to Social Construction*. London: Sage.

Grandori, A. and Soda, G. (1995) Inter-firm networks: antecedents, mechanisms and forms. *Organization Studies*, 16: 183–214.

Kofman, F. and Senge, P. (1993) Communities and commitment: the heart of learning organizations. *Organizational Dynamics*, 22(2): 5–22.

Korte, W. and Wynne, R. (1996) *Telework: Penetration Potential and Practice in Europe*. Amsterdam: IOS Press.

Malhotra, Y. (1998) Tools at work: deciphering the Knowledge Management hype. *The Journal of Quality and Participation*, 21(4): 58–60.

Nelson, R. and Winter, S. (1982) *An Evolutionary Theory of Organizational Change*. Cambridge, Mass: Harvard University Press.

Newell, S. (2002) *Creating the Healthy Organization*. London: Thomson Learning.

Nohria, N. and Eccles, R.G. (1992) *Networks and Organizations: Structure, Form and Action*. Boston, Mass: Harvard University Press.

Nonaka, I. (1994) A dynamic theory of organizational knowledge creation. *Organization Science*, 5: 14–37.

Nonaka, I. and Takeuchi, H. (1995) *The Knowledge-creating Company: How Japanese Companies Create the Dynamics of Innovation*. Oxford: Oxford University Press.

O'Mahony, S. and Barley, S. (1999) Do digital telecommunications affect work and organization? The state of our knowledge. In B. Staw and R. Sutton (eds) *Research in Organization Behavior*, Vol. 21. Greenwich, Conn: JAI Press, pp. 125–62.

Orlikowski, W.J. (1992) The duality of technology: rethinking the concept of technology in organizations. *Organization Science*, 3(3): 398–427.

Orlikowski, W.J., Yates, J., Okamura, K. and Fujimoto, M. (1995) Shaping electronic communication: the metastructuring of technology in the context of use. *Organization Science*, 6(4): 423–44.

Orlikowski, W. (2000) Using technology and constituting structures: a practice lens for studying technology in organizations. *Organization Science*, 11(4): 404–28.

Orlikowski, W. and Barley, S. (2001) Technology and institutions: what can research on information technology and research on organizations learn from each other? *MIS Quarterly*, 25(2): 145–65.

Perrow, C. (1967) *Organizational Analysis: A Sociological View*. London: Tavistock.

Polanyi, M. (1958) *Personal Knowledge*. Chicago, Ill.: University of Chicago Press.

Ruggles, R. (1998) The state of the notion: Knowledge Management in practice. *California Management Review*, 40(3): 80–9.

Scarbrough, H., Swan, J. and Preston, J. (1999) *Knowledge Management and the Learning Organization*. London: IPD.

Scott, W.R. (1995) *Institutions and Organizations*. London: Sage.

Strassmann, P.A. (1998) Taking a measure of knowledge assets. *Computerworld*, 32(4): 74.

Trompenaars, F. (1996) Resolving international conflict: culture and business strategy. *Business Strategy Review,* 7(3): 51–69.

Tsoukas, H. (1996) The firm as a distributed knowledge system: a constructionist perspective. *Strategic Management Journal,* 17: 11–25.

Volberda, H.W. (1998) *Building the Flexible Firm: How to Remain Competitive.* New York: Oxford University Press.

Weick, K. (1995) *Sensemaking in Organizations.* Thousand Oaks, Calif: Sage.

Woodward, J. (1965) *Industrial Organizations: Theory and Practice.* Oxford: Oxford University Press.

6 Community approaches to managing knowledge work

Learning outcomes

At the end of this chapter students will be able to:

■ Define a community of practice and distinguish it from work teams and occupational groups.

■ Identify the effects of communities of practice on knowledge-sharing.

■ Define the organizational conditions which are most likely to favour or inhibit the emergence of communities of practice.

■ Discuss the role of ICT in developing and supporting communities of practice.

Introduction

In Chapter 5, we outlined two major approaches which organizations are taking to the management of knowledge work. The cognitive approach sees knowledge as something which is possessed by individuals, whereas the community approach sees it as the product of social interaction and learning amongst groups. This kind of community is based not on interest or geographical area but on *practice* – this might be a work practice or a hobby, but it involves an activity which others also take part in. And by being a member of that community, individuals are able to develop their practice – sharing experience and ideas with others involved in the same pursuit.

Although there is much evidence for the value of a community approach, it seems to be more difficult for organizations to develop this approach. This is partly because the cognitive approach tends to fit more neatly with established management practices. The emphasis on individuals and on the use of technology to 'capture' knowledge seems to offer a tidier and more predictable solution than a community-based approach. The latter can sometimes seems nebulous to managers who favour a short-term technical fix for their problems. The nebulous quality arises in large part because the term 'communities of practice' does not appear in organization charts or in the different business processes designed by management (Brown and Duguid, 2000).

Even more worryingly for managers, communities of practice do not recognise a boss. They are responsible only to themselves. Individuals become involved voluntarily because they have something to learn and to contribute. This makes them different to teams, for instance. Even though teams are equally unlikely to figure on the organization chart, they are linked into formal systems of goal-setting and accountability. They have goals and leaders, and they are accountable for delivering outputs – reports, new products and so on – within a specific timescale. The team disbands when the project is completed. In contrast, a community of practice is open-ended. It has neither deadlines nor specific 'deliverables'. Brown and Duguid (1998) define such communities by making a distinction between 'know-what' and 'know-how' (also termed explicit and tacit knowledge). They argue that know-how includes the ability to put know-what into practice and is typically found amongst work groups engaged cooperatively in the same work practices.

Becoming a member of a community of practice is usually an informal and self-selecting process, though some organizations (for example, BP in the oil exploration business) are now beginning to formalize community membership. At the same time, a community of practice is not just an informal network based on friendship ties or shared affiliations. Unlike other types of social network, communities of practice support the work process directly by allowing individuals to share experience about their work and thus understand it better. This knowledge-sharing is facilitated by the norms of reciprocity – 'you help me and I will help you' – and the levels of trust generated amongst the community. One consequence is that attempts to create communities of practice in a top-down way often fail because they depend on bottom-up involvement and commitment to be successful.

One further important feature of communities of practice has to do with the way in which knowledge is shared. Because these communities share a common experience of practice, many of the usual barriers to knowledge-sharing are lowered. Community members have typically developed a set of shared meanings deriving from their common experience. One consequence is that they can employ more specialized forms of language such as technical jargon, as well as a more conversational idiom for their communication (Bernstein, 1975). They do not have to spell out the basic assumptions or contextual features that their insight and experience relate to – these are already understood. Consider what is involved in telling a joke, and particularly the shared cultural context and experience involved, and this provides an insight into the way communities of practice facilitate knowledge-sharing.

One result of these features of communities of practice is that story-telling is a more important way of communicating knowledge than codifying it in ICT systems (Brown and Duguid, 1991). Stories are important because:

- They present information in an interesting way – they have a beginning, a middle and an end, and they involve people behaving well or badly.

- They present information in a way that people can empathize with – recounting a situation which each of us might face, so it has greater perceived relevance.

- They personalize the information – instead of talking about situations in the abstract, we hear about the doings of individuals whom we might know or have heard of.

- They bring people together, emphasizing a shared social identity and interests – we 'share' knowledge rather than 'transfer' it.

- Stories express values – they often contain a moral about certain kinds of behaviour leading to either positive or negative outcomes.

In this way, stories link information with interest, values and relevance, giving us a sense of the context in which experience has been developed and helping us to grasp the tacit nature of some of the knowledge being communicated.

The value of communities of practice

Although they may be hard to identify, communities of practice may play a crucial role in sharing learning and knowledge across the organization. According to DiBella and Nevis (1988), there are three essential features of organizational learning:

- New skills, attitudes, values, and behaviours are created or acquired over time.
- What is learned becomes the property of some collective unit.
- What is learned remains within the organization or group even if individuals leave.

According to these criteria, communities of practice can be seen as a vital ingredient in the acquisition and sharing of learning – making knowledge a collective resource for the organization, rather than the property of a particular individual. A good example of this is provided by Orr's (1990) study of customer service representatives ('reps') who repair the photocopiers of Xerox customers. From the management viewpoint, a rep's work is well-defined and largely independent. Customers with problems call the Customer Service Centre, which in turn notifies a rep. He or she goes to the customer's site and, with the help of the error codes displayed and a problem-solving manual, diagnoses the problem and applies the specified fix. When Orr looked at the reps' work more closely, however, he found that they did not operate independently at all. Their working day typically revolved around informal meetings with other reps over breakfast, lunch and coffee. At these meetings the reps would continuously swap war stories about malfunctioning machines that could not be repaired simply by going through the know-what of the repair manual. Orr found that one of these informal conversations would be worth hours of training. While chatting, the reps posed questions to each other, offered solutions, laughed at mistakes and generally kept each other up to date about what they knew and what they had learned on the job. As a result, knowledge was shared extensively amongst the community about ways of dealing with unusual glitches and problems that were simply not covered in the photocopier repair manual.

While the Xerox case highlights the value of the community of practice as a forum for knowledge-sharing, it is important to acknowledge some of the potentially negative implications of such settings for the management of knowledge work. In Chapter 3, for example, we highlighted the problem of 'groupthink' as one of the negative connotations of teamworking. Although communities of practice operate on a much more extensive scale and are not subject to the same group dynamics, the potential loss of objectivity can also be a problem where large numbers of people come to share a similar world-view or perspective (Locke, 1999). The danger inherent in such communities is for a more conservative outlook to dominate, creating barriers against external groups or new ideas. As we will observe in Chapter 8, this can frustrate innovation projects as it inhibits the kind of knowledge-sharing and trust which such projects need to achieve across communities or professional groups.

Managing communities of practice

Communities of practice can be an important factor in improving the performance of an organization. They encourage learning and collaboration and add value to practice. However, communities of practice are difficult to manage because, as noted above, here we have a social grouping which is not formalized and is not sanctioned by management. As such communities tend to emerge spontaneously and are responsible only to themselves, management may even find it difficult to identify them within the organization. As Brown and Duguid (2000) note: 'communities of practice do not necessarily think of themselves as a community in the conventional sense. Equally, conventional communities are not necessarily communities of practice' (p. 96).

A further problem for management is that the cultural features of such communities may run counter to the established norms of the organization. Their implicit values tend to be based on collegiality, reciprocity and influence based on expertise. This may pose a challenge for organizations which have traditionally emphasized efficiency, contractual relationships and influence based on formal roles. A good example of the challenge posed by communities of practice comes from the Xerox case described above. It took some time for Xerox management to recognize the value of the community of practice amongst its customer service reps. Their original attitude, like that of many other management groups, was much more hostile. Informal gatherings of this kind run counter to management's desire to control activities and resources. The typical reaction of managers is to see them as a threat to efficiency. For these reasons, Xerox initially sought to eliminate the reps' informal meetings. This quickly had the apparently beneficial result of increasing the number of calls which reps made to customers. Unfortunately, because knowledge was no longer being shared amongst the reps, the number of repeat calls to deal with the same machine problem also increased. Greater productivity in terms of hours on the job was actually leading to greater inefficiency in terms of solving customer problems. Xerox quickly relented and allowed the informal gatherings to be reinstated.

The Xerox example really shows the limitations of traditional Taylorist approaches when dealing with knowledge-based work. Getting employees to work harder is not the same as getting them to work smarter, and sometimes one may contradict the other. It also suggests that managers need to limit their tendency towards controlling activities. Communities of practice need to be cultivated rather than controlled. This can be done in the following ways (Wenger, 2000):

- *Events*: Companies can organize public events that bring the community together, including formal or informal meetings and problem-solving sessions.
- *Leadership*: Communities of practice depend on internal leadership, and the role of the 'community coordinator' who takes care of the day-to-day work is crucial. A community needs multiple forms of leadership, including 'thought leaders', networkers, people who document practice, pioneers, and so on. These forms of leadership may be carried out by a group or by one or two individuals.
- *Connectivity*: Companies need to facilitate connections between different groups. This may involve brokering relationships and using a variety of communication media.
- *Membership*: A community's members must have critical mass but this should not become so wide that the focus or interest is diluted. Sometimes, sub-communities may develop within a wider grouping.
- *Learning projects*: Communities of practice deepen their commitment when they take responsibility for a learning agenda which pushes their practice further. Relevant learning projects could include assessing tools for practice, building a generic design, and linking with external groups, for example universities, in the same field.
- *Artefacts*: All communities of practice produce their own artefacts such as documents, tools, stories, websites and so on. A community needs to consider what artefacts it needs and who is to produce and maintain them.

In addition, one important feature of any community of practice is *boundaries*. Every community of practice has boundaries in terms of social interaction and membership. This is inevitable. If a community is too open, the value and interest of membership are reduced. However, boundaries can obviously create dangers of exclusivity and insularity. Communities may become inward-looking and unable to recognize the contribution and knowledge of other groups. Boundaries do not just keep knowledge in – they keep it out too. This means that any community-based approach to managing knowledge has to recognize the importance of dealing with these boundaries. This can happen in several ways. First, cross-community initiatives can help to avoid isolation and elitism on the part of one group. Inter-disciplinary projects can help to do this as the learning from the project is disseminated through the communities of practice of team members.

Second, individuals from different communities can play a brokering role which helps all the communities to stay connected. Such knowledge brokers take many different forms (Wenger, 2000):

- *Boundary spanners* – who take care of one specific boundary
- *Roamers* – going from place to place, creating an informal web of connections
- *Outposts* – bringing back news from the front and exploring new territories

Another way of linking different communities of practice together is through the use of information and communication technology (ICT). This may be particularly effective where different groups are geographically dispersed and unable to communicate through face-to-face contacts. In the Xerox case, for example, the group which Orr studied included about a dozen people, whereas the Xerox rep force worldwide numbers around 25,000. The lack of communication across this worldwide range of communities meant that different groups were grappling with problems which had already been solved elsewhere. To overcome this problem and connect these different communities, Xerox initiated the 'Eureka' project to oversee knowledge dissemination. The aim was to create a database which would preserve useful ideas and learning points and make them available globally.

Clearly, there was a danger here, as noted in Chapter 5, of technology being viewed as a solution rather than a support to Knowledge Management. Many knowledge databases are underutilized by the people they are intended to serve. This is often because they are designed top-down with little reference to what users see as useful knowledge. In the case of the Eureka database, the development process was driven not by managers but by the customer service reps themselves. It is reps, not managers, who both supply and vet the tips. A rep submits a suggestion first to a local expert. Together they refine it, before submitting it to a centralized review process in each business unit. Here reps and engineers again vet the tips, rejecting some, eliminating duplicates and calling in experts on a particular product line to resolve disputes. Only when a tip has been through this process is it made available on the database to reps worldwide. This ensures that the content of the database is relevant, reliable and up to date. With this kind of content, Xerox has no problems in ensuring that reps make use of the information available – by helping them work faster and better, these tips make their work life easier, not harder. Brown and Duguid (2000) cite a typical example of how the database is used. In one case, an engineer in Brazil was about to replace a malfunctioning high-end colour machine at a cost of $40,000. A quick visit to the database, however, produced a tip from a Montreal rep that led him to replace a 50 cent fuse instead. The result was one less disgruntled customer and a large saving to the company. In fact, Xerox estimate that Eureka has saved the corporation around $100 million already.

On-line communities of practice

The 'Eureka' project at Xerox underlines the point that communities of practice do not have to involve physical co-location. Indeed, there are many communities which are geographically dispersed but which still operate effectively. These communities often depend on access to a shared ICT infrastructure. It would be a mistake, however, to see ICT's role here as simply one of facilitating information exchange. Rather, communications across dispersed communities can help to create shared *cultural objects* around which virtual communities coalesce – even people who have never met each other can share a sense of belonging to a community (Brown and Duguid, 2000). The historical precedent for this is the development of scientific and religious communities around shared texts: the Bible or the Koran, key scientific treatises, mathematical formulae and so on. Groups who share a common interest in these texts are 'invisible colleges' whose membership spans the globe via the dissemination of the written word.

Clearly, ICT can support such virtual communities in a number of ways. The role of ICT is most obvious, however, in the development of on-line or electronic communities where groups and individuals interact exclusively through electronic means. There are four major forms of on-line community:

- Communities of transaction which provide help to their members in buying and selling
- Communities of interest – members participate in specific topics but this does not extend to their personal life
- Role-playing communities where members interact through the roles they play in the game
- Communities of relationships which are centred on shared life experience, for example, cancer sufferers and people who have experienced divorce or infertility

There are also differences in the way these communities exploit electronic media. A recent survey (Williams, 1999) found that over 50 per cent of the sample used web discussions/newsgroups, 25 per cent used e-mail, and 25 per cent used Lotus Notes. Some communities existed solely on-line while others used electronic communications as only one of several integrating tools. Size also varied: 20 per cent reported fewer than 200 members while 33 per cent reported 5000 + members. Perhaps the most important challenge posed by on-line communities, however, is the need to encourage participation from members. Where members of a working community of practice would see participation as part of their working day, members of on-line communities may need to make a conscious effort to participate actively – something which may be harder or easier depending on the quality of the electronic links. Sixty per cent of on-line communities reported that achieving member participation was a significant challenge, and difficult-to-use technology created hurdles for 40 per cent.

One of the reasons for low participation rates in on-line communities was revealed in a study of the use of a groupware system – Lotus Notes – in the product development department of a major multinational food producer (Ciborra and Patriotta, 1996). Although the culture of this department was very supportive of knowledge-sharing, the study found that few people actually used Lotus Notes to share knowledge and ideas. To some extent this was because they preferred to communicate via the traditional media of face-to-face meetings, telephones and written documents. A bigger problem, however, was their reluctance to commit their thinking about 'below the line' work-in-progress to the Lotus Notes system. Instead they would simply use the system to formally record progress 'above the line'. This was partly because they were frightened of placing their messy and incomplete ideas into a semi-public arena, and partly because doing so involved extra effort – thoughts had to be clarified and written down in structured, sensible English to be accessible to other users of the system. This concern about making ideas and insights visible highlights the extent to which knowledge creation is often a rather private act – something that works best in intimate, face-to-face environments rather than in a more public setting. Also, the study suggests that to share knowledge is to change it. Personal insights may have to be turned into something more prosaic to be accessible to a wider audience. This not only changes the insight itself, but may ultimately prove inefficient given the additional time and effort involved.

These kinds of constraints may mean that some on-line communities that lack member participation and interactive communication may only serve as a means of broadcasting information rather than sharing knowledge. On the other hand, there have been important examples of on-line communities playing an important role in knowledge-sharing. One of the most well-known of these examples derives from the experience of the Pentium chip (Uzumeri and Snyder, 1996).

Case Study 6.1   On-line communities: the Pentium chip

In June 1994, the Intel corporation discovered a flaw in its flagship Pentium processor chip. For divisions involving a few specific numbers, Intel's tests showed that the error occurred only in the ninth significant digit of the answer and affected only a small percentage of the possible division combinations. Intel considered the Pentium flaw so minor that it did not notify computer manufacturers or the public and continued to sell the flawed chip. In November 1994,

---

Case Study 6.1 continued

---

however, the flaw was discovered by a mathematician at Lynchburg College, and he posted a message on a Compuserve electronic bulletin board asking other Pentium users if they were aware of the problem. The message was relayed to an Internet discussion group, comp.sys.intel, that specialized in technical discussions of Intel products. The design flaw was quickly confirmed by other users. This prompted Intel to make a qualified offer to replace flawed chips for 'heavy duty scientific users' only. But contributors to Internet discussion groups quickly identified many plausible scenarios where the design flaw could cause serious computational errors – for example, in spreadsheet calculations involving multiplication of thousands of different numbers. These contributions raised the general level of concern about the Pentium chip so far that Intel were forced to make a 'no questions asked' replacement offer. The company estimated that the replacement program would cause a hit of $475 million on its 1994 earnings.

As Uzumeri and Snyder (1996) note, the Internet discussion group provided an important forum for diagnosing the Pentium flaw, bringing together scientific and lay communities in a powerful way. They claim that by integrating scientific and lay knowledge into a tightly knit discussion, the Internet may create a form of 'accelerated science' which will help to identify and deal with future scientific and technological problems.

Case Study 6.1 highlights the way in which on-line communities can become effective through a shared response to 'cultural objects'. ICT systems which enable the development and sharing of such cultural objects – be they texts, stories or symbolic problems – are more likely to facilitate knowledge-sharing because they are helping to construct as well as connect the community. By facilitating conversations amongst groups and individuals, ICT systems can help to extend the experience of shared meanings and understandings beyond the realm of physical co-location into the virtual space of the company intranet or e-mail forum.

Communities of knowing

One of the implications of the more extensive use of ICT-based systems in organizations is the greater possibility for communication between different communities and across organizational boundaries. Different groups within the organization encounter each other in new ways, and new linkages can be developed. Now, it is always possible that the organization will overestimate the role of technology – expecting internal cultural and political divisions to be overcome simply by introducing a company intranet or by adopting Lotus Notes groupware. We described such a situation in the BankCo case in chapter 5, where the development of intranets only served to reinforce internal divisions.

If managers are to avoid the BankCo scenario, they need to develop a better understanding of the way in which different groups and communities interact. In part, this means having an appreciation of the shape and role of informal social networks in the life of the organization. As Figure 6.1 outlines, the scope and accessibility of ICT-based communication networks is very seductive. They seem to offer extensive and uniform linkages between groups and individuals across the organization. However, when we examine the social networks of the organization – the actual paths along which much knowledge, especially tacit knowledge, is most readily shared – we discover a much more uneven pattern. This kind of network analysis highlights not only the oft-made distinction between knowledge and information, but also the extent to which knowledge circulates *within* rather than *across* communities. This tendency for knowledge to flow within the channels developed by social networks was highlighted by a recent in-house study within a major pharmaceutical company. A survey was conducted of knowledge exchange across the company's five R&D centres worldwide. This found that 70 per cent of such exchange took place within the individual centres and only 5 per cent between centres: this despite the fact that groups within the five centres were working on a number of common problems. Top management in the company discovered that the lack of knowledge-sharing was not only caused by the geographical distance between the centres. It also had much to do with the recent restructuring of the firm which had seen the closure of some R&D facilities. As a result, levels of trust between the different R&D centres were relatively low – each centre feeling itself to be in competition with the others.

However, the problems of knowledge-sharing between communities are not simply to do with the internal and external boundaries of social networks. An organization is fundamentally a distributed system of knowledge, in which knowledge is embedded within particular contexts and communities (Tsoukas, 1996). It follows that trying to expand the scope of knowledge-sharing is not just a question of encouraging informal links or even face-to-face contacts. Even these direct contacts often fail to achieve a genuine sharing of knowledge and experience – we might say that there was not a 'meeting of minds' between the groups involved. Such failures are highlighted by a recent study of Hewlett Packard's attempts to raise quality levels in its plants. The aim of capturing and spreading best practice worldwide encountered major internal barriers which were primarily behavioural and organizational rather than technical:

> At HP some divisions would take the lead experimenting with innovative practices.
> . . . They would really think through the meaning and purpose of these activities and
> what needed to change to make them work . . . If they were successful, managers

from other divisions would visit and 'cherry pick' specific practices aiming for the same results but without the deep system thinking that led to initial success. (Cole, 1999, p. 212)

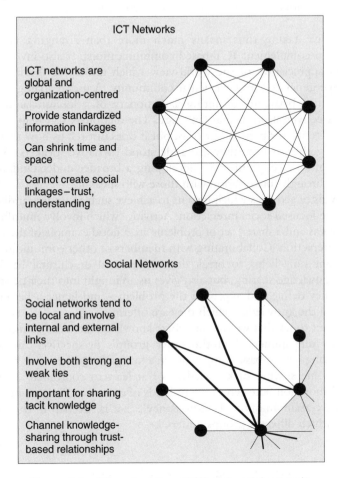

Figure 6.1   Characteristics of ICT and social networks

The reasons for such failures can be explained in terms of the cognitive dimension of communities. Communities of practice are also 'communities of knowing' (Boland and Tenkasi, 1995): that is, the knowledge of the different groups involved is not only socially embedded within informal networks but is also cognitively embedded. It is grounded in particular world-views or perspectives which connect and make sense of the different kinds of knowledge circulating within the community. Boland and Tenkasi (1995) suggest that understanding the other community's perspective is vital to what they term the 'perspective taking' process. This is not something which can be achieved simply by exchanging information. As they put it:

The problem of integration of knowledge in knowledge-intensive firms is not a problem of simply combining, sharing or making data commonly available. It is a problem of perspective taking in which the unique thought worlds of different communities of knowing are made visible and accessible to others. (1995, p. 39)

Perspective taking thus means much more than arranging face-to-face meetings to complement ICT-based communications. It also involves developing an appreciation of the world-view which underpins the insights and knowledge generated by a particular community. A useful analogy might be the difference between consulting a dictionary of a foreign language and holding a conversation in that language. The dictionary can help us identify equivalent terms for particular words, but it does not tell us how these words are put together or how they are understood by native speakers. Acquiring this kind of knowledge involves developing a broader understanding of the language through conversation with those who speak it.

The kinds of activities which help us to achieve such an understanding typically involve focused social interaction. Activities which involve multifunctional project teams and a shared set of problems are a good example of the necessary kind of interaction. Collaborating with members of other communities in this context not only helps to break down the social or cultural barriers that prevent knowledge-sharing, but also gives us an insight into their perspective – the way they define and approach the problem – and hence a better understanding of the knowledge which they are offering.

This is not to say that we can only share knowledge between communities by becoming fully immersed in the other group's perspective. An adequate understanding – like a basic competence in a foreign language – may be sufficient to allow some sharing of knowledge, or at least to coordinate activities to allow collaboration between different kinds of expertise. This can be achieved through a certain amount of 'redundancy', that is, overlap in the tasks and activities which different groups undertake.

Conclusions

This chapter has highlighted the role which communities of practice can play in enabling the organization to learn from the experience of its members. Traditional hierarchical structures are designed to control activities and often militate against the easy sharing of knowledge and learning. Communities, however, help to foster relationships based on mutual trust – 'social capital', in short – which are the unspoken and often unrecognized channels through which knowledge is shared. It follows that communities of practice have profound implications for the management of knowledge work. First, they highlight the limits of management control. Communities are voluntary entities, depending entirely on the interest and commitment of their members.

They cannot be designed or imposed in a top-down manner. Knowledge does not circulate through them in the officially prescribed form of rules, procedures and targets. Rather knowledge is disseminated through stories, jokes and anecdotes which enlighten, or just lighten, a shared experience.

The importance of story-telling also provides a further insight into the limits of technology for managing knowledge. For, while the design of ICT systems is often based on a cognitive model of Knowledge Management, studies of communities suggest that this is a misapprehension about the most important function of ICT-based communications. Such systems work best when they are used to *connect* communities, not to *transfer* knowledge. Because much knowledge is embedded in particular communities or contexts, developing a shared understanding and a degree of trust is often the most critical step towards sharing knowledge. ICT-based networks can complement but not replace the importance of social networks in this regard. Such networks can, however, support the development of new communities through problem-solving interactions that allow individuals to appreciate the different perspectives which others bring to their work. In particular, ICT networks can sustain the development of communities by allowing them to develop and exchange shared cultural objects – texts, stories and images – which help to reinforce the meaning and purpose of a particular group.

One of the implications of this chapter, therefore, is the need to link the management of knowledge work to the *purpose* of a particular activity. Rather than making broad assumptions about the way in which knowledge is being created or shared, we need to look more carefully at the particular groups involved and the intentions which they are pursuing in the situation at hand. This point is further underlined in Chapter 7 when we examine the different 'episodes' of the innovation process and the consequent implications for our ability to manage knowledge for specified purposes.

Case Study 6.2   Buckman Labs

At the time of this study, Buckman Laboratories was a $300 million chemical company serving industries in 102 different countries selling 1000 different specialist chemicals (see www.knowledge-nurture.com for details). It was established in 1945 as a manufacturer of specialist chemicals for aqueous industrial systems. The business grew rapidly under the hard driving leadership of Dr Stanley Buckman. The management philosophy was to change radically, however, in 1978. When his father died from a heart attack at his office, Bob Buckman resolved that from now on management and responsibility had to be devolved throughout the business. As he later commented: 'I knew I didn't want to do it Dad's way. Every single business decision had to be approved by my father. I thought, this is too much work.'

Case Study 6.2 continued

He also recognized that the business world was changing and that from now on knowledge would be the basis of his company's competitive edge. During the 1980s, this led to a greater emphasis on the customer and an increase in the sales force. It was also reflected in significant efforts to make information more widely available throughout the firm. In March 1992, these efforts culminated in the merger of the firm's Information Systems and Telecommunications departments to create the Knowledge Transfer Department (KTD). Within the KTD, an R&D technical information centre which was formerly used as a clearing-house for technical questions from worldwide offices was renamed as the Knowledge Resource Center (KRC). Together with the KRC, the KTD became responsible for the design and ongoing management of the network.

By the end of 1992, Buckman Laboratories had invested $8 million to lay the groundwork for its new knowledge transfer system. For a total investment of $75,000 per month in access charges and the provision of an IBM ThinkPad 720 with modem to each employee, all Buckman staff were able to make a single phone call that established on-line contact with headquarters and provided the necessary real-time access to global information services. With this infrastructure in place, management developed a global knowledge transfer network which they termed K'Netix. Seven discussion forums were established (three customer-focused forums and four regional-focused forums) to allow employees to share experience in particular areas. By March 1993, every employee was able to access K'Netix, and this made it possible to deliver knowledge-based services to customers in over 90 countries worldwide.

The K'Netix Knowledge Management system was divided into two basic parts: organizational forums and codified databases. The focus, however, was very much on connecting individuals rather than stockpiling knowledge for its own sake. The system enabled the electronic sharing of knowledge both between associates themselves and between associates and customers. The most knowledgeable experts at all levels of the organization were therefore kept in touch with each other, encouraging group problem-solving and the sharing of new ideas and knowledge (Buckman, 1998). All 1300 of the organization's associates worldwide were given CompuServe IDs and passwords and they used the network for both intra- and inter-company communication. This single knowledge network aimed to encompass all of the company's knowledge and experience, encouraging Buckman associates to focus on customer needs and problems.

The development of a culture for knowledge-sharing

While the technological infrastructure was being established, an equally important development was the attempt to foster a knowledge-sharing culture at Buckman Labs. In many respects, this attempt to change 'hearts and minds' was an even bigger challenge as established ways of thinking and working tend to be both culturally and politically embedded within organizations. Not only are they intertwined with long-established values and assumptions, they are also defended fiercely by powerful groups who see change as an assault

Case Study 6.2 continued

upon their interests. In this respect, Buckman Labs was no exception. Bob Buckman, in particular, sought to overcome such resistance within the firm. He believed that many associates had developed their expertise within environments such as school and university which encouraged the hoarding, not the sharing, of knowledge. Within the education system, he argued, knowledge-sharing is termed plagiarism and is punished. Copying from others is frowned upon. It is the individual's ability to accumulate knowledge in their own right which is rewarded. In contrast, Buckman sought to create a culture in which associates who shared their knowledge would be the most influential and sought-after individuals within the company.

Resistance to this knowledge-sharing vision came in large part from middle management who had been traditionally perceived as information gatekeepers in the company. The radical cultural change introduced by Bob Buckman had major implications for the power structure of middle management. In the past, middle management had sought to control the flow of information to employees in order to protect their own roles in the organization.

It took some years for these attitudes to change – learning the new norms and values involved painfully unlearning the old culture. To help associates understand the expected behaviour, Buckman sought to put in place a new Code of Ethics. This was issued on a wallet-sized laminated card to every employee. Buckman's Code of Ethics was presented as the 'glue' that would hold the company together. It was seen as providing the basis for the respect and trust that are necessary in a knowledge-sharing environment. In presenting this new model of culture, Bob Buckman asked his employees to think about the company as a ship, with the Code of Ethics as the waterline of the ship. The message to associates was simple: 'You do not shoot below the waterline, because you can sink the ship. However, you are free to be as innovative as you wish in changing the superstructure of the ship to meet the needs of the customer.' This concern with culture reflected Buckman's belief that creating new knowledge involved not only objective, external information, but also tacit and highly subjective individual insights, intuitions and hunches. He sought to ensure that creating and sharing knowledge was no longer seen as the exclusive responsibility of the R&D department but rather a responsibility of all employees.

Buckman Labs' Code of Ethics

Because we are separated – by many miles, by diversity of cultures and languages – we at Buckman need a clear understanding of the basic principles by which we will operate our company. These are:

That the company is made up of individuals – each of whom has different capabilities and potentials – all of which are necessary to the success of the company.

That we acknowledge that individuality by treating each other with dignity and respect – striving to maintain continuous and positive communications among all of us.

Case Study 6.2 continued

> *That we will recognize and reward the contributions and accomplishments of each individual.*
>
> *That we will continually plan for the future so that we can control our destiny instead of letting events overtake us.*

But the cultural change wrought at Buckman Labs rested on more than the issue of laminated cards. Leadership, and in particular Bob Buckman's stern resolve to 'manage the managers', was of paramount importance. The experience here arguably highlights another side of leadership – that is, the selective use of sanctions as well as rewards in order to reinforce certain kinds of behaviour. In this instance, the desire to encourage knowledge-sharing led Bob Buckman to write personally to all of those associates who were deemed to be unwilling to participate in the sharing activities. These letters conveyed the following blunt message: 'If one is not willing to contribute or participate, then he or she should understand that many opportunities offered in the past will no longer be available.' Whatever the success of the more subtle attempts to engineer the right kind of culture, this blunt approach seems to have been effective at least in overcoming resistance to change and dismantling barriers to communication across the organization and between different levels of management. What Buckman termed the 'smokeblowers' in middle management were effectively marginalized. The visible result of this effort to stigmatize knowledge-hoarding was the creation of a global Knowledge Management system in which employees were for the first time encouraged to speak freely about their opinions outside the chain of command. As one manager observed: 'With the global network in place, it does not matter if you are a sales associate, a regional or district manager or a corporate VP [Vice President] – everybody talks to everybody.'

Communities of practice

In the last ten years, communities of practice have evolved informally within the company to share knowledge for specific customer problems as well as to gather knowledge for wider corporate use. According to a scientist from the R&D Department:

> These are small sub-groups of people who have mutual respect, share some common values and generally get the important work done. They are not necessarily a team, a task force or any other authorized group. Their bonding is social as well as technical, and is built around informed participation.

These communities developed around the problem-solving forums that were established through the K'Netix system. The community knowledge base is maintained by 'forum specialists'. Any technical or customer queries relating to a particular area that cannot be answered by the technical–sales person are posted on the forum. Usually the request for help is picked up and

---

Case Study 6.2 continued

---

answered by anyone who has expertise in the related subject area. If the request is unattended for a few hours, however, the forum specialist will pick up the request, identify the potential experts and informally forward it to them for attention. Alternatively, the more formal route involves bringing in 'section leaders' – that is, a group of experts who have volunteered to tackle some of the more stubborn problems in particular areas.

The request for knowledge will be kept on the forum as long as there is an active discussion of it. When it is considered 'dead' or finally resolved, forum specialists and section leaders process it further. For example, the knowledge generated is usually overlapping and sometimes inaccurate. Forum specialists and section leaders organize, validate and verify the knowledge before it is uploaded into the knowledge base to be ready for distribution and use/reuse if a similar query is presented in the future. This knowledge-processing ensures that the tacit knowledge of the experts is shared within the organization on a worldwide basis. More importantly, it allows front-line employees to continue serving customers while the specialists devote their time to capturing their knowledge in a reusable form. The forums, which are accessible only to company associates, are each divided into sections based on Buckman's lines of business, such as water treatment and leather. Codified databases come from a number of sources: valuable knowledge generated from discussions on the forums (industry experts within individual sections advise forum specialists on which exchanges or 'threads' are worth saving), and uploaded external secondary material and any materials that are helpful to associates are also included (for example, competitive intelligence).

One of the first challenges to the development of the K'Netix system came with the problem posed by the different language communities within such a worldwide organization. In total, Buckman employees across the world speak over fifteen different languages. Top management agonized for some time over the question of allowing the development of forums in languages other than English. There was a concern that this would impede the free flow of knowledge across the business. However, when management gave the go-ahead for the development of regionally focused forums – TechForum, Euroforum (for European associates who prefer using European languages), LatinoForum (used mainly by Latin American associates) and AAAForum (for Asian, Australian and African associates) – it was discovered that many employees who were uncomfortable in expressing themselves in English were much happier to share knowledge in their own native language. The provision of language interpreters to monitor forum threads means that valuable knowledge can be rapidly transferred from one regional forum to another.

Thus, what we see at Buckman is the interaction of different communities of practice to share knowledge and to help each other solve specific technical problems. The K'Netix system helps to support that knowledge-sharing, but what is crucial is the way that members of different groups and business units work together through the system. To illustrate this cooperative knowledge-sharing, we can take a fairly typical example of how the system operates in practice. This example has to do with a need for specialist knowledge on

Case Study 6.2 continued

'pitch control'. Pitch control involves working on removing or minimizing the effect of pitch in the paper-making process. Pitch is made up of sticky materials left over in the pulp fibres used in the paper-making process or derived from adhesives or plastics in recycled fibres. Given the increasing range of Buckman Labs' technical activities, there are frequent demands for knowledge of new or esoteric domains. In this instance, knowledge of pitch control was required for a work programme in an Indonesian pulp mill. When Dennis Dalton, who is based in Singapore as Managing Director of all company activities in Asia, was proposing this programme, he circulated a message through the K'Netix system requesting help on how he could go about preparing it: 'I would appreciate an update on successful recent pitch-control strategies in your parts of the world', he wrote.

A response came within a matter of a few hours from Phil Hoekstra in Memphis, including a suggestion for the specific Buckman chemical to use as well as a reference to a Master's thesis on the pitch control of tropical hardwoods, written by an Indonesian student attending North Carolina State University. A further response came only fifty minutes after the first, this time from Michael Sund in Canada. This offered his experience in solving the pitch problem in British Columbia. Then in quick succession Nils Hallberg logged in with examples from Sweden; Wendy Bijiker offered details from a New Zealand paper mill; Jose Vallcorba cited examples from Spain and France; Chip Hill in Memphis contributed scientific advice from the R&D Department; Javier del Rosal included a detailed chemical formula and specific application directions from Mexico; and Lionel Hughes wrote about his experience in South Africa. In total, Dalton's request for suggestions generated eleven replies from six different countries. It stimulated new discussions, generated new knowledge, and put him into a position to secure a $6 million order from the Indonesian pulp mill (Buckman, 1998).

The role of human resource factors

Since 1996, the Buckman Laboratories Learning Center (Bulab Learning Center) has developed an emphasis on allowing associates to manage their own personal and career development, and on bringing new knowledge and skills to its employees in a cost-effective manner. While its knowledge-transfer mechanism has been effective in creating and sharing its organizational knowledge, training and education at Buckman Laboratories continued until recently to be delivered in the traditional hierarchical 'teacher and student' classroom fashion. Based on its maturing platform of a knowledge-sharing environment, Buckman Laboratories decided in 1996, with the help of information technology, to give its associates greater opportunity to receive electronic learning events and opportunities to grow. Buckman Laboratories began experimenting in 1996 with Lotus's novel educational product Learning-Space™. The experiment led to the creation of a multilingual on-line Learning Center. The Learning Center's content ranges from short training and reference materials to advanced academic degrees. The content provided is drawn

---

Case Study 6.2 continued

---

from leading universities, and also includes custom-designed tools to help with employees' day-to-day duties. The responsibility for personal development is thus transferred to the individual associate, reinforcing Buckman's concern to make the individual accountable for their own performance.

Buckman Laboratories does not offer regular financial rewards for sharing knowledge. However, a careful selection of rewards has been utilized at different times. Thus, a one-off event at a fashionable resort was arranged for the 150 employees who had contributed the most widely used knowledge. At the event, employees helped to plan the future of the Knowledge Management initiatives. Those chosen also received new laptop computers and participated in a number of Knowledge Management-related discussions. Although some of those who were not selected for the event were left feeling disappointed, overall participation in the knowledge-sharing forums rose immediately.

So far, at Buckman Laboratories the results and outcomes of knowledge-sharing activities are being measured against the percentage of new products sold as the ability to sell new products has always been a key performance indicator. The successful efforts of knowledge-sharing there have been credited with the company's 250 per cent growth in sales in the past decade. Specifically, its global knowledge-sharing effort has helped increase the percentage of sales from products less than five years old from 14 per cent in 1987 to 34.6 per cent in 1996.

Questions

1. Identify three key factors which encouraged the development of communities of practice at Buckman Labs.
2. Evaluate the roles played by ICT and management respectively in promoting knowledge-sharing.

We gratefully acknowledge the authorship of Shan Ling Pan in relation to the original version of this case study.

Summary of key learning points

- Communities of practice are important in sharing tacit knowledge based on experience.
- Tacit knowledge is shared through story-telling and social networks.
- Organizations find it difficult to manage communities of practice because they are more nebulous than other entities and tend to emerge from the bottom up.

Summary of key learning points continued

- Communities of practice need to be cultivated, not controlled, and rely upon boundary spanners to maintain effective relations with other communities.

- On-line communities have a problem in creating user participation because of the greater visibility of contributions and need for the standardization of language.

- On-line communities are effective where they create shared cultural objects which provide a focus for problem-solving, and where ICT is used to connect groups and individuals.

- Knowledge tends to flow through social networks and within communities. This can create barriers to innovation where change requires the involvement of a number of different groups.

- Overcoming barriers to knowledge-sharing between communities involves shared experience which allows one group to appreciate the world-view of another.

References

Bernstein, B. (1975) *Class, Codes and Control: Towards a Theory of Educational Transmissions.* London: Routledge & Kegan Paul.

Boland, R.J. and Tenkasi, R.V. (1995) Perspective Making and Perspective Taking in Communities of Practice. *Organization Science,* 6(4), 350–63.

Bressand, A. and Distler, C. (1995) *La Planète relationelle.* Paris: Flammarion.

Brown, J.S. and Duguid, P. (1991) Organizational learning and Communities-of-practice: towards a unified view of working, learning and innovation. *Organization Science,* 2, 40–57.

Brown, J.S. and Duguid, P. (1998) Organizing knowledge. *California Management Review,* 40(3): 90–109.

Brown, J.S. and Duguid, P. (2000) *The Social Life of Information.* Boston, Mass.: Harvard Business School Press.

Buckman, R. (1998) Knowledge sharing at Buckman Laboratories. *Journal of Business Strategy,* January/February: 11–15.

Ciborra, C. and Patriotta, G. (1996) Groupware and teamwork in new product development: the case of a consumer goods multinational. In C. Ciborra (ed.) *Groupware and Teamwork.* New York: Wiley.

Cole, R.E. (1999) *Managing Quality Fads.* Oxford: Oxford University Press, p. 239.

DiBella, A. and Nevis, E. (1988) *How Organizations Learn: An Integrated Strategy for Building Learning Capability.* San Francisco: Jossey-Bass.

Locke, E.A. (1999) Some reservations about social capital. *Academy of Management Review,* 24(1): 8–9.

Orr, J. (1990) Sharing knowledge, Celebrating identity in War stories and Community memory in a service culture. In D. Middleton and D. Edwards (eds) *Collective Remembering: Remembering in a Society.* Beverly Hills, Calif: Sage.

Pan, S.L. and Scarbrough, H. (1998) A Socio-technical view of knowledge sharing at Buckman Laboratories. *Journal of Knowledge Management*, **2**(1): 55–66.

Tsoukas, H. (1996) The firm as a distributed knowledge system: a constructionist approach. *Strategic Management Journal*, **17**, 11–25.

Uzumeri, M.V. and Snyder, C.A. (1996) Information technology and accelerated science: the case of the Pentium (TM) flow. *California Management Review*, **38**(2), Winter: 44–8.

Wenger, E. (2000) Communities of practice and social learning systems. *Organization*, **7**(2): 225–46.

Williams, R.L. (1999) Managing an on-line community. *Journal for Quality and Participation*, **22**(6): 54–5.

7

Managing knowledge for a purpose: Knowledge Management and innovation

Learning outcomes

By the end of this chapter students will be able to:

■ Appreciate the importance of linking the management of knowledge to tasks and objectives by considering the task of innovation.

■ Outline the characteristics of innovation: (i) as an episodic process that relies centrally on the creation and application of knowledge to develop new ways of working; (ii) where the outcomes are mediated by cognitive, social, and organizational features of the context in which it occurs.

■ Describe and explain the links between knowledge, Knowledge Management and innovation.

■ Identify appropriate ways of managing knowledge in order to facilitate different episodes of the innovation process.

■ Experience the difficulties of managing knowledge first-hand by engaging in a simulated innovation process involving a group of actors with different perceptions and interests, and suggest how these difficulties can be resolved.

Introduction

The previous chapter showed how developing a community approach can be more useful for managing knowledge work than the 'capture, codify and control' strategies associated with the cognitive model. However, an important point is that neither of these approaches should be thought of as universally applicable to all tasks and situations. As earlier chapters have highlighted, knowledge is situated – its development and application depend crucially on the social context in which it is deployed. This means that attempts to manage knowledge should also be sensitive to social context. The dangers, then, of replacing one set of generalized prescriptions (for example, around the development of communities) with another (for example, around the development of IT systems) should be recognized. Previous chapters have started also to introduce the idea that a firm's approach to Knowledge Management may need to be customized for particular tasks and purposes. This chapter uses the example of managing knowledge where the purpose is innovation to develop this idea further.

Why is innovation an important issue for Knowledge Management?

The answer to the above question is because managing knowledge for its own sake adds little, if any, value to organizations – the value-added comes only when knowledge is applied in order to improve, change or develop specific tasks and activities (McDermott, 1999). In short, innovation is frequently a primary purpose for Knowledge Management (of course there are others, such as improving efficiency and tightening control). Buckman Labs, for example, claimed that the major benefits as a result of the introduction of their Knowledge Management initiative came through improvements in their capacity to innovate (Pan and Scarbrough, 1999).

However, as this chapter will show, innovation can be a complex, uncertain and highly political activity. It involves people with different expertise and experience working together – often over extended periods of time – and combining their knowledge in order to generate more effective work practices, usually in the form of new products or processes. Innovation is not just about R&D – it also occurs through mainstream work activities. For example, at Unilever major cost savings were made when a network was set up around core technologies that allowed individuals with expertise in packaging to work together with chemical process engineers to develop new, still safe, but less complex and more standardized forms of packaging household products. Moreover, the knowledge needed to develop and implement innovation is often widely distributed – for example, across individuals, groups, structural divisions within the firm, even nations and cultures. Therefore bringing this distributed knowledge together, and getting people to buy into the innovation process, is a major challenge for innovation. Innovation, then, is a good example of knowledge work and one that is relevant, not just to knowledge-intensive and high-tech firms, but also to a wide range of private and public sector organizations. Clearly, then, if innovation is dependent on the creation and application of knowledge, Knowledge Management has a critical role to play.

Innovation is also inherently uncertain – it is difficult to know at the outset quite what will be achieved when knowledge is combined in new ways. Therefore, while it is easy to talk about managing knowledge to achieve innovation, it is less easy to do. The major objective of this chapter, then, is to provide an understanding of ways of managing knowledge for innovation. This requires, first, a broad understanding of innovation and, second, an understanding of the links between Knowledge Management and innovation.

Structure of the chapter

The chapter begins by highlighting the importance, more broadly, of linking knowledge, and the management of knowledge, to work tasks and activities. The nature and characteristics of innovation are then outlined. This highlights two critical features of innovation that run through the chapter:

- Its dynamic, processual, episodic nature
- Its implications for the deployment and management of knowledge

Students who have the opportunity to work in syndicate groups will also be able to engage in a role-play, designed to simulate part of an innovation process. It focuses on technological innovation – a task that typically involves changes in the way people work as well as in the application of technical systems, and therefore poses major challenges for the management of knowledge (Clark and Staunton, 1989). A more forensic examination of the different dimensions of the innovation process and the ways in which knowledge might be managed more effectively is possible through the role-play.

This scrutiny of innovation reinforces the conclusions drawn in earlier chapters that a single (in the universalistic sense) 'best practice' approach to Knowledge Management is problematic. What is more useful is to think about the particular purpose that the practice of managing knowledge needs to serve over the varied and sometimes discontinuous life cycle of an innovation process (that is, what is knowledge being managed for?). The chapter therefore provides a further challenge to the pursuit of 'best practice' in managing knowledge that is a feature of much existing work, and presents the case for a more contingent approach. This takes into account the different ways in which knowledge is being deployed at different points of time in the innovation process.

Building from the cognitive and community approaches introduced in Chapter 5, three approaches to managing knowledge for innovation are outlined. These are referred to as the *networking* approach, the *community* approach and the *cognitive* approach. These reflect, respectively, the relative emphasis in different phases of the innovation process on knowledge acquisition, knowledge application and creation, and knowledge reuse. To illustrate these approaches we refer again to the case study of LiftCo, detailed in Chapter 4. This provides a useful example of the ways in which actual practices for managing knowledge can be tailored – albeit perhaps unconsciously – to different episodes of the innovation process.

The problems of 'purposeless' knowledge

A problem with many approaches to knowledge and, correspondingly, managing knowledge work is that, whilst they assume a positive relationship between the accumulation of knowledge and improvement in innovative capability and organizational performance, this relationship is rarely explored in much detail. Frequently knowledge is treated as valuable in its own right and is divorced from the social action and tasks that actually generate changes in performance. Thus, as knowledge has come to be viewed as a 'critical resource' (as outlined in Chapter 1), there has been a tendency towards what might be termed a 'quantity approach' to managing knowledge in much of the literature. According to this, knowledge (however difficult to define) is assumed to have a direct and positive relation to firm performance. The role of Knowledge Management initiatives is therefore to enhance the creation, capture and exploitation of knowledge. The assumption often is that if ever-greater quantities of knowledge are captured, stockpiled and transferred, improvements in the firm's innovative capacity – and therefore its perform-ance – will automatically follow. This is often without really understanding what knowledge is or how it links to innovation. The idea seems to be 'we don't know what knowledge is but it seems to solve problems in a functional way so let's use it anyway' (Alvesson and Karreman, 2001, p. 999).

This quantitative approach has led to numerous general and prescriptive models aimed at increasing the knowledge available to the firm (Prusak, 1997). Yet knowledge can only generate performance advantages if it is linked to concrete actions, tasks and purposes that actually stand to offer some organizational advantage. Leonard-Barton likens 'purposeless' knowledge to the misfortunes of Sisyphus in the Greek fable:

> For all eternity, Sisyphus was sentenced to haul an immense boulder painfully to the top of a hill only to see it repeatedly crash back down to the bottom. Too often, the researchers and engineers on development projects harness their mental and physical creative powers to achieve the almost impossible – often at consider-able personal cost – only to wonder, at the project's end, whether and why the corporation needed that particular boulder moved, or to speculate that they were climbing the wrong hill and the work was in vain. (Leonard-Barton, 1995, pp. 88–9)

What is often missing, then, is an understanding of exactly *what knowledge is being managed for* – the aims and objectives, or the *purpose* of Knowledge Management.

Linking Knowledge Management to tasks and purpose

The recent period of writing on knowledge work has seen a critical reaction to the 'quantity' approach to knowledge (for example, see special issues of the *Journal of Management Studies*, 2001; and the *Journal of Information Technology*, 2001). A number of writers have pointed out that too great an emphasis on knowledge *qua* resource risks divorcing it from concrete actions and outcomes (McDermott, 1999). This may lead to:

● Excessive stockpiling of knowledge (or, perhaps more accurately, information) at the expense of important organizational tasks

● Increased bureaucracy in the form of an emphasis on routines to capture knowledge (regardless of whether that knowledge is applied)

- A supply-led approach to Knowledge Management that emphasizes the supply of information but neglects users' requirements and demands

- Problems associated with information overload (Schultze and Vandenbosch, 1998)

These writers argue that knowledge should not be seen as valuable in itself, but as adding value only where it is created and applied for specific tasks and purposes (McDermott, 1999). Moreover, many tasks are themselves complex, posing different requirements for the deployment of knowledge. This has led to the development of more sophisticated contingency theories that link different strategies for managing knowledge to specific aspects of the tasks at hand. For example, Hansen (1999) looked specifically at the different ways in which knowledge was deployed in 120 product innovation projects across 41 divisions of a large electronics company. He found that, where tasks required the transfer of complex (often tacit) knowledge, then strong network relationships needed to be built between the parties involved (referring in this case to the sub-units within the firm). In contrast, weak ties were more efficient for knowledge transfer where the knowledge involved was less complex (often explicit). Thus Hansen linked Knowledge Management strategy (that is, the development of strong or weak network relations) to specific purposes (that is, the transfer of different kinds of knowledge for product innovation tasks). These findings demonstrate that a single 'best practice' approach to managing knowledge work is untenable – rather, different strategies and approaches need to be tailored to different tasks and purposes.

The remaining sections of this chapter develop this alternative perspective by exploring the deployment and management of knowledge for different aspects of innovation. Whereas the quantity approaches above assume a direct and linear relationship between knowledge stocks and flows and innovative outcomes (Amidon, 1998), we argue for a need to understand the relation between knowledge and innovation as both processual (that is, episodic) and embedded in social relations and context. This theme has run throughout our approach to knowledge work.

In particular, we highlight the ways in which the deployment of knowledge in organizational tasks is driven by actions connected to a specific purpose. We also underline the need to take into account the processual and dynamic nature of such action when developing appropriate approaches to Knowledge Management. Innovation is seen, then, as a cumulative process involving different episodes where multiple actors, multiple forms of knowledge and organizational tasks interact (Clark and Staunton, 1989). The use of the term 'episodes' (rather than 'stages', for example) reflects the sporadic, iterative, recursive and sometimes discontinuous nature of innovation processes (Van de Ven, 1986). In our view, and in contrast with more broad-brushed prescriptive models, the effective deployment and management of knowledge are seen as critically contingent upon the different episodes of innovation as well as upon the cognitive, social and organizational/political features of the context in which those episodes unfold.

Characteristics of innovation

In order to understand how to manage knowledge for innovation, it is important to have some understanding of what innovation entails. Innovation is an extremely broad-ranging subject. Probably the one thing that studies agree upon is that there is no single best way of understanding or achieving innovation (Wolfe, 1994). We could not hope to do justice to the numerous studies of innovation here. Instead, we focus on outlining a processual view of innovation as it is the dynamic, social and knowledge-intensive characteristics of innovation that seem to pose the biggest challenges for managing knowledge work.

Invention, diffusion and implementation

The first point to make about innovation is that it is more than just about coming up with good ideas (that is, invention), it is also about putting them to practical use. Whilst the creation of new knowledge and ideas (invention) is an important part of the innovation process, so too is the process of bringing these ideas into widespread use (diffusion) and applying them to solve real organizational problems (implementation). Thomas Edison was not just a prolific inventor, he also had a keen interest in seeing his ideas become commercially exploitable. Similarly, Ray Kroc did not simply recognize the inventiveness of the five-spindled 'Multimixer' milkshake machine, he also recognized the importance of diffusing this idea and increasing its commercial impact via the fast-food restaurant chain McDonald's. Simply focusing on innovation as invention is therefore a very partial view of innovation. If the concept of innovation is considered more broadly, then important issues regarding knowledge include not just the creation of new knowledge, but also the diffusion and application of existing knowledge to new contexts in ways that change work practices.

Knowledge deployment in product and process innovation

Writers on innovation also make a distinction between 'product' and 'process' innovation: (or 'technical' and 'administrative' innovation: Damanpour, 1987). Broadly speaking, product innovation involves the application of knowledge to the development of tangible new products or services. For example, Grindley *et al.* (1989) described how the Richardson organization managed to buck the trend of the declining Sheffield cutlery industry in the 1970s by applying specialist knowledge of metallurgy to the development of a new type of knife blade – the 'Laser' range. This new blade, with its lifetime sharpness guarantee, was a result of continued commitment to product innovation that was said to have helped turn sales from £1 million in 1974 to £23 million in 1989.

Process innovation, in contrast, involves the development of new management and work or organizational practices (Tidd *et al.*, 1997). Richardson's success resulted not only from the development of new products but also from the development of core competencies in manufacturing process technologies. Whilst much work in innovation has focused on the design and development of products, process innovation is equally important:

> Being able to make something no-one else can, or to do so in ways that are better than anyone else, is a powerful source of advantage . . . the Japanese dominance in several sectors – cars, motorcycles, shipbuilding, consumer electronics – owes a great deal to superior abilities in manufacturing – something which results from a consistent pattern of process innovation. (Tidd *et al.*, 1997, p. 5)

Increasingly the boundaries between product and process innovation are blurred – the two go hand in hand. For example, Direct Line Insurance's major successes from the development of new products and services could not have occurred without radically new ways of organizing their delivery also having been developed. That said, it is worth noting that product and process innovation tasks do pose potentially different problems for the management, capture and transfer of knowledge. Knowledge creation in product innovation projects, for example, tends to converge around the product itself – diverse sources of knowledge are integrated within a single product or service specification. Therefore, much knowledge produced through product innovation can arguably be captured and transferred in relatively tangible forms (for example, as product design templates).

In contrast knowledge produced through process innovation is largely intangible, tacit and context-dependent. It includes, for example, knowledge relating to changes in work practices, changes in roles and responsibilities, and changes in attitudes and cultural values. This knowledge is difficult to capture in explicit forms, at least in ways that could be easily understood when transferred to new contexts. Social and behavioural processes are therefore likely to be as, if not more, important to the capture and transfer of knowledge in process innovation projects than practices (for example, the use of ICTs) aimed at codification. For example, Hansen *et al.* (1999) found that 'personalization' strategies (the development of intensive personal relationships and social networks) were more effective than codification strategies where the knowledge to be transferred was largely tacit in nature. This broad difference between product and process innovation highlights the need to be sensitive to the nature of the innovation task when devising strategies and approaches to Knowledge Management.

Notwithstanding the importance of product innovation, the examples in this chapter focus on process innovation as this is being seen as increasingly critical to organizations across a wide range of sectors. For example, many public and private sector organizations see their major market advantage occurring through the introduction of innovation in technologies and processes. As indicated above, it also seems to pose difficult problems for the management of knowledge. Widespread attempts to introduce process innovations such as Business Process Reengineering, Electronic Commerce, Advanced Manufacturing Technologies, Customer Requirements Management, or even Knowledge Management itself, have been met with varying degrees of success (Bessant, 1991). These kinds of innovation processes involve profound changes in the ways work is carried out, and require a blending of technological expertise with knowledge about organizations and the wider business context (Scarbrough and Corbett, 1992; McLoughlin, 1999).

Traditional views on innovation

There is a popularly held view that the innovation process corresponds to the kind of linear sequence depicted in Figure 7.1 (see, for example, Rogers, 1995).

Innovation is likened to a rational model whereby decisions are made about the adoption of new forms of best practice based on a rational assessment of their technical efficiency over existing techniques and practices. According to this perspective, once a new best practice has been created, and rules for its

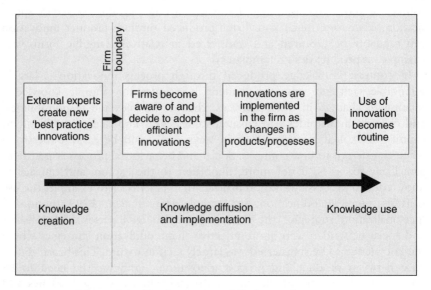

Figure 7.1   The linear view of the innovation process

implementation have been defined, the only problem is to make firms aware of it. Prescriptions about Business Process Reengineering or Customer Requirements Management as essential 'best' practices are good examples. Research shows, however, that this is a misleading and potentially dangerous view (Ettlie and Bridges, 1987) that greatly downplays the problems of implementation and the knowledge requirements of innovation. Most innovation is simply not like that. Box 7.1 summarizes the key limitations of this traditional view.

Box 7.1   Limits of traditional views on innovation

- The innovation process is not linear – pivotal modifications in the innovation introduced during its implementation, for example, feed back into its design (Fleck, 1988).

- The innovation process is not rational (in the traditional sense) – choices about innovation are based as much on claims made about their efficiency (for example, by consultants, experts or different players within firms) as evidence of efficiency *per se* (Abrahamson, 1996).

- Innovation is not a 'thing' or entity with fixed and definable parameters that can be simply inserted into different organizational contexts. Implementation of technological innovation, for example, often involves significant reworking of the initial idea or technology so that it is blended and adapted together with features of the organization (Clark and Staunton, 1989).

- Most innovation cannot, therefore, be introduced as a 'technical fix' with predictable outcomes.

- Innovation is not discrete but has an impact on many different areas of the organization and on many individuals and social groups within it. Effective implementation depends, then, on changes in knowledge, skills and organizational practices that lie outside the remit of the technical expert.

- The notion of a universally applicable 'best practice' is, in any case, misleading. Innovation is highly context-specific – what works in one context may not be applicable in another because of the different knowledge, skills and understandings of the social groups involved (Swan *et al.*, 1999b).

Processual views on innovation

Research on innovation suggests that organizations that consciously or subconsciously follow the linear model are more likely to meet with failure than success. Instead of a linear sequence, a more accurate view of innovation is summarized in Box 7.2.

Box 7.2　Assumptions of processual views on innovation

- Innovation is a dynamic design and decision process that is by nature both iterative and recursive and mediated by a range of cognitive, social and organizational factors.

- This process is influenced not simply by judgements about technical efficiency, but also by the cognitions (knowledge, subjective beliefs and perceptions) of different social groups and actors both inside and outside the organization.

- Political interests, power and influence (Utterback, 1994) also have an impact on innovation. For example, firms may adopt innovations that are technically not the most efficient for political reasons, or professional groups will promote those new techniques and practices that enhance their own claims to knowledge, status and power (Swan and Clark, 1992).

- The innovation process is inherently uncertain and often sporadic. Unintended outcomes are common as different groups inside and outside the organization attempt to mobilize innovation in directions that suit their particular interests.

- Knowledge relevant to innovation may be widely distributed, both inside and outside the organization. Implementation of new organizational and technological solutions involves the gathering of both specialist expertise and tacit knowledge about existing practices from a wide range of sources, people and locations.

- The integration of relevant knowledge through the development of social processes and networks is crucial for innovation. Such networks are also important for encouraging the buy-in and commitment that helps innovative ideas to be actually implemented in practice.

- The ability to effectively integrate knowledge – and innovation – is often inhibited by structural, functional, occupational, and status or hierarchical barriers (McLoughlin, 1999).

In sum, innovation can be more realistically characterized as a complex, iterative design and decision process involving the creation, diffusion (spread), blending and implementation of new ideas in different contexts. Research on innovation (especially innovation in work processes) demonstrates that success depends on constructing a process that can draw upon widely distributed knowledge, is open to the views of the different groups involved and is capable of gaining their commitment.

Defining innovation

In keeping with the processual approach depicted above, a working definition of innovation is: 'the development and implementation of new ideas by people who over time engage in transactions with others in an institutional context' (Van de Ven, 1986 p. 591). This is also in keeping with the approach to Knowledge Management outlined in earlier chapters. This definition implies that the social construction of knowledge and the process of sharing knowledge across social communities are central to innovation.

This definition also highlights the *context specificity* of innovation. Innovation is seen as fundamentally influenced by social networks and social interactions including, for example, interfirm networks, educational systems, professional and occupational groups, regional networks and so on. The nature of these interactions also varies according to the local organizational and institutional context (Clark, 2000). These networks play an important role as trend-setters – legitimizing particular new approaches over others as 'the best practice'. For example, the design and diffusion of advanced manufacturing technologies in the 1980s was heavily influenced by networks of professions (such as the American Production and Inventory Control Association – APICS) and consultants (such as IBM and the US Oliver Wight consultancy). Through these networks knowledge about a particular technology (Manufacturing Resources Planning, or 'MRP2') was diffused selectively as *the* new best practice despite other, arguably more efficient, technologies being available at the time (Swan and Newell, 1995). Therefore to understand the links between knowledge and innovation it is important to consider the networks through which knowledge in specific fields is produced and communicated.

Identifying episodes of the innovation process

Taking the process perspective, innovation is depicted as a set of recursive and overlapping 'episodes', which move from initial awareness of new ideas to the selection (or rejection) of particular ideas, through to implementation (Clark *et al.*, 1992) – see figure 7.2. If implementation is successful, new ideas are utilized in the form of new products, services or ways of organizing and become used routinely in the organization (at which point they would no longer be referred to as innovation: Clark and Staunton, 1989; Rogers, 1995).

Looking in more detail at the process, the first episode, *agenda formation*, concerns the initial awareness of new ideas and of the problems that they may help to address. *Selection* then relates to the further processing and promotion of ideas within the organization such that particular ideas are chosen to go forward for further development because they are seen as matching the problems the organization is currently experiencing. *Implementation* describes the process of actually introducing the selected ideas to the organization and applying them to the local context in the forms of new products, services, technologies or processes. The final episode is *routinization* and describes the situation where the understanding of the innovation has developed to a point at which its use has become routine and it is now seen as a standard working practice to be adopted in other parts of the organization where relevant (Rogers, 1995).

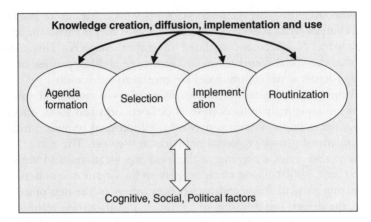

Figure 7.2   A processual view of innovation (after Clark *et al.*, 1992)

Rather than occurring in a linear sequence, these different aspects of innovation are iterative, overlapping and ultimately conflated (Swan and Clark, 1992) – hence the term 'episodes' as opposed to 'stages'. For example, lessons learned during implementation may refine definitions of problems or may influence the design and further diffusion of new ideas and technologies (Fleck, 1994; Leonard-Barton, 1988). The linear model sees innovation as a fairly straightforward process of implementing predefined 'best practice' with relatively certain successful outcomes. However, as we know, many innovation processes fail (in which case they are usually referred to as mistakes). The process-oriented approach notes the inherently uncertain and open-ended nature of innovation. Unintended outcomes are common as different groups and individuals who get involved at different times attempt to own and influence the process in ways that suit their particular interests.

Linking knowledge and Knowledge Management to innovation

As seen, the innovation process entails a number of different episodes ranging from agenda formation through to routinization. It is important to understand that all of these episodes to some extent entail the creation, sharing and application of knowledge. However, each episode emphasizes somewhat different aspects of knowledge and, correspondingly, Knowledge Management. For example, the episodes of agenda formation and selection emphasize knowledge search and acquisition while the implementation episode emphasizes the application of knowledge to specific contexts and local organizational problems. Routinization is more about the standardization of newly developed knowledge so that it becomes an accepted form of work practice.

This suggests that different approaches to managing knowledge will be more or less useful for different episodes of the process (Swan and Newell, 2000). These approaches, and their links to innovation episodes, are summarized in Table 7.1. This is presented in a schematic and stylized way. An important caveat is that this should not be taken as yet another prescriptive model about how to manage knowledge (we noted earlier the limits of broad-brush prescriptions). However, it may be a useful device for beginning to think about the alignment of Knowledge Management with specific tasks and activities – in this case where the purpose is innovation.

Table 7.1 Summary of different approaches to Knowledge Management for innovation

	Agenda formation *networking approach*	*Selection and implementation* *community approach*	*Routinization* *cognitive approach*
Understanding of knowledge	Knowledge is located external to the adopting unit in explicit or implicit forms	Knowledge is constructed socially and based on experience	Knowledge is objectively defined and codified as concepts and facts
Primary activity with respect to knowledge	*Knowledge acquisition.* Knowledge is acquired through access to external networks and sources of information (weak ties important). Information and communication technologies may play a central role	*Knowledge creation and application.* Knowledge is created and applied through development of social communities including project groups and teams (strong ties important). Information and communication technologies play a peripheral role	*Knowledge reuse, capture and storage.* Knowledge is captured through text-based, searchable archival sources. Information and communication technologies play a central role
Primary aim of KM	To keep abreast of new developments	To encourage knowledge-sharing (including tacit knowledge) amongst and between groups and individuals	To codify and capture explicit knowledge and information
Primary gains from KM	Greater awareness of external developments	Greater application of internal and external sources of knowledge to create new management practices	Better recycling of knowledge and the standardization of systems
Dominant metaphors	The network; Linking/joining	The human community; Building/constructing	The human memory; Digging/mining
Critical resources	Social capital	Social and intellectual capital	Intellectual capital
Critical 'success factors'	Boundary spanning	Trust and commitment	Technology

Agenda formation: the networking approach

The agenda formation episode primarily concerns *knowledge acquisition* – that is, the initial acquisition of new ideas from sources external to the innovating unit (including other firms and/or other units in the wider organization). In this way firms can become aware of and choose to adopt new management practices where they are relevant (Rogers, 1995). Here, then, a model of Knowledge Management aimed at increased networking may be most appropriate.

In agenda formation the primary aim of Knowledge Management is to locate and create awareness of new developments. 'Boundary spanning' individuals (Tushman and Scanlan, 1981) who are able to link into external networks and acquire new ideas which they can then share within their own organization play a central role. The development of social capital (as discussed in Chapter 6) through network relations is therefore a crucial aspect of managing knowledge for this episode (Nahapiet and Ghoshal, 1998) – practices and technologies that encourage organizational members to access information and to engage in networking may be helpful. For example, ICTs (such as the Internet and intranets) may help organizational members tap these external sources of knowledge. However, there will also be many non-IT-based practices that may facilitate knowledge acquisition. For example, encouraging employees to actively participate in professional associations, to take educational courses, or to network with consultants may be useful since these are forums where new ideas are disseminated (Swan *et al.*, 1999a).

The dominant metaphor here for Knowledge Management is the network that connects widely dispersed sources of knowledge. The development of weak ties (distant and infrequent relationships: Granovetter, 1973) may be particularly critical because weak ties provide access to novel information by bridging otherwise disconnected groups and individuals. As Hansen (1999) showed, in his study of product innovation projects, weak ties are particularly efficient for information-searching.

Selection and implementation: the community approach

The selection and implementation episodes require knowledge acquired through networks (often presented in explicit forms) to be further developed, shared internally and blended with locally situated (often tacit) knowledge about organizational practices and processes (Scarbrough and Corbett, 1992). These episodes require key individuals and groups with relevant knowledge and expertise to work together in *(re)creating and applying* knowledge in new and appropriate ways at local level. In this way, initial ideas are developed into new work practices. Critical problems here concern:

- The engagement of actors with relevant tacit knowledge (Alavi and Leidner, 2001)

- The development of social cultures and communities of practice (for example, through project teams (Orlikowski *et al.*, 1995))

- The development of trust and shared meanings and understandings (Weick, 1990)

- The politics of decision-making and change (Scarbrough and Corbett, 1992)

Here, then, the community becomes a more appropriate metaphor for Knowledge Management. As seen in previous chapters, the community approach highlights the importance of developing close relationships, shared understandings and positive attitudes to knowledge formation and sharing. This may occur, for example, through the development of multifunctional project teams. Strong ties (close and frequent relationships) are especially important as these generate the redundancy necessary for members of heterogeneous social groups to understand and build from what each other knows (Hansen, 1999).

IT may have a role to play in community-building but this role is likely to be secondary rather than primary. For example, various types of groupware, including intranets and Lotus Notes, may support the development and functioning of social communities. But technology is unlikely, on its own, to encourage effective knowledge-sharing, especially where the membership cuts across organizational, disciplinary or geographical boundaries. This is supported by studies on the introduction of technologies such as Lotus Notes that find that organizational members who communicated frequently or infrequently without the technology continue to communicate on the same basis with it (Vandenbosch and Ginsberg 1996). Moreover, relying solely on this kind of technology may, far from encouraging knowledge-sharing, actually reinforce existing boundaries with 'electronic fences' and fuel 'turf wars' across social groups (remember the case of BankCo in Chapter 5). Where social communities are composed of heterogeneous members, as is often the case in innovation projects, then Knowledge Management practices that encourage the development of trust, commitment and shared understandings are more central. Personal contacts, face-to-face interaction and dialogue are likely, then, to be as important as IT, if not more so.

Routinization: the cognitive approach

Once an innovation has been fully developed, the goal of routinization is to *capture and store* the newly created knowledge and to establish it as an accepted part of organizational practice and culture (Clark and Staunton, 1989). For example, the knowledge embedded in a newly implemented technology – a blend of generic and explicit knowledge with specific and situated (often tacit) knowledge – may be captured and stored so that it can be recycled later, or in other parts of the organization. Establishing standardized rules for quality assessment in different parts of a firm would be an example.

In this episode, the key issue is to ensure the efficient *reuse* of knowledge through *capture and storage* mechanisms. An important way of achieving this is to make explicit and codify the rules, procedures and processes surrounding its use. Here the cognitive approach may be useful with the dominant metaphor being the human memory. As seen in earlier chapters ICTs may play a central role in the exploitation of knowledge where there is sufficient commonality of understanding. For example, data warehouses and data mining tools can be used to facilitate access to and use of information where the knowledge about how to interpret and apply that information has been sufficiently well-developed and accepted.

An Illustration of Managing Knowledge for innovation

These three approaches to Knowledge Management, and their links to innovation episodes, are illustrated by returning to the case example of LiftCo in Case Study 7.2. It is important to note, however, the dangers of over-simplification. For example, it is not likely that these approaches to Know-ledge Management operate discretely or that the organization shifts from one approach to another – indeed research does not support such an assumption. As noted earlier, innovation episodes are conceptualized as overlapping, iterative and ultimately conflated. This means, for example that whilst the focus at a particular point in time may be on implementation (for example, when LiftCo actually begin to test software), political agendas continue to form in parallel. Rather, what we propose is simply that at any particular moment, one approach may be more focal that others. Given the iterative nature of the innovation episodes, and the almost continuous need to look for new oppor-tunities to innovate, an organization must be constantly 'ready' to activate different approaches for specific purposes (Swan *et al.*, 1999c).

Case Study 7.1   Knowledge Management for innovation: LiftCo

LiftCo, the third largest manufacturer and service provider of specialized materials handling equipment with its headquarters in Sweden, has around 3400 employees and a turnover of 4.9 billion krona. The European operation is structured around geographically dispersed business units operating with a high degree of autonomy. While this provided advantages in flexibility, problems were arising in the service side because businesses were failing to share knowledge and information relevant to customer service. Global

Case Study 7.1 continued

customers complained that they were unable to get the same level of service across countries. Traditionally each LiftCo business had gone its own way in terms of systems development. The need to provide common services to global customers led LiftCo to launch an innovation project aimed at improving the uniformity of service delivery through the introduction of common, integrated IT platforms and information systems – an Enterprise Resources Planning system (ERP). This represented a major cultural change for LiftCo in the way people thought about, and managed, IT. The 'Business Information Systems' (BIS) project was launched in 1996 with overall responsibility resting with the corporate IT function in Sweden. Millennium problems with existing systems meant this was to be completed within a strict two-year time schedule.

Although he did not specifically use the term, the BIS project leader recognized at the outset that managing knowledge would be a critical issue. Corporate IT had very limited resources (only 14 people) and imposition of systems from the Centre would likely be met with resistance. Further, there was no 'off-the shelf' package that matched LiftCo's multisite, multifunctional requirements. Key Knowledge Management issues then were: to identify people in the businesses with the right skills, expertise and interests to be involved in systems design and to manage implementation at local level; and to collaborate with an external software supplier which had relevant expertise. Despite the ambitious nature of the project it was completed within one month of the initial target date. With minor exceptions the new software delivered the functionality needed, the project team developed a relatively good long-term relationship with their software supplier and there was high satisfaction among those involved. The ways in which knowledge was managed to achieve this are considered next.

Agenda formation and selection: networking approach

The BIS project began from a study of business processes. This entailed intensive networking (face-to-face meetings every week for four months) among a small group of LiftCo senior managers ('Process Owners') representing different businesses and different functional specialisms (parts, rental, service, finance and so on) working together with external consultants. A network of Process Owners and 'Process Owner Support Staff' was established who had responsibility for following through to systems implementation strategic issues raised in the Business Process study. Following this a small group of senior managers with some systems expertise were brought together to review and evaluate available software. This group actively sought information about available products through external sources (for example, from software suppliers, Internet searches, documentation, training events, other firms). Two suppliers offered products that could deliver most of LiftCo's functionality requirements and these were invited to bid for the contract. Ultimately, Consense were chosen to partner LiftCo in their innovation project. Although Consense's product did not provide the closest functionality match, there was a perception that this supplier (also Swedish) would be more likely to work in a close collaborative, networking arrangement providing opportunities for

Case Study 7.1 continued

knowledge exchange. This would benefit both LiftCo (who would get a product designed to match their business needs) and Consense (who would
design a new product that they could market more widely using LiftCo as a
reference). The most central Knowledge Management practice in agenda
formation, then, was intensive and extensive intra-organizational (among senior
managers from across different parts of the business) and inter-organizational
networking (among LiftCo and external suppliers and consultants). Through
these networks knowledge was acquired about business processes and
problems as well as different software solutions. Knowledge exchange was
mostly face to face and informal apart from written material describing software products.

Implementation: community approach

Implementation began with an intensive design and development phase to
redesign Consense's core package to match LiftCo's business portfolio. The
project leader aimed to develop a community across LiftCo with IT and business expertise who would be able to generate ownership and commitment to
the BIS project at local level. As seen in Chapter 4, selection, recruitment and
commitment of the project team were seen as critical. Consense consultants
worked alongside selected LiftCo managers from different parts of the business on one site in Sweden for around three days a week over a 12-week
period. In addition four graduates with business and IT skills were recruited to
work on the BIS project. These enjoyed a novel employment contract that
gave them the option of working either with Consense or LiftCo when the project ended. Working partly on-site at LiftCo and partly at Consense, these
graduates played an important role as 'brokers', bridging the social communities of LiftCo and Consense.

The roll-out of the new system again emphasized local ownership and commitment through the development of a community of 'key users' trained and
facilitated by the BIS project team at the Centre. Implementation was
managed by three coordinated implementation teams, each responsible for
roll-out at two to four European sites. Each implementation team comprised
around nine people seconded to the BIS project. These included a Consense
consultant, a member of the central BIS project team, and local business
managers who (where possible) were those that had been involved during
the design phase. Importantly, then, the teams involved representatives from
most of the different social communities that would be affected by the system
and whose local knowledge was important. They were also selected to
comprise different 'personality' types and status. The implementation teams
travelled to their allocated sites to 'kick off' implementation and to provide
training and advice. Beyond this, implementation was managed locally by 'key
users' identified at each site. These were not necessarily IT experts but were
those with business knowledge and power at local level. Knowledge exchange
was primarily through face-to-face 'sharing of experiences' and 'learning by
doing', supported by mobile phone and e-mail – there was relatively little reliance

Case Study 7.1 continued

on formal documentation at this stage. The three implementation teams were coordinated such that, where possible, they would travel in parallel to their allocated sites for two weeks and then, every third week, would return to the Swedish headquarters where they could meet and share experiences and lessons learnt through respective implementations. This allowed a strong *esprit de corps* to develop within but also across teams and provided a solid base for the sharing of knowledge and ideas. Implementation teams provided each local business with hands-on training in both the system and its philosophy. This was delivered to 'end users' from different functional areas, trained together in the same room for four weeks. This allowed users to share knowledge about the system while they were discovering it through practice. This was important because the system needed to operate in an integrated way – by being trained together, when users experimented with new parameters on their own parts of the system (for example, for finance or parts) they were able to see immediately the impact on other functions' modules. The implementation episode therefore focused around the development of a community of practitioners from different functions and different businesses who had not previously worked closely together to generate commitment to the implementation of an integrated system.

Routinization: cognitive approach

Once the system went 'live' there was an increasing reliance on codification, using IT to support more documented forms of knowledge communication. For example, routines were introduced to document errors so that when a user encountered a problem they could see if this had been logged before and, if so, how it had been resolved. An e-mail site was developed (initially informally) for 'frequently asked questions'. This became increasingly formalized and provided an important mechanism for users at local sites to exchange information about systems usage at other sites. Similarly, to maintain system integration, where changes to any particular module were likely to affect the operation of other parts of the system, a strict procedure was developed to assess, control and approve all requests for change. An important point here, though, is that this codified information was only useful to people because they already had a good practical understanding of the system through being involved in actually using it. This gave them the tacit knowledge necessary to add to and/or interpret the documentation in a meaningful way.

Cognitive, social and organizational issues in innovation

As seen, innovation depends upon the involvement of a range of individuals or groups within and across organization: 'innovation occurs at the boundaries between mind sets, not within the provincial territory of one knowledge and skills base' (Leonard-Barton, 1995, p. 64). Regardless of what broad approach (e.g. cognitive, community, networking) is taken to manage knowledge, this raises specific *micro-challenges* in terms of the ways in which the knowledge and interests of different stakeholders can be brought together in order to achieve successful innovation. This is because individuals and groups have different roles in the company (for example, manager, operative, technical specialist), different types of knowledge and expertise (for example, in systems, production, finance, sales) and different political agendas and interests. The traditional linear view tends to assume that innovation is all to do with collecting and processing information. However, often the problems of innovation are less to do with the amount of knowledge or information that an organization has at its disposal, and more to do with the *distribution* of knowledge across different individuals and groups (Tsoukas, 1996). Knowledge Management for innovation, then, is as much to do with managing conflict as with collaboration: 'Business is conflict. That's the creative process. You don't get excellence by saying yes. You get love but you don't get excellence' (Richard Snyder, former CEO, Simon & Schuster, cited in Huseman and Goodman, 1999, p. 196).

In order to devise a strategy for managing knowledge for innovation, it is important, then, to understand the features of the social context that mediate the innovation process. These can be described as three sets of factors:

- *Cognitive factors* to do with the distribution of knowledge, information and perceptions and beliefs
- *Social factors* to do with the development of social relations and networks
- *Organizational factors* to do with organizational politics and perceptions in different parts of the organization (for example, across levels, functions, and occupational groups: Swan, 1995).

Recognizing these factors is a major step towards more effective and successful management of knowledge when the primary purpose is innovation.

Cognitive factors

The linear model treats innovation as a self-contained 'thing' or package that was invented elsewhere and simply has to be installed. This ignores the importance of the users' own knowledge and beliefs in actively interpreting and redesigning innovation. Critical to the exploration and exploitation of knowledge for innovation is an understanding of the various kinds of knowledge (for example, business or technical) required. However, cognitive issues do not just include technical skills and expertise – the subjective beliefs, hunches, intuitions and perceptions of different individuals and groups also mediate the ways in which information relating to innovation is shared, constructed and interpreted, especially in contexts characterized by high levels of uncertainty: 'If an issue arises that feels odd, sounds odd, looks odd, or my stomach gets upset, I want to back off immediately. When something doesn't feel good inside, your inner sense is telling you something is wrong, and you have to listen' (senior Vice-President at Cornish and Carey Residential real estate, cited in Huseman and Goodman, 1999 p. 113).

The implementation of innovation both depends on, and in turn influences, the distribution of knowledge and expertise across functions, levels and occupational groups. This includes not only expertise about the relationships between the organization and its suppliers and markets, but also detailed or tacit knowledge about the operation of existing systems which will be required to dovetail with the new technology (Fleck, 1994).

Social factors

Also critical to innovation are social relationships and networks through which relevant knowledge can be acquired, shared and developed and through which support for innovation can be mobilized (von Hippel, 1988). These networks may include developing formal relationships with external experts (for example, consultants and IT suppliers) and sources of expertise (for example, professional courses and publications), and informal relationships (for example, with friends and colleagues). Robertson *et al.* (1996), for example, found that the interplay among these kinds of networks was critical in shaping the design and implementation, and ultimate success, of new manufacturing process control technologies in automotive firms.

Organizational factors

Earlier chapters have demonstrated how organizational factors (for example, structure, culture, organizational environment and context) can influence the exploration (creation) and exploitation (use) of knowledge (March, 1991). Similarly innovation processes cannot rely on knowledge alone for success. They also depend on converting knowledge into organizational action. This involves mobilizing power to overcome organizational inertia and motivating individuals to overcome resistance. It is important, then, to create organizational conditions to ensure that relevant knowledge is actually put into action. For example, Kodak's philosophy emphasizes the need for world-class organizations to continuously seek knowledge and technology wherever they reside: 'a culture of "not-invented here" is a prescription for second-class citizenship in the global marketplace' (Tidd *et al.*, 1997, p. 226).

The decision processes that influence innovation are themselves influenced by the distribution of power and influence within the organization. Engaging in innovation processes that involve changes in technology and organization often disrupts or threatens established power and authority structures, and this may generate conflict and resistance. For example, Clark and Fujimoto (1992) note the importance of 'heavyweight' project managers for complex innovation projects – people who have the organizational power to coordinate the process and push it through. Equally, there may be internal political reasons why some individuals or groups within organizations attempt to assassinate innovation attempts by others. For example, in their study of MRP2 innovation, Robertson *et al.* (1996) describe how in one firm a powerful Purchasing Manager effectively helped to kill off the project by placing a very junior member of his department on the implementation team.

The more groups and interests affected by a particular innovation, the wider the range of perceptions and views on the technology, and the greater the possibility of conflict. It is important, then, when introducing Knowledge Management initiatives, to understand the politics of the innovation process so that stakeholders feel motivated and emotionally committed, and so that conflict can be used constructively rather than destructively (Scarbrough and Corbett, 1992). In this way, those with relevant knowledge and expertise will be more likely to share it.

These cognitive, social and organizational issues influencing innovation are complex, dynamic, often intangible and difficult to appreciate. They will also mediate any attempts to manage knowledge for innovation regardless of what approach (networking, cognitive or community) is taken. The role-play of 'Innovation at Oakland Furniture' provided at the end of this chapter offers students the chance to experience an innovation process in a particular (simulated) organizational context. Working through this role-play in syndicates should 'bring to life' the major issues outlined above and demonstrate their centrality to managing knowledge in the uncertain and political context of innovation.

Conclusions

The examination of knowledge and innovation presented in this chapter emphasizes the point that a single 'best practice' approach to Knowledge Management is problematic. To gain performance advantages knowledge must be related to purposes and action – the relevance of particular forms of knowledge, and corresponding approaches to Knowledge Management, can only be defined in relation to the tasks at hand (McDermott, 1999). This is a feature that has sometimes been glossed over in mainstream accounts, where the processing of knowledge (for example, from tacit to explicit forms in Nonaka's (1994) 'spiral' of knowledge creation) is viewed independently of purposeful action. Endless debates in the literature to date about the epistemology and ontology of knowledge itself (for example, about whether knowledge is tacit or explicit, individual or collective) risk divorcing the discussion from concrete tasks and purposes.

This tendency to neglect the links between knowledge and its purpose reflects an assumption that there is a relatively linear relationship between knowledge creation and accumulation, and outcomes. The Nonaka account, where ideas are progressively and seamlessly translated into products, is a good example of this perceived linearity. It is questionable, however, how far this focus on knowledge conversion is generally appropriate for innovation processes. This chapter suggests a more contingent approach to managing knowledge work that takes into account the purpose for which knowledge is deployed and also the process through which this occurs. The main conclusion, then, is that those Knowledge Management practices and processes that will be helpful are likely to vary across different episodes of the innovation process because these episodes have different requirements in terms of their treatment and application of knowledge.

In this chapter the creation and application of knowledge have been considered in relation to specific innovation tasks or projects. This represents an attempt to locate different ways to approach the management of knowledge within specific tasks and contexts. However, even if this is possible, it still leaves the problem of how to transfer the learning and knowledge that is created within one task or context to other relevant tasks or contexts. The problems of transferring knowledge across different tasks and contexts (for example, across different innovation projects) is addressed in the next, and concluding, chapter.

Summary of key learning points

■ Knowledge should not be seen as valuable in itself but as adding value when created and applied for specific tasks and purposes. Performance improvements do not directly follow from amassing ever-greater quantities of knowledge.

■ Organizational tasks and purposes have different requirements for knowledge – the notion of a tightly prescribed, universally applicable 'best practice' to Knowledge Management is flawed.

■ An organization's approach to Knowledge Management needs to be customized for particular tasks and purposes – that is, to consider the question: 'What is knowledge being managed for?'

■ Where the purpose of Knowledge Management is innovation then it is important to understand the nature of innovation as: (i) an episodic process that relies centrally on the creation and application of knowledge in order to develop new ways of working; (ii) a process where the outcomes are mediated by cognitive, social and organizational factors.

■ Effective innovation can be seen as an example of knowledge work, where there is a heavy reliance on changes in knowledge, skills, perceptions *and* organizational practices.

Summary of key learning points continued

- Knowledge relevant for innovation may be *distributed* across a wide range of sources, people and locations, both inside and outside the organization. *Integration* of knowledge (for example, through the development of social processes and networks) is therefore crucial.

- Innovation involves different episodes. These can be identified as: agenda formation, selection, implementation and routinization. These are not linear and sequential but are, more often, overlapping, iterative and recursive. Moreover they have different requirements with respect to the deployment of knowledge.

- Approaches to Knowledge Management (e.g. networking, community, cognitive) are contingent upon different episodes of the innovation process (e.g. formation and selection implementation routinization).

- Regardless of the approach, outcomes of innovation are mediated by: (i) *cognitive factors* to do with the distribution of knowledge, information and perceptions and beliefs; (ii) *social factors* to do with the development of social relations and networks; (iii) *organizational factors* to do with organizational politics, roles and structures. Recognizing these factors is a major step towards more effective and successful Knowledge Management when the primary purpose is innovation.

- It is critical to understand the politics of the innovation process when managing knowledge for innovation so that stakeholders in the process are willing to engage and share what knowledge they have, and so that conflict can be used constructively rather than destructively.

Group exercise: innovation at Oakland Furniture – a role-play*

This role-play simulates the early episodes (agenda formation and selection) of an innovation process. These episodes involve a consideration of the problems facing Oakland, a furniture manufacturing company, and a decision about whether or not to select a particular new technology – an Enterprise Resources Planning (ERP) system (earlier versions of this technology were referred to as Manufacturing Resources Planning systems – MRP2). Nine different players are involved – eight work within Oakland with different functional role responsibilities, the ninth is an external consultant and an expert in ERP technology. Managing knowledge is therefore critical to this decision.

The company

Oakland Furniture Ltd is located on a single site near a town in England called High Wycombe, where many other furniture companies, some very small, are also based. Oakland is quite large in furniture industry terms and employs 300 people. There are 210 employees on the shop floor, of whom 144 are skilled (65 machine operators and 79 cabinet makers and finishers). The remaining 66 are semi-skilled or unskilled, and work on general handling jobs, packing and unpacking, and so on. There are 90 other staff: 25 production people including foremen and women, supervisors and managers; 25 sales field staff and managers; and about 40 clerical staff. Most shop-floor workers and some staff are members of the furniture industry trade union, the FTAT (Furniture, Timber and Allied Trades).

Oakland specializes in high-quality 'English' furniture, using oak, beech and yew solid timber stock and veneers. Their present product range is quite restricted. It is focused on the dining and occasional furniture (that is, living room cabinets, coffee tables and so on) sectors of the market. It grew very rapidly some 25 years ago, largely due to one particular dining-room range, the 'Oakland', which gave the company its name. This sold very well in high street retailers up and down the country. Oakland Furniture now produces five coordinated ranges and a few 'specials' – such things as one-off tables and matching sets of chairs for town halls, university council chambers and company boardrooms. Oakland's major competitors are firms such as Stag, Parker Knoll, Meredith and McIntosh.

The company was purchased more than ten years ago at the peak of its earnings by a major conglomerate. But it languished, declining into losses four years in a row. This opened the door for a management buy-out two years ago, organized by the present Managing Director, Alex Rheingold, in close association with Rowan Gregory, the Chief Designer.

Technological change at Oakland

In the enthusiasm unleashed by the buy-out, and the injection of cash made available, various opportunities for improving Oakland's operations were implemented and others were being closely examined. Several numerically controlled machine tools were bought second-hand. A major new machine, designed with expert contribution from Rowan Gregory and produced by a German manufacturer, was obtained on special terms. Various marketing initiatives were also launched. These certainly improved the situation, and the company was breaking even, despite having to cover the heavy burden of interest on the loans used to finance the buy-out.

However, though fundamentally sound in market position, product range and quality, it was clear that the company desperately required improved means of stock control and production planning. It was in this general context that Alex Rheingold was impressed by a presentation on the benefits of Enterprise Resources Planning by a consultant, Sandy Corbett, at a furniture industry conference. ERP is sold as an integrated computer-aided system for materials handling and production scheduling. The latest version of such systems links production planning to other functional areas of the firm and more broadly to manufacturing strategy on a company-wide level. As a result of the consultant's presentation, Alex suggested that Oakland should look into the pros and cons of introducing ERP technology (including software to support it).

The meeting

Alex has convened a meeting (to last around one hour) of a working group to discuss the pros and cons of introducing ERP technology, and to decide on a way forward for the company in terms of technological innovation. The aim of the meeting is to decide whether or not to pursue the development of an ERP system in Oakland. Because of the company-wide potential for ERP a group of eight key Oakland employees has been called together. In addition, Sandy

Group Exercise continued

Corbett, the external consultant, has also been invited to advise the company and is ready to answer any questions that members of the working group might have. Those invited to join the meeting include:

1. Alex Rheingold: Managing Director. Chairs the meeting. Knows about the furniture industry. The driving force behind the recent management buy-out. Impressed by a recent conference presentation by the ERP consultant, Sandy Corbett. Initiated the present event.

2. Chris Duncan: Financial Director. Knows about the turnover and profitability of the firm. Tough on the payback of proposals. Suspicious of any control system not under the Financial Director's direct control.

3. Jan Pettigrew: Operations Director. Worked entirely within the furniture industry, and believes it to be unique and distinct. Took a course about ERP but unsure whether it would work in Oaklands.

4. Rowan Gregory: Chief Designer. Ambitious to promote a quality 'Oakland's style'. Technologically progressive but concerned that ERP might restrict the design scope and force excessive standardization.

5. Sam Newton: Sales and Distribution Manager. Responsible for sales and customer care, and worried about the company's present bad image over delivery times.

6. Jo Armstrong: Purchasing Manager. Responsible for maintaining adequate stocks of quality timbers. Also knows something about just-in-time.

7. Robin Johnston: Production Scheduler. Time-served, with excellent intuitive judgement but sceptical about computer-based systems. Are they going to make the scheduler's special skills redundant?

8. Jean Lamont: Systems Administrator. Knows about the existing computer systems and about data-handling practicalities. Very enthusiastic about ERP but might leave a 'time bomb' if not respected.

9. Sandy Corbett: Outside Consultant. Knowledgeable about the ERP approach. Does not directly sell software but can recommend a supplier. Knows little about the furniture industry but believes that any manufacturing environment would benefit from ERP software and its philosophy for production planning.

To perform the role play in syndicate groups you should go now to pp. 190–200 to see your tutor-allocated role brief in full (note: you only need to read and prepare your own role brief for the role-play).

Questions

Having performed the role-play syndicate groups can discuss the following questions:

1. What factors (cognitive, social and organizational) were important in influencing the innovation decision process in your groups?

Group Exercise continued

2. What approach(es) to Knowledge Management might help with this innovation process?
3. What were the main barriers to knowledge-sharing and what specific Knowledge Management practices could be introduced to overcome these?

* This role play is an abridged version of the original produced by James Fleck (Professor in Innovation at the University of Edinburgh) with two of the authors (Jacky Swan and Harry Scarbrough). The original was part of an initiative funded by the Economic and Social Research Council (ESRC) to develop training materials in innovation. The full original version provides more detailed role information and is intended to run over a longer session (approximately three hours). This can be found at http://omni.bus.ed. ac.uk/opsman/oakland/oak1.htm. The case of Oakland is a fictional one but the information about the company is based upon a number of real research cases.

References

Abrahamson, E. (1996) Management fashion. *Academy of Management Review*, **21**: 254–85.

Alavi, M. and Leidner, D. (2001) Knowledge management and Knowledge Management systems: conceptual foundations and research issues. *MIS Quarterly*, **25**: 107–36.

Alvesson, M. and Karreman, D. (2001) Odd Couple: Making Sense of the curious concept of Knowledge Management. *Journal of Management Studies*, **38**(7): 995–1018.

Amidon, D.M. (1998) The evolving community of knowledge practice: the Ken awakening. *International Journal of Technology Management*, **16**: 45–63.

Bessant, J. (1991) *Managing Advanced Manufacturing Technology: The Challenge of the Fifth Wave.* Oxford: Blackwell.

Clark, K. and Fujimoto, T. (1992) *Product Development Performance.* Boston, Mass.: Harvard Business School Press.

Clark, P. (2000) *Organizations in Action: Competition between Contexts.* London: Routledge.

Clark, P. and Staunton, N. (1989) *Innovation in Technology and Organization.* London: Routledge.

Clark, P., Newell, S., Burcher, P., Bennett, B., Sharifi, S. and Swan, J. (1992) The decision-episode framework and computer aided production management (CAPM). *International Studies of Management and Organization*, **22**: 69–80.

Damanpour, F. (1987) The adoption of technological, administrative and ancillary innnovations: impact of organizational factors. *Journal of Management*, **13**: 675–88.

Ettlie, J.E. and Bridges, W.P. (1987) Technology policy and innovation in organizations. In J.M. Pennings and A. Buitendam (eds) *New Technology as Organizational Innovation.* Cambridge, Mass.: Ballinger, pp. 117–37.

Fleck, J. (1988) *Innofusion or Diffusation?* Edinburgh: University of Edinburgh, Department of Business Studies.

Fleck, J. (1994) Learning by trying: the implementation of configurational technology. *Research Policy*, **23**: 637–52.

Granovetter, Mark S. (1973) The strength of weak ties. *American Journal of Sociology*, **78**: 1360–80.

Grindley, P., McBryde, R. and Roper, M. (1989) *Technology and the Competitive Edge: The Case of Richardson Sheffield*. London: London Business School.

Haney, C., Banks, C. and Zimbardo, P. (1973) Interpersonal Dynamics in a Simulated Prison. *International Journal of Criminology and Penology*, **1**, 69–97.

Hansen, M.T. (1999) The search transfer problem: the role of weak ties in sharing knowledge across organizational sub-units. *Administrative Science Quarterly*, **44**: 82–111.

Hansen, M., Nohria, N. and Tierney, T. (1999). What's your strategy for managing knowledge? *Harvard Business Review*, 77(2): 106–17.

Huseman, R.C. and Goodman, J.P. (1999). *Leading with knowledge: The Nature of competition in the 21st century*. Thousand Oaks: Sage.

Leonard-Barton, D. (1988) Implementation as mutual adapation of technology and organization, *Research Policy*, **17**: 251–67.

Leonard-Barton, D. (1995) *Wellsprings of Knowledge: Building and Sustaining the Sources of Innovation*. Boston, Mass.: Harvard Business School Press.

McDermott, R. (1999) Why information technology inspired but cannot deliver Knowledge Management. *California Management Review*, **41**: 103–17.

McLoughlin, I. (1999) *Creative Technological Change*. London: Routledge.

March, J.G. (1991) Exploration and exploitation in organizational learning. *Organization Science*, **2**: 71–87.

Nahapiet, J. and Ghoshal, S. (1998) Social capital, intellectual capital and the organizational advantage. *Academy of Management Review*, **23**: 242–66.

Nonaka, I. (1994) A dynamic theory of organizational knowledge creation. *Organization Science*, **5**: 14–37.

Orlikowski, W.J., Yates, J., Okamura, K. and Fujimoto, M. (1995) Shaping electronic communication: the metastructuring of technology in the contest of use. *Organization Science*, **6**(4): 423–44.

Pan, S. and Scarbrough, H. (1999) Knowledge management in practice: an exploratory case study. *Technology Analysis and Strategic Management*, **11**: 359–74.

Prusak, L. (1997) *Knowledge in Organizations*. Oxford: Butterworth-Heinemann.

Robertson, M., Swan, J. and Newell, S. (1996) The role of networks in the diffusion of technological innovation. *Journal of Management Studies*, **33**: 333–59.

Rogers, E. (1995) *Diffusion of Innovations*, 3rd edn. New York: Free Press.

Scarbrough, H. and Corbett, J.M. (1992) *Technology and Organization: Power, Meaning and Design*. London: Routledge.

Schultze, U. and Vandenbosch, B. (1998) Information overload in a GroupWare environment: now you see it, now you don't. *Journal of Organizational Computing and Electronic Commerce*, **8**(2): 127–48.

Swan, J.A. (1995) Exploring knowledge and cognitions in decisions about technological innovation: mapping managerial cognitions. *Human Relations*, **48**(11): 1241–70.

Swan, J. and Clark, P. (1992) Organizational decision-making in the appropriation of technological innovation: cognitive and political dimensions. *European Work and Organizational Psychologist*, **2**: 103–27.

Swan, J.A. and Newell, S. (1995). The role of professional associations in technology diffusion. *Organization Studies*, **16**(5): 847–74.

Swan, J.A. and Newell, S. (2000). Linking knowledge management and innovation. *Proceedings of European Conference on Information Systems*, Vienna, July: 591–8.

Swan, J.A., Newell, S. and Robertson, M. (1999a) Central agencies in the diffusion and design of technology: a comparison of the UK and Sweden. *Organization Studies*, **20**: 905–32.

Swan, J.A., Newell, S. and Robertson, M. (1999b) The illusion of best practice in information systems for operations management. *European Journal of Information Systems*, **8**: 284–93.

Swan, J., Newell, S., Scarbrough, H. and Hislop, D (1999c) Knowledge Management and innovation: networks and networking. *Journal of Knowledge Management*, **3**: 262–75.

Tidd, J., Bessant, J. and Pavitt, K. (1997) *Managing Innovation: Integrating Technological Market and Organizational Change*. Chichester: Wiley.

Tsoukas, H. (1996) The firm as a distributed knowledge system: a constructionist perspective. *Strategic Management Journal*, **17**: 11–25.

Tushman, M. and Scanlan, T. (1981) Boundary spanning individuals: their role in information transfer and their antecedents. *Academy of Management Journal*, **24**: 289–305.

Utterback, J. (1994) *Managing the Dynamics of Innovation*. Boston, Mass.: Harvard Business School Press.

Van de Ven, A.H. (1986) Central problems in the management of innovation. *Management Science*, **32**: 590–607.

Vandenbosch, B. and Ginsberg, M. (1996) Lotus notes and collaboration: plus ça change. *Journal of Management Information Systems*, **13**: 65–82.

von Hippel, E. (1988) *The Sources of Innovation*. Oxford: Oxford University Press.

Weick, K.E. (1990) Technology as equivoque: sensemaking in new technologies. In P.S. Goodman, L.S. Sproull *et al.* (eds), *Technology and Organisations*. Oxford: Jossey-Bass.

Weick, K.E. (1995) *Sensemaking in Organizations*. London: Sage.

Wilson, F., Desmond, J. and Roberts, H. (1994) Success and failure of MRPII implementation. *British Journal of Management*, **5**: 221–40.

Wolfe, R.A. (1994) Organizational innovation: review, critique and suggested research directions. *Journal of Management Studies*, **31**: 405–31.

8 Conclusions: key challenges in the management of knowledge work

---

Learning outcomes

At the end of this chapter students will be able to:

- Draw together the lessons from other chapters.
- Understand the barriers and facilitators influencing the management of knowledge.
- Develop an awareness of the relationship between knowledge creation or generation and knowledge transfer.

Introduction

We have seen in previous chapters that the attempt to 'manage knowledge' within organizations is not new. Indeed, if we go back to traditional craft industries, young people entering an industry learnt their trade by serving an apprenticeship. This was effectively a system of managing knowledge that involved watching and learning from a skilled craftsperson. While the apprenticeship system left the knowledge and skill with the individual craftspeople, Taylor's Scientific Management was a break from tradition in that it attempted to separate decision knowledge from action knowledge. As we saw in Chapter 1, Taylor wanted managers to have the knowledge about how, why and when to carry out the various production activities in order to maximize productivity. Workers were to be the 'hands' and managers the 'brains'. To some extent this approach is still prevalent, especially in jobs and industries based on a mass production and mass consumption philosophy. So a worker in a fast-food restaurant is following a set of clearly defined procedures in making a hamburger, and a person working in a call centre is following a script in responding to a customer enquiry. In both cases, where a customer requires a service that falls outside the defined procedures the worker is not able to deal with this situation. Indeed, if they did attempt to service the customer by ignoring standard procedures they would be reprimanded.

Such an approach to managing work may well still be appropriate in some jobs and in some industries. However, as we saw in Chapter 7, divorcing knowledge from concrete tasks and actions (that is, the brain from the hands) risks major problems. While the disciplines of Scientific Management spread rapidly from the car industry into other mass-production industries before and after the Second World War, the years since the 1970s have seen managers in many industries – including the car industry itself – realize the limitations of this approach. This realization was stimulated by the success of Japanese forms of work organization such as quality circles and 'just-in-time' production which made much greater use of the tacit knowledge of the shop-floor workforce – knowledge which even the most rigorous kinds of Scientific Management had been unable to eliminate.

Moreover, as we saw in Chapters 1 and 2, the environment in many sectors is increasingly dynamic and globalized. Organizations need to respond rapidly to such environments, using all available knowledge to develop new products, services and organizational processes to suit changing circumstances. To seek to concentrate decision-making power and authority in 'the brain'– the managerial technostructure – while the major part of the organization, 'the hands', simply obeys its commands, is slow and cumbersome. Worse, it ignores the extent to which much of the most important knowledge within the organizational domain simply cannot be concentrated at the centre. Very often, the employees who are closest to the rapidly changing business environment are not the managers, but the rank-and-file sales people and production operatives. It is their experience and tacit understanding which are most relevant to making decisions. It follows that in this kind of environment, power and authority need to be decentralized – indeed they will almost inevitably be so to some extent – so that empowered workers can use their knowledge and experience to develop solutions to problems and opportunities that confront them. This trend is apparent across a range of industries, jobs and tasks. It is most advanced, however, in the jobs, tasks and industries that we have characterized as knowledge-intensive. Here, we see a very different approach to managing knowledge work.

Job design for knowledge-intensive work

In these dynamic and global environments, it is not possible to expect managers to do all the thinking – in other words, the separation between thinking and doing (or decision and action knowledge) is no longer appropriate. Success depends, rather, on harnessing the intellectual capital of all employees. Moreover, in such situations people will often work together in teams to create new solutions, integrating their knowledge and experience to develop new products and services. Both the structural and cultural conditions within organizations will play an important part in creating an environment in which knowledge workers demonstrate responsible autonomy (as we saw in the ScienceCo case in Chapter 2). However, we also saw in Chapters 3 and 7 that this synergy among groups of experts is actually more difficult to achieve in practice than is often suggested, since individuals will have different agendas and will use political tactics to influence the team process. Moreover, given the different backgrounds of individual team members, creating the necessary trust and shared understanding between team members is often problematic, as demonstrated by the ResearchTeam case and the Oakland role-play.

This focus on teamworking also highlights another issue that has been discussed in earlier chapters – that is, the importance of social capital (Nahapiet and Ghoshal, 1998). It is becoming increasingly apparent that, especially in complex situations, an individual or even a team will not have all the required knowledge to design a new product or develop a new service. This means that knowledge-intensive jobs cannot be seen in isolation. Rather there is a need to focus on the network of interpersonal relationships which can be used by the knowledge worker. The configuration and quality of these networks help to influence the kinds of knowledge which the individual or group is able to draw on, as well as the ability to transfer this knowledge to other groups. Strong network ties are important for the sharing of tacit knowledge, while weak ties are more important for accessing explicit knowledge in other parts of the organization (cf. Hansen, 1999). At the same time, the value of personal networks also has to be balanced against the possible limiting effect of strong or redundant ties on information flows. So in the ResearchTeam case, the selection of one of the research officers (ROs) was based on an existing strong tie but this had a negative impact on the project, culminating in the exit of this RO from the project team. These issues of networking and communication and their relation to managing knowledge work were discussed more fully in Chapters 6 and 7.

The design of knowledge-intensive work is, therefore, very different from that advocated by Taylor. We can characterize this as a change from specialized, clearly defined and individualized job design to complex, problem-oriented, loosely defined, and team-based job design. Moreover, developing and supporting workers engaged in the latter kind of complex knowledge-intensive work requires a very different management approach and form of control. As we saw in Chapters 2 and 4, the characteristic 'carrot-and-stick' command-and-control approach of Scientific Management is not appropriate. Instead, close attention needs to be paid to the development of human resource practices that engender commitment and engagement from knowledge workers. In particular, we have stressed the importance of recruitment and selection practices, training and development opportunities and reward systems. These policies have important long-term effects on the extent of knowledge-sharing within an organization (Scarbrough and Carter, 2001).

Although the precise mechanisms through which Human Resource Management (HRM) policies influence knowledge-sharing are still open to some debate, the fact and importance of HRM's impact are not, and through research it is possible to identify some of the key characteristics of its influence. These include, in particular, the degree of 'fit' between HRM policies and the wider strategy for exploiting knowledge. As we noted in our discussion of 'personalization' and 'codification', for example, placing the emphasis on individual experience or on collective knowledge bases has dramatic implications for the kinds of selection, career development and reward policies that will be effective for the organization. At the same time, there are also longer-term and more insidious effects from HRM policy which have their impact on the fundamental quality of trust and relationships through which knowledge is shared. The focus of our discussion here was the notion of social capital. Although this is something that emerges 'bottom-up' out of informal interaction – not something, therefore, which can be enforced in a top-down way – the HRM policies of the firm are crucial in shaping the environment for such interactions. An obvious example is the influence of payment and promotion systems. While the 1990s saw a major shift in HRM policies towards individual performance as the basis for pay, this was happening at the same time as a shift towards teamworking which demanded greater knowledge-sharing amongst team members. As many organizations quickly realized, focusing too narrowly on the individual placed trust and collaboration within teams in great jeopardy – and with it the collective willingness to exchange ideas and experience which is critical to effective Knowledge Management.

While we have, in this book, been at pains to emphasize these human resource practices and the behavioural aspects of the management of knowledge work, we have also seen (in Chapter 5) that, as yet, this is not the initial reaction of many organizations. Rather, the predominant response to the perceived 'Knowledge Management problem' has been to introduce information and communication technologies (ICTs) to supposedly encourage and support knowledge-sharing and knowledge creation. However, we also saw how this solution was problematic, especially in relation to tasks that require the sharing of tacit knowledge – in particular between people from different backgrounds, be it different functions, divisions or geographical locations. Certainly ICTs have a role to play but, as Chapters 5 and 7 demonstrate, this role must be considered both in terms of what the aims and purposes of Knowledge Management are and the social context in which it occurs.

Offering a counterbalance to the overwhelming emphasis in Knowledge Management on ICTs, we have focused instead on the importance of developing knowledge-sharing communities, contrasting the community approach with the cognitive approach to the management of knowledge work. Whilst the creation of communities is now increasingly called for in the literature on Knowledge Management and organizational learning, there has been relatively little attention to the actual practices and issues that this entails. Practices and strategies for developing effective knowledge communities were explored more fully in Chapter 6, where we highlighted the role played by 'communities of practice' in the sharing of tacit knowledge. The value of such communities, as well as the social capital on which they are based, is often understated by organizations. Indeed, it may only become visible when the community has been dispersed and some taken-for-granted knowledge is no longer available. Many of the companies which experienced BPR (Business Process Reengineering) in the 1990s, for instance, often had cause to rue the loss of valuable capabilities associated with the delayering of middle management. In many cases, this had less to do with an individual's expertise than with managers' ability to access vital knowledge through their informal networks.

All this is not to say that 'communities of practice' are a panacea for the management of knowledge work. As demonstrated in the previous chapter, the notion of 'best practice' in relation to Knowledge Management is extremely problematic. Further, since they tend to emerge out of informal interaction, communities cannot be managed in conventional ways – they require assiduous cultivation, not heavy-handed control. They can also represent sites of conservatism, inertia, entrenchment and resistance – for example, their social boundaries and restricted codes may retard innovation projects that cut across different communities. This said, however, it is already clear from existing research that purely cognitive, ICT-based approaches to the management of knowledge work are unlikely to succeed because so much of the working knowledge of any organization is socially embedded in its different communities.

A contingency approach to the management of knowledge work

It is important to reiterate the point made in the previous chapter that neither the cognitive nor the community approach is inherently preferable to the other. Nor are they mutually exclusive. Rather, they are more or less appropriate in different situations. The cognitive approach may be appropriate for the sharing of explicit information, where those involved have enough common understanding to make the passing of information from person to person relatively straightforward. So, for example, a group of software engineers who have already developed a common language for software development may well be able to use e-mail to jointly develop a new software program. They may have little requirement for any face-to-face contact in this process. Similarly documentation strategies in LiftCo were quite useful at the point where the innovation had become sufficiently well-routinized and a common set of languages and understandings had developed around the innovation. This meant that the documentation could be interpreted.

The cognitive approach may also be more applicable where the objective of knowledge-sharing is the creation of a tangible entity (for example, in product innovation projects – see Chapter 7). For example, in the Buckman Labs case (Chapter 6), the sharing of knowledge about pitch-control strategies was possible because the knowledge effectively became codified and embodied in the technology itself. This knowledge was then able to be shared across the global organization, at least among people with a basic understanding of the technology. Similarly, and using an example closer to many people's experience, knowledge about how to use Windows software applications (for example, the ability to open, save, edit and drag files) is effectively codified and communicated in the form of technology itself. This embodies strict rules over what actions are permissable, or advisable, and we are reminded of these in very explicit ways – for example, with error messages, beeps, and 'helpful' paperclips and dogs. In other words knowledge on how to use the technology (or product) is effectively codified into the design of the technology (or product). This means that, once users learn the basic codes for operating in a Windows environment, they can learn new Windows applications relatively quickly.

The community approach, on the other hand, is appropriate where the sharing of tacit knowledge is central and those involved do not share a common frame of reference or context. For example, in a situation where a group of IT specialists is designing a software program for a group of business analysts, there may be little common understanding or context between the two groups. Moreover, much of the knowledge on both sides is likely to be tacit and difficult to articulate. In this situation, considerable face-to-face contact will be necessary before each side understands the issues confronting the other and so can develop a solution that is feasible and useful. This will involve what has been termed 'perspective taking', such that one group can begin to appreciate the world-view and context that underpin the knowledge and experience of the other (Boland and Tenkasi, 1995).

The community approach is also more appropriate in situations where the goal of the joint activity is relatively intangible and context-dependent. This applies particularly to interdisciplinary projects that focus on both technical and organizational change, such as the process innovation projects described in the LiftCo and BankCo cases. In these situations, knowledge is much more tacit and difficult to capture in explicit forms. The BankCo case described in Chapter 5 illustrates this very well, with the focus on the technology precluding the sharing of tacit knowledge and experience that might have produced a more integrated response. In LiftCo, on the other hand, the project managers were able to combine the use of technology with a community approach at crucial moments during the innovation project, and were considerably more successful in achieving their objectives. In projects with broad or hard-to-specify objectives, therefore, the community approach to managing knowledge work is likely to be more applicable where the development of strong interpersonal network ties is a crucial mechanism.

This contingency approach to the management of knowledge work can be developed further. It is not simply that different activities or project tasks are more suited to one or another approach. It was also suggested in Chapter 7 that, even within the context of a single project task or activity, different approaches will be more or less applicable, depending on the particular purpose being pursued at different points in time. In Chapter 7, then, the focus was on considering how knowledge could be effectively managed to support innovation – an example of knowledge work. In that chapter we argued that different approaches to the management of knowledge would need to be used depending on the episode of the innovation process that was central at any particular point in time. In considering this a third approach to managing knowledge, encapsulated in the networking approach – with an emphasis on the development of broad, weak social networks (possibly also using ICTs) – was introduced to supplement the cognitive and community approaches discussed earlier. This showed that at the point in time where knowledge search and acquisition are a main priority, a networking approach may be more applicable. The major point is that these, and possibly other, approaches to the management of knowledge work need to be applied flexibly, depending both on the purpose being pursued and the process through which this evolves over time. The importance of context, and of recognizing the different kinds of knowledge mobilized for different tasks, means that there is unlikely to be a single approach that is effective. The relevance of any particular approach will depend on its fit with these requirements, and particularly on its ability to promote knowledge-sharing amongst the different groups involved.

Creating a knowledge-sharing culture

In the earlier chapters a range of factors were identified which were shown to influence the success of knowledge-sharing. Attention to these factors will help an organization to develop an organizational culture that is supportive of knowledge-sharing (rather than knowledge-hoarding). Summarizing these, we can identify the following factors as key:

- *Appropriate incentives and motivation*: Incentive structures are important in the individual's willingness to share or exploit knowledge (Scarbrough and Carter, 2000; Robertson and O'Malley Hammersley, 2000; Keegan, 1998). While some literature exaggerates the problem of knowledge-hoarding, it is certainly the case that knowledge-sharing will be more likely if individuals are rewarded (intrinsically or extrinsically) for this, as was discussed more fully in Chapter 4. In the cases used in this book, problems have arisen where no attention was paid to this issue of reward and incentive systems, for example, BankCo, while success is apparent where this has been considered, for example, ScienceCo and Buckman Labs.

- *Adequate resources*: Given the importance of developing a shared under-standing, it is important that individuals are given the time to share ideas and information with others as well as the tools to facilitate this. This may be time to codify experiences for others to read, time to read about the experiences and ideas of others, and/or time to engage in debate and dialogue with others in order to further understanding. This issue of time provision can be related to Cyert and March's (1963) notion of 'organiza-tional slack'. In this respect ScienceCo and LiftCo certainly made more resources available for the projects compared to the resources made available at BankCo or ResearchTeam. For example, in the ResearchTeam case, given the diversity of backgrounds, not enough time was spent interacting and sharing information and ideas whereas in the LiftCo case 'spaces' for social interaction were built into the project plan.

- *Appropriate breadth and depth of skills and expertise*: As emphasized in Chapter 3, in order to share ideas with others, there has to be some common understanding. This demands a degree of knowledge redundancy or know-ledge overlap (Nonaka, 1994). Knowledge redundancy affects a team's 'absorptive capacity' (Cohen and Levinthal, 1990) – that is, the ability to recognize the value of new knowledge, assimilate it with existing knowledge, and apply it to commercial ends. This kind of redundancy can only be achieved if individuals are provided with a broad range of opportunities and experiences so that a breadth of understanding is developed. Knowledge 'brokers' who are able, effectively, to bridge social spaces and understandings (for example, the graduate employees seen in LiftCo) may be useful in creating necessary redundancy (Aldrich and von Glinow, 1992). At the same time, given the knowledge-intensive nature of the work, there is also a requirement for deep knowledge and understanding so that high levels of expertise are achieved in particular areas. This suggests that training and development opportunities are important for encouraging knowledge-sharing. These issues were illustrated in the ScienceCo case and in the LiftCo case.

- *Linking-pin/boundary-spanning individuals*: It is also important to have individuals who encourage knowledge-sharing across organizational boundaries, both internal and external. Different groups within and across organizations often fail to share knowledge, not because they are particularly resistant, but merely because they operate in different 'life worlds' with different understandings, priorities or 'logics of action' (Cyert and March, 1963). Consequently, they may simply not see the point of sharing knowledge. Boundary-spanning individuals are important in translating the experience of particular individuals or groups into the language understood by others in the wider organization (Brown and Duguid, 1998; Grandori and Soda, 1995). In the LiftCo case, again, the students who worked for both the company and the software consultants performed this linking-pin role. On the other hand, the administrator in the ResearchTeam case, who could potentially have acted as a linking pin between those involved at the three different universities, failed to play this boundary-spanning role, instead immersing herself in the one organization where she was based.

- *A committed project champion*: In the Buckman case, Bob Buckman himself acted as the project champion for the successful development of the knowledge-sharing culture. On the other hand, in the BankCo case, where knowledge-sharing was so problematic, there was no such project champion. The importance of a project champion has been illustrated by others (for example, Ginsberg and Abrahamson, 1991). Such champions are important, not just in terms of what they actually do, but also in terms of how they are seen by others – they act as symbols for celebrating successes (hence terms like 'champion') and thereby catalyse learning from a complex and uncertain situation. The case later in this chapter illustrates the importance of this symbolic role.

Knowledge transfer

One final issue that has been implied in previous chapters and in the section above, but not explicitly considered, is that of knowledge transfer. Knowledge transfer is a key objective behind many Knowledge Management initiatives, with organizations keen to prevent individuals and groups 'reinventing the wheel'. This was, indeed, the specific objective of the Knowledge Management initiative at BankCo. Knowledge transfer thus relates to the extent to which reusable products of individual or group learning are made available to, and applied by, other individuals and groups within the wider organization.

While knowledge transfer has been an important motivation for the development of Knowledge Management Systems – the recycling of knowledge being highly cost-efficient – it is often difficult to achieve in practice. As we noted in Chapter 6, the use of ICTs is often most effective when used dialectically, helping to connect, engage and develop communities rather than to simply transfer information. Moreoever, where knowledge transfer does happen, it often takes place accidentally or through the transfer of embodied knowledge that accompanies movements of personnel between project teams and between assignments, as illustrated in the ScienceCo and LiftCo cases. This suggests that staff rotation and career development systems may be key in facilitating knowledge transfer. Yet these elements often remain unrecognized in initiatives to manage knowledge work, maybe because they appear unexciting or mundane compared to new ICTs. However, such staff movements crucially impact on personal networks, widening the range of contacts of an individual, and thus increasing his or her social capital (Nahapiet and Ghoshal, 1998). These personal networks influence knowledge transfer in at least two ways. First, personal networks can be important in identifying and accessing the knowledge needed for a given activity. Second, personal networks can enhance the informal transfer of learning by helping to develop the relationships and trust that underpin it, as discussed in Chapter 3.

Knowledge transfer can also take place, of course, via the transfer of documentation and through electronic means (intranet and e-mail). However, we have already discussed how such codified knowledge transfer is only effective in situations where there is some common understanding and a sufficiently well-defined task. Given this, ICTs may link geographically diverse teams but may inhibit knowledge transfer if it becomes a substitute for face-to-face interaction, as demonstrated in the BankCo and ResearchTeam cases.

The importance of the wider social context for knowledge transfer

Aside from these questions of the mode of knowledge transfer, the organizational, political and wider societal context will also crucially influence the effort placed on knowledge transfer. For example, at the organizational level, the time horizons of management objectives and political agendas exert a strong influence on the willingness of individuals and groups to capture learning and share knowledge across internal boundaries. This was seen in relation to BankCo, where individual departments were not willing to engage in global knowledge-sharing because in the short term this would distract from the goals and objectives against which they, as a department, would be judged. Similarly a common outcome in the Oakland Furniture role-play is that individuals representing different departments fail to share relevant knowledge, or even conceal knowledge, because it is in their particular interests, and /or in the political interests of their department, to do so. On the other hand, in Buckman Labs, global knowledge-sharing occurred because this was promoted from the top by a powerful CEO and managers were rewarded for this activity, rather than simply for improving the profitability of their own particular unit.

The very different outcomes of attempts to manage knowledge work that we see in all our cases have been explained for the most part in terms of management practices and approaches. However, it is also clear from reviewing these cases that there are significant societal influences at work here too. Consider, for instance, the strong HRM orientation that we see in developments at LiftCo – a company with a strong Swedish base – or the problems of decentralization in the highly multinational BankCo organization.

There is also a large body of research that demonstrates the ways in which wider institutional arrangements, such as the organization of professions, educational systems and social and science policy, both structure and channel the production and consumption of knowledge (Nowotny *et al.*, 2001; Clark, 2000; Aldrich, 1999). This research lies mainly outside the scope of this book, but it is important to be aware of it because it underlines the influence of the societal and institutional context on the management of knowledge work. Although this influence is often diffuse and difficult to specify, its importance is not to be underestimated. It is perhaps not very surprising, for example, to discover that many of the organizations which are cited as leading exponents of Knowledge Management are Japanese companies (Fruin, 1997). Thus the classic account of knowledge creation is based on a Japanese firm, where, as described by Ijuiro Nonaka, a knowledge spiral translates tacit knowledge into innovative products (Nonaka, 1994). What is often forgotten in descriptions of the knowledge spiral is how far it depends on the sheer dedication and collective team spirit which are characteristic features of large Japanese firms – and which depend (or, arguably, depended) on the wider cultural norms, institutions and systems of control in Japan. It is debatable whether the same willingness to share knowledge would be found in the more uncertain, hypercompetitive and individualistic environments found in some Western societies.

These questions of the influence of the national and institutional context on knowledge transfer are amply underlined by the case in this final chapter: Midlands Hospital NHS Trust. As in previous chapters, following the Conclusions section, the case is described. This is followed by a set of questions for analysis.

Conclusions

The points in this chapter, along with the case analyses, exercises and discussions in previous chapters, support those who are arguing for a shift in thinking about managing knowledge work. This shift is from strategies that emphasize dissemination and imitation (that is, 'first-generation Knowledge Management') to those that promote education and innovation (that is, 'second-generation Knowledge Management': McElroy, 2000). In second-generation Knowledge Management the focus moves from the supply of knowledge to satisfying the organizational demand for knowledge, and to creating and maintaining the conditions required for the production of knowledge. Second-generation Knowledge Management recognizes that knowledge is context-dependent, since 'meanings' are interpreted in reference to a particular paradigm. As Shariq (1998) notes, in order to make sense, or create understanding, humans bring prior knowledge and context to information. He goes on to note that without the human context information by itself has no meaning. Second-generation Knowledge Management, then, reconnects knowledge with social context, social purpose and social action. It recognizes, given differences in contexts, that alternative interpretations, meaning and understandings are inevitable, even when people are presented with the same information (as you will have found for yourselves if you have been involved in the role-play provided in Chapter 7). Not only are they inevitable, but alternative interpretations are also desirable, being a great source of innovation and change – provided, that is, that conflict can be used constructively rather than destructively.

Recognizing that the value of knowledge is relative to the context of its application leads to a much more sceptical view about one of the most widespread aspirations of Knowledge Management initiatives. This is the idea that templates for 'best practice' (including 'best practice' Knowledge Management) can be identified in one part of an organization, captured in some form or other and transferred to other parts or to other organizations. While a seductive idea in theory, not least because it avoids reinventing the wheel, it often founders on the context-dependent nature of what is best at any point in time. Simply put, what works in one department or one organization may not work in another, not simply because the context is different, but also because the 'best practice' template which is transferred cannot capture all of the knowledge involved in actually making it effective. Thus, templates and practices presented as 'best' will be interpreted differently in each context of application. Indeed, in many cases, what is considered to be a 'best practice' in one context may be deemed unworkable in another, because the sense-making in these other social contexts remains bounded by traditions and assumptions that are anchored in history. As Dervin (1998) observes, reading about a best practice, makes little sense without an understanding of the struggle and gaps it was designed to overcome.

This concluding point is well-illustrated in the final, Midlands Hospital Trust case study that follows. This case provides an example of a team that was actually quite successful in sharing knowledge in order to design a new 'best practice' form of treatment for patients. This new treatment may well prove beneficial in other locations and contexts. However, a close analysis of the process that the team went through to produce this new treatment also suggests that the knowledge about the treatment could not be easily transferred to another organizational context in the form of a set of templates or guidelines. This is because to apply this knowledge (the 'know-what') in the new context, it would also need to be accompanied by the transfer of knowledge about the social processes and conditions needed to interpret it, legitimate it and act upon it (that is, the 'know-how' and, especially, the 'know-who'). In other words, a key feature of managing knowledge work is to transfer not just knowledge about a 'best' (or perhaps more appropriately 'good') practice, but also knowledge about how to develop the social processes and conditions needed to endorse and act upon it in a new context.

This final case draws together major themes of this book, and highlights the importance for managing knowledge work, not just of sharing or transferring knowledge about facts and things, but also of creating a 'shared context for knowing' (Blackler, 1995; Ciborra, 1999). This does not mean that the role of management is to create an environment where everyone thinks the same. Rather it means adopting a more *pluralist* approach to managing knowledge work – one that recognizes the importance of diverse cultures, understandings and 'logics of action' and develops a social context where these can both coexist *and* learn from one another (Scarbrough, 1999). The key issues in creating a 'shared context for knowing' have been a major theme in this book. Such an approach helps to redress the reification of knowledge – evident in much of the literature on Knowledge Management – and makes its successful application to organizational tasks, purposes and actions more promising. If we really take seriously the notion, that knowledge is not developed in isolation from the social context and culture (Tsoukas, 1996) then this would seem essential for managing knowledge work.

Case Study 8.1: Midlands Hospital NHS Trust

Midlands NHS Trust Hospital is one of a large number of trusts that together make up the National Health Service of the United Kingdom. Developed in the postwar period as a means of providing affordable, quality healthcare to all UK residents, the National Health Service has, in recent years, been plagued with a series of shortages with respect to staff, theatres and beds, as well as untenably long lead times for non-life-threatening procedures. This has led to a public backlash against the system and the formation of a dual system of public and private health care to which many more affluent UK residents subscribe.

Case Study 8.1 continued

One of the areas targeted by the government as in need of change is the cataract diagnosis and treatment procedure. Cataract surgery, which is a 20-minute procedure, represents 96 per cent of the ophthalmology workload. Traditionally, cataract diagnosis and treatment involved a number of visits to various specialists. For example, the patient would begin at the optometrist (the local high street optician) who would diagnose that the patient had cataracts that were significantly reducing vision, and then refer that patient to his or her general practitioner (GP) for further treatment. After a visit to the local GP who, not being an eye specialist, would generally rely on the diagnosis of the optometrist, the patient was forwarded on to the hospital for further examination. At that time, the patient would meet briefly with the consultant and, in a separate appointment, meet with the hospital nurse for a physical examination. Only when all of these visits were complete would the patient get in the queue for obtaining a date for the cataract surgery. In many trusts, the lead time for cataract surgery was over 12 months. Post-surgery, another visit to the consultant was scheduled to check on the patient and then the patient was referred back to the optometrist for a new pair of glasses. Therefore, it took patients at least six visits and often well over a year to have a routine, 20-minute, outpatient, surgical procedure.

Given the complex and long-drawn-out nature of this existing process, a new reengineered cataract diagnostic and treatment process was seen as potentially beneficial. To facilitate that change, a designated member of the hospital's transformation team was assigned to the process. This was a team that was unique to this particular hospital. Their remit was to facilitate organizational change within the hospital, both identifying where change might provide most benefit and encouraging the relevant groups to design and implement changed processes. In this instance, the transformation team member gathered a team of eye experts from both the hospital and the community to discuss ways in which to cut surgery lead times and improve patient satisfaction. Members of the cataract team included the head nurse in the eye unit, a hospital administrator, general practitioners, a set of optometrists from the local community, and a surgical consultant who was instrumental in championing the need for change and in leading the change process. Team meetings were held in the evening to facilitate attendance, and were led by the transformation team member. Minutes, flow charts and other necessary documentation for the process were produced by the transformation team member, and distributed to all team members after each meeting. In total, approximately five project team meetings were held over a six-month period.

At these meetings the various professionals involved shared information about their current roles and procedures so that all gradually came to a collective understanding of the diagnosis and treatment process. Based on this understanding, plus an increased awareness of the competencies and skills of the various groups involved, they were able to see alternatives to the traditional process. In doing this, each individual in the team drew upon their own experience and knowledge, but also used their personal networks to find out what was happening in other hospitals. For example, the project team went to

Case Study 8.1 continued

look at procedures in a leading eye surgery where they felt they might learn something useful to apply to their own context.

A number of changes to the existing process were made. Non-essential visits to the general practitioner, the consultant and the nurse were eliminated. Instead, optometrists were empowered to decide if a patient needed cataract surgery. In doing so, they were required to fill out a detailed form that provided the consultant with specific information about the nature and severity of the cataract, and to call the hospital and book a time for the patient's surgery. This form was developed by the project team through an iterative process of design and testing. For their additional responsibility, the optometrists were given some extra training and received a small financial incentive from the trust.

The preliminary pre-operation physical was replaced with a self-diagnostic questionnaire that each patient was required to fill out and return to the hospital before surgery. This self-diagnostic questionnaire was again developed by the project team; but in this instance they had access to a similar form that had been developed elsewhere. The project team did not, however, simply use the form that had been previously developed by others. Rather, they used this existing form as the starting point to develop a new questionnaire which suited their particular requirements, as perceived by the project team.

Immediately before surgery, nurses were to telephone each patient to check the patient's details and answer any questions. Post-operation consultant appointments were also replaced with follow-up telephone calls. One indication of how much the process changed was the traditional post-operation meal. Under the traditional method, before discharge, each patient was treated to a plate of hospital food; under the new system, they were given a cup of tea and a biscuit and were then sent home.

The new cataract procedure resulted in a number of efficiency gains. Lead times were radically reduced from over 12 months down to six to eight weeks. In addition, theatre utilization rates improved due to the addition of an administrator whose sole responsibility lay in scheduling theatres. Finally, and most importantly, according to follow-up phone conversations with cataract project patients, patient satisfaction improved dramatically.

The new cataract process had significantly altered roles and responsibilities, particularly for the optometrists, who could now diagnose and directly refer patients. This process, however, was not entirely straightforward, and considerable learning was necessary among those involved. The consultants had worked with the optometrists, so that the optometrists could learn how to make diagnoses that were acceptable to the consultants. The consultants provided the optometrists with regular feedback on the patients they had referred and also answered their questions. For example, one optometrist explained that at times he had needed to clarify issues with the consultant in order to ensure that a particular patient was actually suitable for the cataract operation. The optometrist claimed that this would be very difficult for consultants

Case Study 8.1 continued

who had not been involved in the project because they undervalued the knowledge of optometrists:

> When patients eventually find their way to hospital any comment that the optometrist has made that is relayed to the hospital staff is usually treated with contempt – 'what do they know about it', that sort of attitude. (Project member)

While there were, then, many advantages of the new system there were pockets of resistance. Previously, theatre scheduling had been done by each consultant's secretary on the basis of the consultant's availability. As part of the reengineering project, this secretarial support had been centralized and theatre scheduling defined as a separate activity. The secretaries had resisted this change, insisting that they were far too busy to be assigned to more than one consultant. In order to overcome this resistance, one of the nurses on the project team, aware of another hospital that had successfully introduced a centralized secretarial pool, took the secretaries to see this pool working. While this helped to weaken the resistance it did not eliminate it. For example, initially the new administrator in charge of theatre scheduling was not provided with the theatre schedules from the secretaries and therefore she was unable to perform her role. However, when it became clear that this was not going to be acceptable, the secretaries revised their strategy and all sent in their schedules together so that the new administrator was overwhelmed by the workload. As one project member put it, 'they were wanting her to sink'.

There was also some resistance from local optometrists who refused to get involved in the redesigned diagnosis process. This resistance was gradually overcome, however. For example, the transformation team member recounted the story of an optometrist with a large local practice, who refused to participate in the fast-track cataract process. As luck would have it, the transformation team member happened to need a new pair of glasses and so decided to visit the reluctant optometrist. She sang the praises of this new cataract procedure throughout her eye exam. By the time her glasses were ready, the optometrist had reconsidered his position and had decided to participate in the project.

While the redesigned cataract process was thus considered to be highly successful in the hospital where it had been developed, the transfer of this newly designed process to other hospitals was proving to be extremely problematic. For example, in one hospital which had looked at the new process in Midlands Hospital the idea had been rejected, because it was seen as 'too radical':

> We had some interest from one of the ophthalmologists [from another region] who wanted to start a similar project, so we sent them our paperwork and documentation. We had some interesting discussion and feedback from people but they didn't like the idea. (Project member)

Indeed, even within Midlands Hospital itself, consultants who had not been involved in the reengineering project still assumed that optometrists could

Case Study 8.1 continued

not properly diagnose cataracts and continued to want to see all patients themselves to make the diagnosis:

> There are a lot of other departments where people express reservations about the skills of optometrists who will be referring patients to them and they are not prepared to go down that route [that is, the new cataract process] because of that. (Project member)

Questions

1. What are the key factors that encouraged the success of this team in redesigning the cataract diagnosis and treatment processes?
2. How useful was codified knowledge in designing the new cataract diagnosis and treatment process?
3. Why was it proving difficult to transfer knowledge from this hospital trust to other hospitals where it would also be relevant?

Summary of key learning points

■ Attempts to manage knowledge are not new, but the classical approach of separating 'the brains' from 'the hands' (decisions and actions) is no longer appropriate in situations where an organization needs to respond to dynamic, global and highly competitive environments.

■ For knowledge-intensive work, job design needs to change from the classical specialized, clearly defined and individualized job design to complex, problem-oriented, loosely defined and team-based job design.

■ A contingency view of the management of knowledge work is helpful. In some situations the cognitive approach is applicable while in other situations the community approach is more appropriate.

■ The approach to the management of knowledge work and knowledge workers needs, therefore, to be flexible, with different approaches suiting different purposes.

■ Three different approaches have been identified in this book – the cognitive, community and network approaches. These are not considered to be exhaustive but illustrate the need for a flexible approach to the management of knowledge work and knowledge workers.

■ Attempts to manage knowledge work, especially where the objective is knowledge transfer, need to focus not just on transferring knowledge about facts and things but also on creating a 'shared context for knowing'.

Summary of key learning points continued

■ All approaches to the management of knowledge work and knowledge workers will be facilitated by the development of a supportive organizational culture.

■ Attention to incentives and motivation, the provision of adequate resources, the development of individuals' breadth and depth of skills and expertise, the provision of linking-pin roles and the emergence of committed champions can help to facilitate the development of such a culture.

■ Knowledge transfer is facilitated by the movement of personnel and by ICTs. However, in some situations, ICTs can impede the transfer of knowledge, especially if ICTs are used as a substitute for face-to-face contact.

References

Aldrich, H.E. (1999) *Organizations Evolving*. London: Sage.

Aldrich, H.E. and von Glinow, M.A. (1992) Personal networks and infrastructure development. In D.V. Gibson, G. Kozmetsky and R.W. Smilor (eds) *The Technopolis Phenomenon*. Rowman & Littlefield.

Blackler, F. (1995) Knowledge, knowledge work and organizations: an overview and interpretation. *Organization Studies*, 16(6): 1021–46.

Boland, R.J. and Tenkasi, R.V. (1995) Perspective making and perspective taking in communities of knowing. *Organization Science*, 6(4): 350–63.

Brown, J.S. and Duguid, P. (1998) Organizing knowledge. *California Management Review*, 40(3): 90–109.

Ciborra, C. (1999) A theory of information systems based on improvisation. In W. Currie and B. Galliers (eds) *Rethinking Information Systems*. Oxford: Oxford University Press.

Clark, P. (2000) *Organizations in Action: Competition Between Contexts*. London: Routledge.

Cohen, M. and Levinthal, D. (1990) Absorptive capacity: a new perspective on learning and innovation. *Administrative Science Quarterly*, 35(1): 128–52.

Cook, S.D.N. and Brown, J.S. (1999) Bridging epistemologies: the generative dance between organizational knowledge and organizational knowing. *Organization Science*, 190: 381–400.

Cyert, R.M. and March, J.G. (1963) *A Behavioral Theory of the Firm*. Englewood Cliffs, NJ: Prentice-Hall.

Czarniawska, B. and Joerges, B. (1996) Travels of ideas. In B. Czarniawska and G. Seven (eds) *Translating Organizational Change*. Berlin: De Gruyter, 13–48.

Dervin, B. (1998) Sense-making theory and practice: an overview of user interests in knowledge seeking and use. *Journal of Knowledge Management*, 2(2): 36–45.

Fruin, W. Mark. (1997) *Knowledge Works: Managing Intellectual Capital at Toshiba*. New York: Oxford University Press.

Gherardi, S. and Nicolini, D. (2000) The organizational learning of safety in communities of practice. *Journal of Management Inquiry*, 9(1): 7–18.

Ginsberg, A. and Abrahamson, E. (1991) Champions of change and strategic shifts: the role of internal and external change advocates. *Journal of Management Studies*, 28(2): 173–90.

Grandori, A. and Soda, G. (1995) Inter-firm networks: antecedents, mechanisms and forms. *Organization Studies*, **16**: 183–214.

Granovetter, M. (1973) The strength of weak ties. *American Journal of Sociology*, **78**(6): 1360–80.

Hansen, M.T. (1999) The search transfer problem: the role of weak ties in sharing knowledge across organizational sub-units. *Administrative Science Quarterly*, **44**: 82–111.

Keegan, A. (1998) Management practice in knowledge-intensive firms: the future of HRM in the knowledge era. Presented at British Academy of Management Conference, Nottingham, September.

McElroy, M. (2000) Integrating complexity theory, knowledge management and organizational learning. *Journal of Knowledge Management*, **4**(3): 195–203.

Nahapiet, J. and Ghoshal, S. (1998) Social capital, intellectual capital and the organizational advantage. *Academy of Management Review*, **23**(2): 242–66.

Nonaka, I. (1994) A dynamic theory of organizational knowledge creation. *Organization Science*, **5**: 14–37.

Nowotny, H., Scott, P. and Gibbons, M. (2001) *Rethinking Science: Knowledge and the Public in an Age of Uncertainty*. Cambridge: Polity Press.

Robertson, M. and O'Malley Hammersley, G. (2000) Knowledge management practices within a knowledge intensive firm: the significance of the people management dimension. *Journal of European Industrial Training*, **24**(4): 241–53.

Rowley, J. (2000) From learning organization to knowledge entrepreneur. *Journal of Knowledge Management*, **4**(1): 7–15.

Scarbrough, H. (1999) The management of knowledge workers. In W. Currie and B. Galliers (eds) *Rethinking Information Systems*. Oxford: Oxford University Press.

Scarbrough, H. and Carter, C. (2001) *Investigating Knowledge Management*. Research Report. Chartered Institute of Personnel and Development, London.

Shariq, S.Z. (1998) Sense making and artifacts: an exploration into the role of tools in knowledge management. *Journal of Knowledge Management*, **2**(2): 10–19.

Tsoukas, H. (1996) The firm as a distributed knowledge system: a constructionist perspective. *Strategic Management Journal*, **17**: 11–25.

Appendix 7.1: Innovation at Oakland Furniture – the role players

Alex Rheingold: Managing Director

In a few minutes, you will be chairing a meeting of a working group you have established to discuss the possible adoption of ERP in Oakland. During this meeting – which you will ensure keeps to time as is your usual practice – the group will be addressed by a consultant, Sandy Corbett, on the benefits of ERP. You saw Sandy (of Corbett Consulting) giving an impressive talk at a recent industry conference on this topic – hence the invitation. You want to give people in Oakland an opportunity for discussion before the final decision has to be made. Knowing Oakland's propensity for inertia you are keen that some decision is made to take the company forward. ERP seems to have great potential for Oakland. You have a keen personal interest in this since you were the driving force behind the recent management buy-out, which at one point involved taking out a second mortgage on your family home. Although this brought you close to your Chief Designer, Rowan Gregory, some other members of the management team have criticized you in the past for not really trusting them. They have suggested that you sometimes go in and do things to suit you that are properly their responsibility.

You are highly knowledgeable about the furniture industry and about Oakland's place in it. You appreciate the variety of products in the industry (including upholstery, bedding, and bedroom, kitchen, dining, occasional and office furniture) and are aware of trends in the industry. These include: the increased importance of fitted kitchens and other fitted furniture over the last decade or so; the 'furniturization' of many industrial and consumer products (such as TV cabinets, DVD/CD/video storage, gas and electric fires, refrigerators and dishwashers); the emergence of 'minimalist Scandinavian-style' kitchen and bedroom furniture; the growth of a bespoke sector; and increased competition from firms across Europe. You are also aware that different products necessitate quite different design parameters. Even where ergonomically similar, furniture is manufactured to different severity grades as specified by FIRA (the Furniture Industry Research Association). Oakland has focused on dining and occasional furniture, both of which have been slower-growing. It has suffered somewhat as a result, leading the firm into losses after its initial very successful early growth. Nevertheless, since the buy-out two years ago and the minor restructuring which took place then, the basic quality of Oakland's products has enabled it to break even on annual sales of around £15–20 million. This represents about 10 per cent of the relevant UK market. Moreover, there are indications that if lead times could be improved and stock levels reduced, the firm could move to healthy profits and be well-set for growth, especially with the introduction of new ranges.

Chris Duncan: Financial Director

In a few minutes, you will be attending a meeting of a working group chaired by Alex Rheingold (your MD) to discuss the possible adoption of an ERP system in Oakland. The meeting will include a consultant's presentation. You joined Oakland Furniture not long after the management buy-out had established the company's independence. Not being part of the original buy-out team means that you sometimes feel left out in the cold in decision-making. However, as a fully qualified accountant, you are the company's expert on the turnover (currently around $15–20 million) and profitability of the firm and the capital investment in the machinery. Oakland has just returned to an operating profit since the buy-out. Normally, one would expect profits in the industry to be running at some 6 per cent of sales. Prior to the management buy-out, funding had been a mixture of inter-company loans from the holding company and bank borrowings. When Oakland was purchased by its management from the parent group that had owned it, the financial structure of the company was altered with the introduction of outside finance. The existing management purchased the ordinary shares in the company assisted by a specialist finance institution. This institution also provided dividend preference shares and arranged both new overdraft facilities and a term loan. Fortunately interest rates are currently favourable. However, the strength of UK sterling is further squeezing Oakland's exports and profit margins.

You are always interested in anything that can improve the present situation, characterized, as you see it, by an endemic lack of control, but not at any price. You have to be very tough on the payback of proposals, especially given the recent disappointing performance of the company. At present, despite improving their performance since the buy-out, the company has no scope for funding investments and is scarcely breaking even. They have major cash-flow worries. Long and uncertain lead times presently result in delays of nearly a year in many cases between paying for the raw materials and the receipts for the final goods. You are consequently rather suspicious of any significant new control system unless it is going to be under your own personal control. Currently, you have established a control target of $60,000 worth of production every day to keep the company on an even keel financially. You believe that simple payback within two years is a perfectly adequate criterion. If an investment proposal requires any fancy number-juggling, then clearly it cannot be that good. In particular you are rather concerned about a recent deal that Rowan Gregory, the Chief Designer, managed to swing. This involved the purchase of a very sophisticated machining centre. This was partly because of the initial buy-out conditions (Gregory was one of the principals), and partly because of special payment terms. These were in recompense for Gregory's design contribution to the new machine's development. You are not entirely satisfied that

that investment was properly scrutinized. Worse still, you have yet to be satisfied that it was in reality a good deal for the company, since it does not seem to be producing the savings promised. You will need some persuading that further costly expenditure on production systems can really help the firm.

Jan Pettigrew: Operations Director

In a few minutes, you will be attending a meeting of a working group chaired by Alex Rheingold (your MD) to discuss the possible adoption of an ERP system in Oakland. The meeting will include a consultant's presentation. Since you started way back as a shop-floor lathe operator, you have always worked in the furniture industry. It is unique and distinct, partly because of the heterogeneity and special character of wood (the major material) and partly because of the design/fashion element and the resulting intensity of craft skill. Wood is a natural material so one piece is never quite the same as the next. It is also hydroscopic (absorbs and retains moisture), causing it to swell and shrink with obvious implications for production. This offers certain problems for mass production. Fewer problems are offered by the manufactured items such as blockboard and chipboard. These are also used extensively, faced with veneer and finished with suitable edgings, to make surfaces and panels.

The manufacturing process follows a fairly logical path. First a range of furniture is designed, and drawings, dimensions and the appropriate fabrication processes specified. Prototypes are made up in the craft area with visits to the appropriate machine lines, to 'prove' the design. This information is then passed on in standard paper forms to the machine shop and assembly processes when the production schedule requires. You have been on an IOM (Institute of Operations Management) course on ERP, but would it really work in Oakland? However, the improved production planning and control claimed for these systems is certainly very attractive and you know at present you do have problems with inventory levels, quality control and scrap. This is in part because you are fighting a running (but friendly) battle with the Chief Designer, Rowan Gregory. Rowan keeps fiddling about with the product specifications for no good reason. These changes necessitate slightly different machining operations and mean that the shop floor have to be continually given new instructions. It also means that a plethora of different piece parts exist, ostensibly for the same bit of furniture. This is a monitoring and control nightmare, and has caused some horror stories: once a batch of tables was assembled with the wrong legs! You also know that Sam Newton, the Sales and Distribution Manager, puts in inflated sales forecasts to try to speed up the assembly process and hence delivery times to customers. This unfortunately causes huge inventory holding costs, and so you don't take Sam's sales too seriously. It's better to keep the shop floor busy and working on reasonable-sized batches. The present company monitoring systems don't help either. They run in purely monetary terms, with a target of $60,000 value of production a day (in terms of ultimate sales prices). You are concerned that the present production control system depends too much on Robin Johnston, the Production Scheduler. Robin quite clearly enjoys the influence afforded by special knowledge of the finished goods inventory and makes the most of it. But what would happen if he fell under a bus? Or took a dislike to one of your policies? You shudder to think.

Rowan Gregory: Chief Designer

In a few minutes, you will be attending a meeting of a working group chaired by Alex Rheingold (your MD) to discuss the possible adoption of an ERP system in Oakland. The meeting will include a consultant's presentation. As an ambitious designer, you are keen to make a name for yourself in the industry. You would like to challenge the quality image of Scandinavian design with a distinctive English 'Oakland style'. Oakland presently produces five major ranges: the York, the Winchester, the Westminster, the Salisbury and the Coventry. These are distinguished by their overall style, by the wood used (variation in wood is part of its natural beauty), by hardware, and by the elements available within the range. This leads to many possible permutations. You want to continue to create successful, established ranges, with new and imaginative product introductions within these ranges. This contrasts with the current policy of continual turnover of established ranges and a more or less standard range of products within each range. You are also very keen on bespoke opportunities. Indeed the company has established quite a reputation in this respect, mainly thanks to your creative efforts. You think new technology is a great thing in general – the computer aided design system in the Design shop is brilliant. But will a standardized ERP software platform restrict your scope for refining designs? Will it force the company even more down a standards route?

You became involved in the management buy-out to increase creative scope, not diminish it. You were the main driver and ideas person behind the recent investment in a new computer-controlled panel machining centre and were able to get special terms from the German machine tool firm which developed the machine. This automated machine greatly facilitates the production of high-quality, complex (and ornate) designs of panels, surfaces and doors. It allows complicated cuts to be made in panels, enabling the automatic replication of, for example, surface carving. Your contribution was to help devise a 'clever' adaptive randomization program. This enables variation in replication to be achieved. It is also able to cater (up to a point at least) for variations in the natural characteristics of the wood being machined. Together, these features enable the machine to provide a convincing emulation of the unique variation found with hand carving. It is also very flexible: once the complicated programs had been developed, machine set-up time was quite fast. The acquisition of this machine is an essential part of your longer-term plans for CAD/CAM (computer aided design and manufacturing). Unfortunately these benefits have not yet shown up clearly, as they could only come to the fore with smaller jobs than Oakland is currently running. This has led to a difference of opinion with the Financial Director, Chris Duncan. Duncan has no imagination and makes no secret of his opinion that you are indulging yourself with expensive and useless toys.

Sam Newton: Sales and Distribution Manager

In a few minutes, you will be attending a meeting of a working group chaired by Alex Rheingold (your MD) to discuss the possible adoption of an ERP system in Oakland. The meeting will include a consultant's presentation. You are responsible for sales lead times and customer care. You are very worried about the image the company gives to customers. There is total confusion over delivery times at present, partly because Oakland's products are in demand. There are often 1000 telephone calls a day enquiring when orders are going to be delivered. This absorbs a lot of unproductive time just chasing things up. When an irate customer phones to enquire about their order, one of the sales clerks has to go down to the assembly shop floor and literally *look* for the items of furniture, going round all the work benches asking the people there if they had completed that order. Sometimes it is a matter of checking even further back, to see if the piece parts required are available. Meanwhile the customers hanging on the phone are not always too impressed.

Oakland is currently quoting 20 weeks' lead time (an improvement on our previous 25 weeks), but it often seems more a matter of luck than planning if they are able to achieve that. This leads to constant interruptions of fabrication work, and ties up a team of ten people who do little else other than progress-chase and expedite crucial orders. However, Oakland is highly regarded for quality, and all of the ranges sell well. Indeed you could probably sell much more if lead times were reduced to a level similar to those of our competitors, some of whom are quoting ten weeks. In this connection, Oakland's bespoke and 'specials' service is a nice sideline (very much Gregory's baby) and certainly gives you market prominence, contributing significantly to the firm's reputation for high quality. You are also well-aware of increasing demand for such products. But it does add to the confusion on the shop floor, sometimes interrupts other standard batched jobs (fitted bedroom and kitchen furniture is a big seller), and tends to take raw material unpredictably, thus leading to shortages. Other competitors have similar problems, although some have reduced their lead times to ten weeks, while others try to offer a guarantee on the lead time they quote. As a result of the lead times problem, you tend to inflate sales order forecasts, so that more piece parts stock is held. Then the final assembly stages can be more quickly carried out. In this context, ERP is an intriguing proposition. From talking to sales colleagues in companies that have introduced some form of ERP system, it has both positive and negative possibilities. Speaking positively, the ERP system is driven to some extent by 'demand management' where forecasts of future sales are important. This may gave you more strategic influence within the company. On the other hand, it becomes more difficult to massage sales forecasts as these feed the system. This limits your room for manoeuvre and the ability to play the role of 'cheerleader' in the management team.

Jo Armstrong: Purchasing Manager

In a few minutes, you will be attending a meeting of a working group chaired by Alex Rheingold (your MD) to discuss the possible adoption of an ERP system in Oakland. The meeting will include a consultant's presentation. You are responsible for controlling the raw materials stock levels. The maintenance of adequate stocks of quality timbers is a particular concern. You are interested in what you see as Japanese-style management technologies and ideas such as just-in-time, although you don't know how to go about introducing them. You are not sure how relevant JIT is to your timber stocks; timber requires conditioning before it can be processed. But, you feel that a simple JIT system might be more appropriate for Oakland than ERP. You think this is because JIT is based on a 'pull system' – pulling production through based on orders received at the shop floor. In contrast, ERP seems to be no more than an elaborate name for the conventional Western approach or push system that people used to call MRP2 (Manufacturing Resources Planning) – pushing through production to meet anticipated sales controlled by a centralized production plan. OK, so ERP is broader, but what's the real difference? Currently Oakland tries to operate a simple reorder point system for raw materials. This is certainly possible with the manufactured items such as hardware and chipboard. As far as possible, you negotiate bulk discounts through competitive tendering. This can lead to substantial cuts in purchase prices, but it does mean that you have to carry very large stocks of certain items. However, Oakland's manufacturing suppliers (who provide chipboard, blockboard and the like) will only deliver in certain minimum batches, for example, 10 tonnes of ply – 10,000 square metres or so. The purchase of solid timber is particularly problematic.

You know a lot about timber, especially in choosing high-quality stock. Here it is very rare for large purchases to be made. The variation in wood as a natural material and the selection necessary means that unpredictable and varying amounts will be purchased as and when timber stock of the appropriate quality and type becomes available. Moreover, because of the natural characteristics of wood, timber stocks have to be held under controlled conditions sufficiently long for the material to stabilize. In some cases the company takes an option on wood still standing. In these cases, of course, the final yield is difficult to estimate. There are also occasional opportunities to purchase excellent specimen timber stocks in small quantities, for instance following gales or storms which inevitably bring some trees crashing to the ground unexpectedly. You are always on the lookout for such opportunities. In such cases, you keep close contact with Rowan Gregory, the designer, who will come up with 'specials' which incorporate the specimen timber as a feature.

Robin Johnston: Production Scheduler

In a few minutes, you will be attending a meeting of a working group chaired by Alex Rheingold (your MD) to discuss the possible adoption of an ERP system in Oakland. The meeting will include a consultant's presentation and then there will be a further meeting to take a decision. You are a time-served craftworker, and everyone knows you have excellent intuitive judgement about scheduling and keeping things running smoothly in the factory. They all depend on you. You know all there is to know about wood (a naturally variable material) and its production. Your main task is to ensure that enough of the correct furniture parts are available so that complete assemblies can always be made up from the machined parts store. The assembly kits are made up to meet firm customer orders first, subject to a minimum batch of 25. If the order is for less than 25, the balance goes into the finished goods store. You have what seems to outsiders an uncanny memory for everything that is in the finished goods store and are rarely wrong. This provides a considerable measure of influence in running operations and you know that your boss, Jan Pettigrew (the Operations Director), very much relies on your skills in this regard. The task of remembering exactly what is in the machined parts store is, however, altogether more formidable: the company produces some 400 products requiring more than 20,000 separate parts. Many of these are left-or right-hand versions of the same piece, which often (but not always) go together in pairs (for example, table legs). To further complicate matters, due to the particular difficulties of machining and matching wood, there is usually quite a high rate of rejects. This means that although you might have started out making 100 left- and right-hand pairs you could easily end up with 96 of one and 91 of the other. Ensuring that enough of the appropriate parts are available for the assembly kits is a major problem. To make life even more difficult, Jan Pettigrew always attempts to meet the Financial Director's control target of $60,000 worth of production per day. To achieve this, the bigger batches are progressed ahead of the smaller ones. These then sit on your shop floor somewhere until eventually someone comes down from Sales chasing up an irate customer's late order. By this time, it is more than likely that the assembly kit has been raided for some piece to replace a damaged part for another assembly, hence leading to further delays.

OK, so you know there are a few problems but nothing you can't handle. And what is this new IT system going to do to your job? You know that Jan Pettigrew is a little bit unhappy over the undoubted influence you enjoy because of your special skills and central role. Is this a ploy to undermine your position? Even if it isn't, it is certainly going to change what you do. The computer system will issue the order releases and make your judgement redundant. What will there be left for you to do?

Jean Lamont: Systems Administrator

In a few minutes, you will be attending a meeting of a working group chaired by Alex Rheingold (your MD) to discuss the possible adoption of an ERP system in Oakland. The meeting will include a consultant's presentation and then there will be a further meeting to take a decision. Currently Oakland has a number of unconnected software systems (for payroll, accounts and sales, and a CAD package). You know all about them and thoroughly enjoy keeping them working in good order. There are three staff working for you in this area. The payroll and accounts systems are standard packages with 'bits added in here and there'. The CAD package has evolved way beyond the original version, largely on account of Rowan Gregory's enthusiasm and predilection for experiment – aided and abetted by you. However, this is now getting very creaky and unwieldy – far more effective packages can be bought on the market. The sales system is a customized one with few problems. This is good for generating the appropriate paperwork for vendors and for linking up with the accounts but it is useless for tracking materials or for stock control within the company. There is no systematic parts numbering system – the present plethora of piece parts (some 22,000 and growing) is described in a vast array of drawings and process specifications that reside in an untidy set of filing chests in the design office. There are good systems available but Robin Johnston, Rowan Gregory and Jan Pettigrew between them hold the information necessary for linking the final products to the raw materials, essentially in their heads!

You are interested in the ERP idea but also understand the practicalities of implementing associated software, like how long it takes to read in data and set up new systems and parameters. This always takes far longer than people expect and they never give you enough resources to do the job properly. Computers and web-based communication technologies are obviously the way forward, the life-blood of any organization, yet they never get taken seriously enough. You are often treated like some sort of semi-skilled mechanic – no one appreciates how good you are really are. Sometimes, when you feel that you are underappreciated, you remind yourself that there are many good opportunities elsewhere. In particular, Alex Rheingold seems insufficiently appreciative of your special skills. Alex is apt to think that buying in new systems or some form of facilities management arrangement would eliminate entirely the need for the systems group. You are always stressing how your group forms the essential link between the systems and actual business processes. Is the consideration of ERP an opportunity for demonstrating the true value of your systems expertise? Or is it just an attempt by Alex to eventually outsource systems development entirely. Well, if so they'd better watch out. There might be a few surprises if they try to get rid of you! It might just be rather difficult for anyone else to take over.

Sandy Corbett: Consultant

You are a consultant with access to the latest technology, the ability to work closely with senior management and a track record of success. In your previous job as a production engineer and manager in an aerospace company, you were directly involved in the implementation of MRP2 – a precursor of ERP. You are very much an enthusiast for this approach to production control. This technology allows the integration of business functions and achieves and sustains tight discipline in shop-floor operations. You know what it can do in terms of: increasing financial control of operations; banishing paperwork from the supply chain; drastically reducing lead times; reducing waste and scrap; providing continuous improvement of supplier performance. All of this, as you tell your clients, leads to enhanced profits and competitiveness. You understand the philosophy of the technology and try to get this over to your clients. ERP is essentially based on the 'push philosophy' of the original MRP2 system that matches the purchasing and scheduling of raw materials and parts to centralized production plans based on sales forecasts so that materials are available when they are needed for production without holding unnecessarily high levels of inventory. ERP though also considers how planning, scheduling and control can be aligned to broader business (enterprise) objectives in particular markets.

Operationally, the planning systems and software needed to achieve ERP break activities into a front end, an engine and a back end. The front end produces the master production schedule (MPS). The MPS plans the production of the goods offered to customers over a given planning horizon based on sales forecasts. The back end handles factory scheduling and manages materials from suppliers. Material requirements planning (MRP) is the *core* of the engine. It takes a period-by-period set of MPS requirements and generates a related set of component parts and raw materials requirements. These MRP data make it possible to generate a *time-phased requirement record* for any part number. This can also drive the *detailed capacity planning* modules – a massive computational task. MRP is therefore the natural starting point for many companies to begin to computerize their overall production control where they are starting more or less from scratch. Then the systems can be developed into a more sophisticated version that provides continual updates of the various components and materials requirements to match changing circumstances. This enables better priority-setting and fine-tuning of shop-floor operations. As well as managing material flows, these enhanced systems can allocate resources (such as machinery and personnel) more efficiently. They can also include financial modules. Simulation techniques allow the examination of various 'what if' scenarios. Such enhanced systems are clearly more company-wide, being less narrowly focused on production control. Indeed, their scope is so much wider than the original concepts of MRP, that the guru Oliver Wight coined the new term – MRP2 – 'Manufacturing Resource Planning'. Later versions are known even more grandly as ERP (Enterprise Resources Planning).

ERP is much more exciting because it allows you to work with clients, aligning their production planning with financial accounting and much broader strategic objectives. It also usually means a much longer-term (and more costly!) relationship with clients. You read a recent study some years ago reporting a large survey of 2000 ERP users that described the benefits and costs of ERP systems. This showed substantial benefits. For example, performance on delivery promises increased from 61 per cent to 88 per cent and lead times reduced from 71 to 44 days (almost 50 per cent). Typically paybacks begin within some six to nine months of 'going live' with the software. It also found that average costs of systems installation were substantial, ranging from as little as $113,000 in small companies to $2,876,000 in the largest companies (you do not usually broadcast the upper end of these costs when asked by potential clients). Interestingly, it did not cost more to achieve high ERP benefits – the degree of computerization, management support and the implementation approach used were more important in predicting benefits than the amount of money spent on the IT system.

You are also aware that a lot of companies have run into problems introducing ERP software but then they didn't have the benefit of your expertise. You are fairly cynical about how good some other consultants in this area are – some say sweet things but don't seem to have much of a clue when it comes to actually implementing systems. Although you know little about the furniture industry, basically all manufacturing businesses are the same. They take in bits, process them, combine them, and then sell them according a broad strategic plan. And in between, the actual flows of all the bits have to be monitored and accounted for. For this, essentially identical systems can be used. The nature of the bits doesn't really matter. You have special links with one software supplier, but of course you do your best to offer impartial advice. It would not serve your interests to recommend a system that will eventually cause problems. Once a company has bought into MRP/MRP2, they will probably continue to invest and upgrade over a number of years before achieving a full ERP system. And you will continue to help them. In making your presentation to the working group at Oakland Furniture, you are very aware of the political dynamics of the situation. Not everyone there is likely to welcome ERP. You only have limited access to key decision-makers (for example, Alex Rheingold) and you need to make the most of it.

Index